DOING SOCIAL SCIENCE

Doing Social Science

Evidence and Methods in Empirical Research

Edited by

Fiona Devine
University of Manchester, UK

and

Sue Heath
University of Southampton, UK

palgrave
macmillan

First published 2009 by
PALGRAVE MACMILLAN

Palgrave Macmillan in the UK is an imprint of Macmillan Publishers Limited, registered in England, company number 785998, of Houndmills, Basingstoke, Hampshire RG21 6XS.

Palgrave Macmillan in the US is a division of St Martin's Press LLC, 175 Fifth Avenue, New York, NY 10010.

Palgrave Macmillan is the global academic imprint of the above companies and has companies and representatives throughout the world.

Palgrave® and Macmillan® are registered trademarks in the United States, the United Kingdom, Europe and other countries

ISBN 978–0–230–53789–7 hardback
ISBN 978–0–230–53790–3 paperback

This book is printed on paper suitable for recycling and made from fully managed and sustained forest sources. Logging, pulping and manufacturing processes are expected to conform to the environmental regulations of the country of origin.

A catalogue record for this book is available from the British Library.

A catalog record for this book is available from the Library of Congress.

10 9 8 7 6 5 4 3 2 1
18 17 16 15 14 13 12 11 10 09

Printed and bound in Great Britain by
CPI Antony Rowe, Chippenham and Eastbourne

To past, present and future students of research methods everywhere!

Contents

List of Tables

List of Figures

Notes on Contributors

Wendy Bottero is Senior Lecturer at the University of Manchester. Her research interests are in the areas of stratification and 'class'; lifestyles and differential association; and social theory, particularly the work of Pierre Bourdieu. She is the author of *Stratification: Social Divisions and Inequality* (2005), as well as numerous book chapters and articles on social mobility, stratification and the 'space of social relations' in *Sociological Review*, the *British Journal of Sociology*, *Sociology*, *Historical Methods* and *Sociological Research Online* amongst others. She previously lectured at the University of Southampton before moving to the University of Manchester in 2006.

Fiona Devine is Professor of Sociology at the University of Manchester. She was Head of Sociology between 2004 and 2007 and is now Head of the School of Social Sciences. Her research interests straddle social stratification and mobility, work and employment, politics and participation, and urban sociology. She is the author of *Affluent Workers Revisited* (1992), *Social Class in America and Britain* (1997), *Class Practices* (2004), *Sociological Research Methods in Context* with Sue Heath (1999), three other edited collections, including *Rethinking Class* (2005) and numerous book chapters and journal articles. Her next book, *Class: A Very Short Introduction*, will be published in 2011.

Sue Heath is Professor of Sociology in the School of Social Sciences at the University of Southampton and is a co-director of the ESRC National Centre for Research Methods. Methodologically, her interests lie in issues of research ethics and the challenges of research with young people, and she has a growing interest in the possibilities of qualitative social network-based research. Sue's substantive research interests are located within the sociology of youth and the sociology of education. Much of her recent research and writing has focused on single young adults, household formation and the redefinition of 'adulthood', reflecting her broader interest in processes of transition to adulthood. These concerns are being pursued as part of the work programme of the new ESRC Centre for Population Change at the University of Southampton, of which she is a co-director. Her most recent book, *Researching Young People's Lives* (with Rachel Brooks, Elizabeth Cleaver and Eleanor Ireland, published in 2009), combines her interests in the sociology of youth and social science research methodology.

Christian Greiffenhagen is British Academy Postdoctoral Fellow at the University of Manchester, currently conducting ethnographic research on mathematical practice. His previous research was a video-based ethnographic study of how a new innovative storyboarding software was embedded in everyday classroom practice. Recent publications have appeared in *Computer Supported Cooperative Work (CSCW)*, the *Journal for the Theory of Social Behaviour* and *Science & Education*.

Graeme Kirkpatrick is Senior Lecturer in Sociology at the University of Manchester. He is the author of *Critical Technology* (2004), which won the 2005 Philip Abrams Memorial Prize from the British Sociological Association, and *Technology and Social Power* (2008), and he is co-editor of *Historical Materialism and Social Evolution* (2002). He has published articles in *Sociological Review*, *Max Weber Studies*, *Thesis Eleven* and several other journals. He is currently writing a book about computer games.

Vanessa May is Lecturer in Sociology and a member of the Morgan Centre for the Study of Relationships and Personal Life at the University of Manchester. She has published on lone motherhood, divorce, contact and residence disputes, and methodology in *Sociological Review*, *Narrative Inquiry*, *Women's Studies International Forum*, *International Journal of Social Research Methodology*, *Child and Family Law Quarterly* and the *Journal of Social Welfare and Family Law*.

Alice Mills is Lecturer in Criminology in the School of Social Sciences at the University of Southampton. She has published in a variety of prison-related areas, particularly mental health in prisons and prisoners' families, notably a chapter in the *Handbook on Prisons* (2007) and recent co-authored articles in the *British Journal of Psychiatry* and the *Journal of Forensic Psychiatry and Psychology*. She is currently involved in research to evaluate the prison mental health in-reach programme and the role of the third sector in the criminal justice system, and is co-authoring an introductory text to prisons and imprisonment (with David Scott and Helen Codd).

Navtej Purewal is Lecturer in Sociology at the University of Manchester. She is working on a project exploring popular and shared religious practices on both sides of the Indian–Pakistan border in Punjab where she is currently based. Her research interests are in the areas of gender, religion and caste marginality in South Asia, focusing on the region of Punjab, and she has published in *Contemporary South Asia*, the *Interdisciplinary Journal of Gender Studies* and the *Journal of Punjab Studies*. Her book *Son Preference: Cultures, Economies and Technologies* is forthcoming.

Dale Southerton is Senior Lecturer in Sociology at the University of Manchester. His research focuses on social change and consumption in

relation to time and space, identity and social networks; interpersonal relat-
ionships, childhood and technological innovation; social practices; and
sustainability. He has published widely on these topics in journals such as
Sociology, the *British Journal of Sociology*, *Sociological Review*, *Time & Society*,
Society & Space, *Acta Sociologica*, the *Journal of Consumer Culture* and the
Journal of Material Culture. He co-edited the book *Sustainable Consumption:
The Implications of Changing Infrastructures of Provision* (2004) and is currently
Editor-in-Chief of the *Encyclopedia of Consumer Culture* (due for publication
in 2010).

Paul Sweetman is Senior Lecturer in Sociology at the University of
Southampton. He has published articles and chapters on fashion, reflexivity
and habitus, body modification, subcultures, and debates within cultural
studies, and he is co-editor – with Caroline Knowles – of *Picturing the Social
Landscape: Visual Methods and the Sociological Imagination* (2004). He is an
associate member of the ESRC National Centre for Research Methods, Co-
convenor (with David Gauntlett) of the British Sociological Association Visual
Sociology Study Group and a former member of the *Sociology* editorial board.

Helen Wood is Reader in Media and Communication at De Montfort University, Leicester, having previously taught at Manchester. Her main academic
interests are in television studies, media theory, gender and social change,
and audience studies. She is author of *Talking With Television: Women, Talk
Shows and Modern Self-Reflexivity* (2009). She has recently co-edited two
volumes of *The Centre for Contemporary Cultural Studies Working Papers*
(2007). She has published a number of articles on television and reception
in journals including *Media, Culture and Society*; the *European Journal of Cultural Studies*; the *Cinema Journal*; and *The Communication Review*. She is also
Assistant Editor of the journal *Ethnographies*.

Acknowledgements

It is pleasing to be approached by a publisher with a view to a second edition of a book. Emily Satz did this on behalf of Palgrave in 2006. But we were now ten years older and had acquired a few more responsibilities along the way. In an ideal world, we would have completely rewritten *Sociological Research Methods in Context* (1999) in keeping with the ethos of critically evaluating recent social science research. Instead, we have chosen to do a second edition of the book in the form of an edited collection, drawing on the expertise of colleagues at our respective institutions: the University of Manchester and the University of Southampton. We are very grateful to Emily for her openness to this suggestion so that this book has come to fruition. We want to acknowledge the day-to-day advice, especially about visual matters, permissions and copyright from Anna Reeve. Thank you both!

Given this preamble, our sincere thanks go to the contributors of this collection: Wendy Bottero, Christian Greiffenhagen, Graeme Kirkpatrick, Vanessa May, Alice Mills, Navtej Purewal, Dale Southerton, Paul Sweetman and Helen Wood. Some of our colleagues have moved institutions: namely, Wendy from Southampton to Manchester and Helen from Manchester to De Montfort. We gave our contributors lots of deadlines. Of course, there was slippage (including by us), as everyone juggled other research projects, teaching duties and administrative responsibilities. We got there in the end. More importantly, as editors, we had a lot to say about first and second drafts of chapters. We are happy to say that everyone responded to us positively and we are firmly of the view that the chapters are excellent as a result of that dialogue. This book is even better than we hoped it would be and all thanks must go to our colleagues for this final product.

We would also like to thank the authors upon whose work the contributors have drawn: Gaynor Bagnall, Vern Bengtson, Timothy Biblarz, Urvashi Butalia, Steven Clayman, Kimmett Edgar, John Heritage, Jonathan Gershuny, Paul Hodkinson, Brian Longhurst, Carol Martin, Ian O'Donnell, Robert Roberts, Mike Savage, T. L. Taylor and Thomas Tufte. As editors of this book, we have been at one remove from the authors of the books that are critically evaluated here. We encouraged our contributors to send drafts of their chapters to the authors of their chosen book. When they did so, the authors were very generous in their remarks. They made careful comments which enhanced our contributors' understanding and evaluation of the material. Nonetheless, the views that are advanced in this book are those of the contributors alone. We are able to report that contact between contributors and authors has led, in some instances, to further conversations about research. We are delighted about this unintended consequence.

Finally, we would like to say a big thank you to our respective partners: Jim and Jayne. We want to thank each other again too! Ten years on from the first edition of this book, and having worked very closely together on this one, we are still the firmest of friends.

FIONA DEVINE
University of Manchester

SUE HEATH
University of Southampton

The contributors, editors and publishers wish to thank the following for permission to use copyright material: The MIT Press for the use of T. L. Taylor's *Play Between Worlds: Exploring Online Game Culture* (2006); Sony Online Entertainment LLC for permission to use the screenshot from multi-player online PC role-playing game, *EverQuest*; Willan Publishing for K. Edgar, I. O'Donnell and C. Martin, *Prison Violence: The Dynamics of Conflict, Fear and Power* (2003); Routledge for reproduction of Figures 3.2 and 3.3 from K. Edgar, I. O'Donnell and C. Martin, 'Tracking the Pathways to Violence in Prison', in R. M. Lee and E. A. Stanko (eds), *Researching Violence: Essays on Methodology and Meas-urement*; Oxford University Press for J. Gershuny, *Changing Times, Work and Leisure in Postindustrial Society* (2000); Sage for M. Savage, G. Bagnall and B. Longhurst, *Globalization and Belonging* (2004); Berg for P. Hodkinson, *Goth: Identity, Style and Subculture* (2002); Sarah Hodkinson for reproduction of photograph on front cover of P. Hodkinson's *Goth*; John Libbey Publishing for T. Tufte, *Living with the Rubbish Queen: Telenovelas, Culture and Modernity in Brazil* (2000); Duke University Press for U. Butalia, *The Other Side of Silence: Voices from the Partition of India* (2000); Palgrave Macmillan for reproduction of Table 8.1 taken from R. Jeffrey, *What's Happening to India? Punjab, Ethnic Conflict and the Test for Federalism*, 2nd edn (1994); Cambridge University Press for V. L. Bengtson, T. J. Biblarz and R. E. L. Roberts, *How Families Still Matter: A Longitudinal Study of Youth in Two Generations* (2002); Vern Bengtson for reproduction of screenshot of home page of the Longitudinal Study of Generations website. Every effort has been made to trace all the copyright-holders, but if any have been inadvertently overlooked the publishers will be pleased to make the necessary arrangement at the first opportunity.

CHAPTER 1

Doing Social Science

FIONA DEVINE AND SUE HEATH

Introduction

This book introduces students to issues of method – not through an abstract 'how to' approach, but by focusing on specific examples of high quality empirical research which have been published since the year 2000. By so doing, we seek to highlight the excitement as well as the challenge of conducting real life research and to demonstrate how the choice and use of particular methods and techniques can critically shape the findings of social science research. Our book consists of a series of critical evaluations of recent research in core and new areas of social science – with themes as diverse as family change, online gaming and the Partition of India; international time-use, Brazilian soap operas and prison violence; and political interviews, goth subculture and attachment to place. We believe that the contributors to this book have identified studies which will provide a benchmark for high quality social science research in the years ahead. In addition to UK-based research, these studies include examples of research on other societies as well as comparative cross-national research. They also embrace a variety of social science disciplines, including sociology, cultural studies, media studies, criminology and social history.

These examples also reflect a number of important developments which have occurred in the world of social science methodology in recent years. In the UK context, there has been an explosion of interest in methodological concerns in social science research, alongside a growing emphasis on interdisciplinary research, which has led researchers from different disciplines, often with very different methodological traditions, to come together to tackle key social research questions. This has contributed more generally to the widespread adoption of mixed methods approaches to research. In addition, we have seen the emergence of new methodological approaches, often linked to the possibilities afforded by technologies such as the internet and other communication technologies, and the development of, as well as enhanced access to, new sources of data, in many cases on an unprecedented scale. The first decade of the twenty-first century has also been marked by an unprecedented level of UK investment in the development of research methods, including the Economic and Social Research Council (ESRC)'s Research Methods Programme, the National Centre for Research Methods, the National Centre for e-Social Science, the Researcher Development Initiative, and the now biennial ESRC Research Methods Festival. All of these factors have led to a renewed interest in research methods as a field of study and have revitalized research in specific subfields. And all of these developments are reflected in the choice of studies included within this book. The methodological map of the UK is very different today than it was even ten years ago.

The Choice of Studies

This book consists of nine separate case studies of exemplary social research representing a broad range of research topics. Each has been chosen by current or former colleagues from the Universities of Manchester and Southampton with interests in these research fields and who are therefore well-placed to develop a critique of their chosen studies from a position of expertise. Certain criteria have been adopted in determining which studies were chosen by our contributors. First, all of the studies have been published in book form since 2000, and should therefore be easily accessible. Second, the chosen studies cover a cross-section of some key areas of social science research: criminology, family life, work, leisure, subcultures, the media, gender divisions, social class, race and ethnicity, to name some of the dominant themes. Each of the studies that has been chosen also taps into an important aspect of people's everyday lives and sheds light on the operation of social divisions and other social processes within contemporary societies. Third, the studies which have been chosen cover a diverse range of research strategies (see Table 1.1). Fourth, they all include an explicit discussion of at least some aspects of their underpinning research design, hence making a detailed critique possible.

Each chapter starts with a short introduction to the chosen study and its broader context, followed by a discussion of where the study might be located in relation to other work and to broad theoretical and methodological traditions within that field of research. As will become clear, in some cases the studies follow very much in the footsteps of earlier research in their respective fields, whilst in other cases they mark a break with, or even a direct challenge to, what has gone before. The main findings of the research are then

Table 1.1   Research methods used in the nine case studies

Author	Title of study	Methods
T.L. Taylor	*Play Between Worlds: Exploring Online Game Culture*	Online and offline participant observation; interviews
Kimmett Edgar, Ian O'Donnell and Carol Martin	*Prison Violence: The Dynamics of Conflict, Fear and Power*	Victimization surveys, interviews, documentary analysis
Jonathan Gershuny	*Changing Times: Work and Leisure in Postindustrial Society*	Time-use diaries
Mike Savage, Gaynor Bagnall and Brian Longhurst	*Globalization and Belonging*	In-depth interviews, local questionnaire survey
Paul Hodkinson	*Goth: Identity, Style and Subculture*	Participant observation, in-depth interviews, media analysis, questionnaire survey
Thomas Tufte	*Living with the Rubbish Queen: Telenovelas, Culture and Modernity in Brazil*	Interviews, participant observation, survey
Urvashi Butalia	*The Other Side of Silence: Voices from the Partition of India*	Oral history interviews, documentary analysis (memoirs, diaries, autobiographies and letters), personal experience
Steven Clayman and John Heritage	*The News Interview: Journalists and Public Figures on the Air*	Conversation analysis
Vern Bengtson, Timothy Biblarz and Robert Roberts	*How Families Still Matter*	Multicohort longitudinal survey design

summarized, before a discussion of two or three key methodological themes raised by the study in question. The link between research findings and research design is crucial, as the methods chosen by a research team can either create possibilities or place restrictions on the nature of the conclusions that can be drawn. Each chapter finishes with an overview of the methods and findings of the study, followed by some guidance on further reading in relation to both the substantive topic and the methods used.

Our contributors' choice of books has influenced the range and nature of issues of method that are addressed in this edited collection. Four issues emerged on numerous occasions across the chapters, although the following discussion highlights just one key issue in relation to each book under discussion. First, the relationship between theories and methods emerges in Wendy Bottero's discussion of *Globalization and Belonging* (2004) by Mike Savage and his colleagues, and in Paul Sweetman's consideration of Paul Hodkinson's book, *Goth* (2002). Second, sampling techniques and measurement issues loom large in Vanessa May's evaluation of Vern Bengtson et al.'s *How Families Still Matter* (2002), in Dale Southerton's critique of Jonathan Gershuny's *Changing Times* (2000), and in Alice Mills's discussion of Kimmett Edgar et al.'s book, *Prison Violence* (2003). Third, research relationships in the field emerge in Graeme Kirkpatrick's consideration of T. L. Taylor's *Play Between Worlds* (2006) and in Navtej Purewal's evaluation of Urvashi Butalia's *The Other Side of Silence* (2000). Fourth, issues of interpretation are raised in Christian Greiffenhagen's discussion of Steven Clayman and John Heritage's *The News Interview* (2002) and in Helen Wood's consideration of Thomas Tufte's *Living with the Rubbish Queen* (2000). These four issues are now briefly introduced with reference to the case studies discussed in detail in each chapter.

The Relationship between Theory and Method

A number of chapters in this book address the relationship between theories and methods in the social sciences. Recently, scholars have expressed their concern about the relationship between theoretical developments and the seemingly growing distance from empirical research on everyday life (Goldthorpe 2007a, 2007b; Savage and Burrows 2007; Smart 2007). On the one hand, theorists stand accused of engaging in grand speculative thinking and making predictions about epic social change uninformed by past empirical research. On the other hand, empirical researchers are criticized for dismissing theory as irrelevant to their needs and are then unable to draw wider conclusions from their work. Carol Smart (2007), for example, has recently described her unhappiness with theories of individualization – associated with Giddens (1992) and Beck and Beck-Gernsheim (1995). Such 'top-down' theories proffer clear and coherent explanations of social life whilst most peoples' everyday lives are messy and complex. The challenge is to develop more 'bottom-up' theories, which are informed by empirical research and capture the richness and complexity of everyday life without being confusing and incomprehensible.

Globalization, with its emphasis on the mobility of people, capital, objects and information, is an obvious example of a grand theory which makes big predictions about how the world is changing. In *Globalization and Belonging*, Savage et al. (2004) conducted large-scale qualitative research in four middle-class suburbs in Manchester to test the theory. They found that local identities are important, although they are not fixed and static. Their study is not without problems as Wendy Bottero astutely notes. The decision to concentrate on middle-class suburbs created limitations for the development of their own theory of 'elective belonging'. It is doubtful whether the same ideas about reflective choices apply to residents of working-class localities. Bottero also considers the limitations of qualitative interviews – which capture people's micro experiences of a particular place – to say things about macrostructures and processes. Moreover, whether qualitative interviews are the best way to explore questions of embodiment, the tacit practices of the habitus and field relations – namely, to articulate aspects of life that are often left unarticulated – is also worthy of reflection.

The relationship between theory and method also looms large in Paul Sweetman's consideration of Paul Hodkinson's book, *Goth: Identity, Style and Subculture* (2002). Critical of the work on youth culture and subcultures by members of the Birmingham Centre for Contemporary Cultural Studies (CCCS), Hodkinson undertook a detailed study of goths by way of a multi-faceted ethnography involving participant observation, in-depth interviews, media analysis and a questionnaire. Goths form a distinctive subculture but its members are not especially subversive. Sweetman approves of Hodkinson's detailed description of how goths live their everyday lives rather than simply conducting a textual or semiotic analysis of aspects of their style for its mean-ing and significance. He is not, however, entirely convinced by Hodkinson's critique and refinement of the concept of subcultures. Is it still useful to retain a concept like subculture when most of its previous meaning has been stripped away? Are social scientists bound by past theory which, arguably, acts as a straightjacket that inhibits new ways of thinking about substantive topics like youth culture and subcultures?

Sampling Techniques and Measurement Issues

Sampling techniques, namely 'the selection of people, places or activities suitable for study' (Lee 1993: 60), are without any doubt crucial issues in quantitative and qualitative research. Different sampling frames affect the representativeness of the sample (the degree to which the sample accurately reflects the characteristics of the broader sample) and the generalizability of the research findings (the degree to which one can say with confidence that the findings from one setting are likely to apply to similar settings). In longi-tudinal quantitative research, the big challenge is attrition when respondents do not want to be reinterviewed in subsequent waves of research. Non-response causes the sample to shrink and to become less representative of the population under investigation. The ability to generalize is compromised. Fortunately, these pressing methodological issues are themselves the subject of research so that attrition is better understood, avoided where possible, circumvented where not and the quality of data is improved (Plewis 2007; Vandecasteele and Debels 2007). The chapters outlined next consider these issues and also wider concerns about the difficulties of measuring social phenomena like time pressures and prison violence.

Vanessa May considers representativeness and generalizability in her discussion of *How Families Still Matter: A Longitudinal Study of Youth in Two Generations* by Vern L. Bengtson, Timothy J. Biblarz and Robert E. L. Roberts (2002). The book is based on the Longitudinal Study of Generations (LSOG) which involved several generations of the same families in the research. Despite claims that families are less important than in the past, Bengtson and his colleagues found that family transmissions have not weakened over time and that contemporary young people are not fairing any worse than previous generations. May notes the limitations of the LSOG. The initial study was not a random probability study and was skewed towards white middle-class American respondents. The study also suffered from attrition problems over time as original sample members were not reinterviewed for various reasons. This is a real problem because any respondent who fails to take part in subsequent waves cannot be replaced and the sample size diminishes over time. Finally, longitudinal data cannot pinpoint *why* a particular change has taken place. The researcher has to provide a contextualized story for why change has occurred and what the contributing factors have been.

Dale Southerton picks up on measurement issues in his review of Jonathan Gershuny's book, *Changing Times: Work and Leisure in Postindustrial Society* (2000). Gershuny analysed 35 time-use studies (comprising a sample of 120,000 respondents filling in time diaries), conducted in 20 different countries between 1961 and the early 1990s. He found changes in the distribution of paid and unpaid work, in the domestic division of labour between men and women, and in the amount of leisure time enjoyed by different socio-economic groups. Southerton notes that measuring time-use is difficult. Coding is far from easy when diary entries are imprecise and the purpose of an activity is unclear. Such difficulties are compounded by comparative research where time intervals are measured differently. If time dairy methodologies, like all survey data, provide only a partial account of everyday life, Southerton considers how it is possible to make the best use of available evidence, overcome shortcomings and remain aware of limitations. These are very important questions to ask if time-use diaries are to be better sources of data in the future and to help us understand social change.

Measurement issues also loom large in Alice Mills's discussion of *Prison Violence: The Dynamics of Conflict, Fear and Power* by Kimmett Edgar, Ian O'Donnell and Carol Martin (2003). The book examines interpersonal violence between prisoners ranging from bullying to assault. It draws on two studies: a 'victimization study' funded by the Home Office and a 'conflicts study' funded by the ESRC as part of a Violence Research Programme.

Mills notes the difficulties of using a victimization survey to study prison violence. Edgar et al. issued an anonymous self-complete questionnaire which they distributed to prisoners while locked in their cells and collected them half an hour later. Given the high levels of overcrowding, Mills wonders how many of the prisoners were alone in their cells and therefore felt free to write about their experiences. She also considers whether prisoners, known to have low levels of literacy, would have able to do such writing satisfactorily. Many prisoners would have needed help in this respect and, though finding themselves in the situation of having individuals to hand – prisoners or staff – who could assist, the very presence of these others might compromise their ability to write what they wanted. The problems of underreportage, in other words, are considered fully.

Research Relationships in the Field

The nature of research relationships in the field is a key methodological issue. When are relationships too close that they lead to bias in the collection and interpretation of research material? Is it possible to eliminate bias in the name of objectivity or are we only able to discuss field relations in order to acknowledge their influence on how research gets done and substantive issues emerge? The latter approach, namely a commitment to a self-critical approach to social analysis – reflexivity – is now common in the social sciences (Heaphy 2007: 48; May 2003). Research relationships in the field are discussed by Sweetman with regard to Hodkinson's study of goth subculture noted above. More recently, critical reflection on the nature of field relations has raised discussion around ethical issues (Lee-Treweek and Linkogle 2000). How should we conduct ourselves with others in the field? Should we always seek informed consent from participants and how do we go about doing so? How much information should we provide on our research? Should vulnerable groups (where issues of power may arise) be treated differently (Heath et al. 2007; Wiles et al. 2006, 2007)?

These questions are extremely important at a time when social research embraces new areas of investigation. One such example is research on the internet, as discussed in Graeme Kirkpatrick's contribution to this volume. Kirkpatrick offers a critical appraisal of T. L. Taylor's book, *Play between Worlds* (2006), which is a qualitative ethnographic study of computer games. Taylor is especially interested in the social and cultural life to be found in this virtual world, including the friends and acquaintances that are developed and sustained. Kirkpatrick rightly notes that Taylor's book is a very exciting sociological exploration of the virtual world and there are new challenges for research ethics in online research. Social scientists are only just beginning to grapple with them.

For example, Kirkpatrick considers the ethics of 'playing' with disclosure and when researchers should reveal that they are conducting research to their unwitting participants (if at all). If researchers disclose their activities, can we tell if participants are then lost or if relationships change as a consequence? What are the implications for the research and research findings if these things happen?

Navtej Purewal explores issues of reflexivity in her discussion of Urvashi Butalia's *The Other Side of Silence* (2000). The book focuses on the partition of India – into modern-day India and Pakistan – in 1947. It explores the human experience of these events – especially of women, children and the lower castes – and the pain and suffering they endured. Butalia's book is an oral history of this period, based on intensive interviews and the reading of diaries, letters and memories over many years. Butalia critically reflects on her 'use of self', from how it motivated her to explore the hidden experiences of the partition to her way of writing the material for her book. The virtue of her approach is that she is explicit about her family experiences, though she is aware of its downsides too. The researcher has to be open to reinterpreting personal experiences, and this can be very uncomfortable. The temptation can be to shy away from such discomfort especially when the issues are close to heart. Reflexivity, therefore, is a considerable challenge for researchers.

Questions of Interpretation

Questions of interpretation figure large in many of the studies included in this book, reflecting the continuing influence of methodological critiques arising out of the postmodern turn in the social sciences. Debates about the dual crises of representation and legitimation upon which these critiques are based (Devine and Heath 1999) often place a question mark over the validity of the interpretations which social scientists can offer when analysing data, and it is not unusual for researchers to emphasize the situated nature of their own interpretations, regardless of whether or not they would identify themselves as postmodernists. This section explores these issues in relation to Christian Greiffenhagen's discussion of Steven Clayman and John Heritage's *The News Interview* (2002) and Helen Wood's consideration of Thomas Tufte's *Living with the Rubbish Queen* (2000).

Clayman and Heritage's book is concerned with the norms and conventions that govern the modern broadcast news interview. Based on conversation analysis (CA), the study focuses on the structural properties of radio news interviews with politicians in order to explore the ways in which the content of such interviews is directly achieved through the interaction between interviewer and interviewee. Greiffenhagen's discussion of their work provides an overview of the practices and conventions that appear to govern the news interview. He notes that conversation analysts consider the types of data which they analyse to be free from distortion, given that their data is not the product of an artificial encounter between a researcher and a research participant, but is instead a source of 'real world' data which can be readily shared with other researchers. Clayman and Heritage claim that this renders the process of interpretation more transparent, claiming further that 'within CA every effort is made to ground any analysis in the understandings and orientations of the participants themselves' (Clayman and Heritage 2002: 19). This position implies that participants' own understandings and orientations are largely self-evident. As Greiffenhagen points out, data do not speak for themselves in this way: the analytical challenge is how to decide between the different possible interpretations that can be placed upon an interaction.

A related set of issues arise in Helen Wood's discussion of Thomas Tufte's *Living with the Rubbish Queen* (2000), an ethnographic study of the impact of Brazilian telenovelas – serialized melodramas broadcast six days a week – on their largely female audiences in low-income urban areas of Brazil. His focus is firmly on how viewers interpret the meanings of these telenovelas and the ways in which they appropriate them as part of their lives, rather than on the interpretations that might have been intended by their producers. Wood quotes Geertz's (1973: 9) argument that 'what we call our data are really our own constructions of other people's constructions of what they and their compatriots are up to', yet she cautions against the assumption that 'anything goes' or that all interpretations meet on equal grounds. Her response is to take into account the extent to which the researcher's own positioning within his or her research might influence the validity of his or her interpretation(s), a consideration which would appear particularly relevant to a study by a middle-class, male, Danish researcher of the everyday lives of low-income Brazilian women. Tufte anticipates the criticism that his own authority to interpret these women's lives might be open to question by positioning himself as someone with a degree of 'insider' expertise; yet Wood is of the view that there is actually relatively little reflection on the impact of Tufte's own presence in the field – especially in relation to his gender – within the descriptions of his findings. She makes the case for the situated nature of any given interpretation, and acknowledges that not all accounts may be equally convincing once we know about a researcher's own positioning.

Some Observations about Our Methodological Coverage

Inevitably, a book of this kind is not as comprehensive as a prescriptive methods text. We are aware of a number of omissions in our methodological coverage, but we will highlight two in particular. First, often having neglected the visual senses in the past, scholars are increasingly aware of the 'visual' character of contemporary culture and how important 'seeing' is to 'knowing' about the world (Jenks 1995; Pink 2006; Prosser 1998). Social scientists are increasingly using visual material – photographs, film, art and other images – as data in empirical research. They are also using visual material as a methodological tool including, for example, as prompts for interviews and generating focus group discussions. Research participants are increasingly being asked to produce visual images as part of research projects too (Knowles and Sweetman 2004; Pole 2004). These developments raise new methodological challenges. What kinds of questions can we ask of visual material? How do we go about sampling such material? How should visual data be analysed? Many of these questions have yet to be answered. There will be much 'learning by doing'. These are exciting challenges for future generations of scholars and students. Second, there are important developments underway in longitudinal research in the UK. In the field of quantitative research, a new panel survey called Understanding Society has been launched, involving annual interviews with approximately 100,000 members of 40,000 households. The survey is the biggest of its kind in the world and will eventually also involve the collection of biometric data as well as some qualitative data. This new survey is being undertaken by the team previously responsible for the British Household Panel Survey, based in the ESRC's United Kingdom Longitudinal Studies Centre at the University of Essex. In the field of qualitative research, the ESRC has recently launched the Timescapes Longitudinal Study, the first major qualitative longitudinal study to be funded in the UK. Timescapes currently consists of seven linked projects, all of which explore the ways in which personal and family relationships change over time. All use a combination of different qualitative approaches to data generation, including interviews, narratives, photographs and other visual documents. Timescapes has a strong methodological strand running through all of the projects, which is concerned with developing new approaches to the use, reuse and sharing of longitudinal qualitative data and the ways in which different studies might be combined for purposes of exploring social change. Both Timescapes and Understanding Society are exciting methodological developments which will facilitate a better understanding of personal, social and historical change.

The ways in which we collect evidence and the methods by which we do so are, then, dynamic issues in the social sciences. Research is an ongoing creative process (Pole and Lampard 2001). New types of evidence and new forms of method pose exciting challenges for current and future generations of both scholars and students. It is our intention that the discussion of the topics in this book will stimulate students to think more explicitly about evidence and methods, and to evaluate critically both how research is done and the substantive findings that are drawn from such research. By avoiding an abstract and dry discussion we have sought to consider methods in a fresh and invigorating way. The welcome consequence of such an endeavour has been to draw on published work which is testimony to the continued strength of theoretically informed empirical research in the social sciences.

References

Beck, U. and E. Beck-Gernsheim (1995) *The Normal Chaos of Love*, Cambridge: Polity.

Bengtson, V.L., T.J. Biblarz and R.E.L. Roberts (2002) *How Families Still Matter: A Longitudinal Study of Youth in Two Generations*, Cambridge: Cambridge University Press.

Bourdieu, P. (1986) *Distinction: A Social Critique of the Judgement of Taste*, London: Routledge.

Butalia, U. (2000) *The Other Side of Silence: Voices from the Partition of India*, Durham, NC: Duke University Press.

Clayman, S. and J. Heritage (2002) *The News Interview: Journalists and Public Figures on the Air*, Cambridge: Cambridge University Press.

Devine, F. and S. Heath (1999) *Sociological Research Methods in Context*, Basingstoke: Macmillan.

Edgar, K., I. O'Donnell and C. Martin (2003) *Prison Violence: The Dynamics of Conflict, Fear and Power*, Cullompton: Willan Publishing.

Geertz, C. (1973) *The Interpretation of Cultures*, New York: Basic Books.

Gershuny, J. (2000) *Changing Times: Work and Leisure in Postindustrial Society*, Oxford: Oxford University Press.

Giddens, A. (1992) *The Transformation of Intimacy*, Cambridge: Polity.

Goldthorpe, J.H. (2007a) *On Sociology, vol. 1: Critique and Program*, 2nd edn, Stanford, CA: Stanford California Press.

Goldthorpe, J.H. (2007b) *On Sociology, vol. 2: Illustrations and Retrospect*, 2nd edn, Stanford, CA: Stanford California Press.

Heath, S., V. Charles, G. Crow and R. Wiles (2007) 'Informed consent, gatekeepers and go-between: negotiating consent in child and youth-oriented institutions', *British Educational Research Journal*, 33(3): 403–17.

Heaphy, B. (2007) *Late Modernity and Social Change: Reconstructing Social and Personal Life*, London: Routledge.

Henderson, S., J. Holland, S. McGrellis, S. Sharpe and R. Thompson (2007) *Inventing Adulthoods: A Biographical Approach to Youth Transitions*, London: Sage.

Hodkinson, P. (2002) *Goth: Identity, Style and Subculture*, Oxford: Berg.

Jenks, C. (1995) *Visual Culture*, London: Routledge.

Knowles, C. and P. Sweetman (2004) *Picturing the Social Landscape*, London: Routledge.

Lee, R. (1993) *Doing Research on Sensitive Topics*, London: Sage.

Lee-Treweek, G. and S. Linkogle (2000) *Danger in the Field: Risk and Ethics in Social Research*, London: Routledge.

May, T. (2003) *Social Research: Issues, Methods and Process*, 3rd edn, Buckingham: Open University Press.

McLeod, J. and R. Thomson (2009) *Researching Change: Qualitative Approaches to Personal, Social and Historical Processes*, London: Sage.

Neale, B.A. and J.J. Flowerdew (2003) 'Time texture and childhood: the contours of qualitative longitudinal research', *International Journal of Social Research Methodology*, 6(3): 189–99.

Pink, S. (2006) *Doing Visual Ethnography: Images, Media and Representation in Research*, 2nd edn, London: Sage.

Plewis, I. (2007) 'Non-response in a birth cohort study: the case of the Millennium Cohort Study', *International Journal of Social Research Methodology*, 10(5): 325–34.

Plumridge, L. and R. Thomson (2003) 'Longitudinal qualitative studies and the reflexive self', *International Journal of Social Science Methods*, 6(3): 213–22.

Pole, C. (ed.) (2004) *Seeing is Believing: Approaches to Visual Research*, London: JAI Press.

Pole, C. and R. Lampard (2001) *Practical Social Investigation: Qualitative and Quantitative Methods in Social Research*, London: Prentice-Hall.

Prosser, J. (1998) *Image-based Research: A Sourcebook for Qualitative Researchers*, London: Routledge.

Savage, M., G. Bagnor and B. Longhurst (2004) *Globalization and Belonging*, London: Sage.

Savage, M. and R. Burrows (2007) 'The coming crisis of empirical sociology', *Sociology*, 41(5): 885–99.

Smart, C. (2007) *Personal Life*, Cambridge: Polity.

Taylor, T.L. (2006) *Play Between Worlds: Exploring Online Game Culture*, Cambridge, MA: MIT Press.

Thompson, R. and J. Holland (2003) 'Hindsight, foresight and insight: the challenges of longitudinal qualitative research', *International Journal of Social Research Methodology*, 6(3): 233–44.

Thomson, R. (2007) 'The qualitative longitudinal case history: practical, methodological and ethical reflections', *Social Policy and Society*, 6(4): 571–82.

Tufte, T. (2000) *Living with the Rubbish Queen: Telenovelas, Culture and Modernity in Brazil*, Luton: University of Luton Press.

Vandecasteele, L. and A. Debels (2007) 'Modelling attrition in panel data: the effectiveness of weighting', *European Sociological Review*, 23(1): 81–97.

Wiles, R., G. Crow, V. Charles and S. Heath (2007) 'Informed consent and the research process: following rules or striking balances?', *Sociological Research Online*, 12(2).

Wiles, R., V. Charles, G. Crow, and S. Heath (2006) 'Researching researchers: lessons for research ethics', *Qualitative Research*, 6(3): 283–99.

CHAPTER 2

Technology:
Taylor's *Play Between Worlds*

GRAEME KIRKPATRICK

This chapter considers issues of method in the virtual world of computer games, which present a new social reality full of interaction and communication. Graeme Kirkpatrick presents a critical overview of T. L. Taylor's book, Play Between Worlds: Exploring Online Game Culture (2006), which is based on ethnographic research on the game Everquest and its fictitious world of Norrath. Two methodological themes are examined. First, Kirkpatrick explores how authenticity is achieved by examining how Taylor defined her research site and how she established the reliability of the material she collected. Second, Kirkpatrick reflects on the ethics of 'playing' with disclosure. When should a researcher reveal that he or she is doing research on unwitting participants, if at all? Kirkpatrick is impressed by the way in which Taylor assembles her field notes and files on avatar activity to assure us of the reliability of her findings. He concurs with Taylor's pragmatic approach of revealing her research activities when the opportunities arose in a carefully considered ethical way. These methodological challenges are important to confront in the growing field of technology research.

Introduction

Massive Multiplayer Games (MMPGs) are three-dimensional computer-supported environments usually populated with characters recognizable from 'fantasy' literary genres. They are persistent, dynamic 'worlds' that can be accessed by thousands of people at a time and they are games in the sense of being rule-bound systems that people play with, using tactics and skill to achieve satisfying outcomes. People also go there to play in the slightly different sense of assuming a fictional role or identity. Players participate in MMPGs by creating and controlling an in-game character or 'avatar' (Klevjer 2006), which they assemble from a series of menus presented at the start of play. They control this character as it enters and explores the game world, and the appearance and actions of the avatar constitute them as they appear there to other players.

According to the economist Edward Castronova (2005), between 10 and 30 million people are involved in this activity worldwide, with particular concentrations in China, South Korea, Japan, the USA and Europe. Players commonly spend upwards of several hours a week playing these games. The activity involves extensive collaboration with other players, including the formation of friendships and associations that may persist for years and which regularly become the basis for connections outside the game as well. The sociological importance of MMPGs cannot be in any doubt. Yet, until recently, very little was known about these places and the kinds of social and cultural life that are going on there. T. L. Taylor's pioneering study of *EverQuest* responds to a gap in sociology's understanding of the modern world. The game's fictional world, *Norrath*, is a sprawling mythical environment; as a player-character you can cast spells, fight monsters, go on raiding expeditions and live (and look) as if you were a character from a story like *The Lord of the Rings* or *Narnia*. Taylor's work is an ethnography, which means that it describes what people do and shows why and how these activities take on and retain the significance they do for those people. As the book's sub-title suggests, it is an *exploration* of *EverQuest*. Fortunately, it is also methodologically rigorous, subtle in its analyses and searching in its exploration of key sociological questions; it is an exemplary piece of qualitative sociological writing.

I will begin this discussion of *Play Between Worlds* by describing some of its precursors in the literature on virtual environments and online culture, and I review the recent work in computer game studies, which clarifies the distinctiveness of the computer game as a cultural form. This is followed by a fuller description of Taylor's work, including an account of her main findings. Then I concentrate on her use of ethnographic methods and the specific problems often associated with such methods when applied to virtual environments. First, I look at the issue of authenticity in the study, which concerns how Taylor defines the site of the research and the reliability of what she finds there. Because her work is a virtual ethnography, its site is both the emergent culture of the game environment and the culture of computer gaming itself: it includes disparate physical and virtual locations and cannot be bounded in the manner of traditional social spaces. Second, I turn to the question of research ethics in online social research, focusing on some specific risks opened up by Taylor's approach and discussing some innovations in our thinking about ethics in research that may be helpful to future researchers working in the area of online games and culture. In conclusion, I will offer a short appraisal of the significance of Taylor's work for our understanding of online research methods.

Studying Online Games

The MMPG *EverQuest* (*EQ*) was created by Sony Online Entertainment in 1999. The game is hosted on multiple servers, and players connect to it via the World Wide Web. To do this they must have a copy of the game software, which they purchase in the form of a CD or download for a fee from the game's home site. For a monthly subscription of £8.99 they are allowed to enter the game and to become a character therein. There are many such games in which players can assume roles, develop their characters and, in the process, form friendships and enter established societies in computer-mediated social space. The historical precursors of these games were Multi-User Domains, or MUDs (Dibbell 1999; Turkle 1995). These resemble contemporary MMPGs in that they combine gamic, fictional and social elements, but they differ from them in being made of text, rather than images and sounds. Visitors construct the visual appearance of the houses, dungeons and castles in the MUD world imaginatively from descriptions generated by a database. The first attempts to understand these environments sociologically, as places that people go to associate with others and to create and exchange meanings, focused on their peculiar communicative dynamics. The emphasis in these early studies tended to be on what was lost in computer mediated communication (C-M-C) as against traditional face-to-face interaction (Hine 2001). Susan Herring's (1994) work on gender and communication, for example, drew attention to the way that male and female communicative styles seemed to carry over into the new, cybersocial context, despite the absence of physical markers of gender difference.

We have known since the work of Mead (1967 [1934]) that individual identity is a product of social recognition and individual effort. The two work reciprocally: we all must try to establish what is distinctive about ourselves and worthy of recognition as such, while, at the same time, if we are to be successful, our unique characters have to be accommodated to the social structure. Different societies may vary the margins of manoeuvre allowed to individuals – with 'traditional' societies allegedly more homogeneous than modern ones, for example – but societies in general can only recognize and accommodate personality types that are functional for the social organism as a whole (Habermas 1992). Individual identity is formed in the complex interplay of these two sets of factors. Viewed as such, it is a struggle in which individuals send out symbolic messages about themselves and hope to find these accepted and reflected back at them as such by the wider environment. Of pioneering significance in using these ideas to develop our understanding of C-M-C was Sherry Turkle's (1995) *Life on the Screen*, which tried to comprehend MUDs and other online spaces as mini-societies in which identity-formation processes were played with in a kind of extended experiment involving individuals and online communities.

These early efforts to comprehend computer-generated environments as social locations tended to be produced by sociologists and psychologists who specialized in what is known as the 'human factors' aspect of computing. Negotiating one's way around a computer system requires very different skills from those of the 'sensitive reading' of texts and the fact that computer games were thought of as technological artefacts for the first 40 years of their existence (Gere 2000) probably deterred many in the humanities from seriously engaging with them. However, with the development of Science and Technology Studies (STS) during the 1980s, sociologists have become used to thinking of technology design as thoroughly social. STS introduced the principle that even the most austere technologies and technical practices are freighted with various kinds of cultural investment (McKenzie and Wajcman 1999). In order for a technology to be taken up and used by human beings it has to be designed in a way that holds out openings for them and works with the grain of prevailing social and cultural expectations. STS scholars have shown that these social pressures shape the design of technology in its innermost recesses and cannot be limited in their explanatory range to the 'front end' or 'user interface'. The very idea of a 'personal computer', for example, is one that is heavily informed by individualism and a culture of free experimentation that was very distinctively American, even Californian (Kirkpatrick 2008; Levy 1984). For STS scholars, technology does not 'impact' upon society from 'outside', but is itself profoundly shaped by social and cultural factors.

For a long time computer games have tended to be seen by humanities scholars, including sociologists, as merely an extension of a well-understood, low-brow, visual culture and therefore unlikely to repay serious study (Stallabrass 1996). In common with most computer games, MMPGs offer fantasy environments presented in a cartoonish visual style. Much of the game-play action centres on fighting monsters and searching for gems and magic items, and these activities tend to be perceived as childish at best. This situation has changed in the years since 2000, which has been described (Aarseth 2001) as 'Year One' for the new discipline of Computer Game Studies. In the first decade of the twenty-first century there has been a succession of serious-minded, scholarly works whose cumulative impact has been to overturn the negative and complacent impressions of computer games that previously held sway. There are now several excellent textbook introductions to the field (Egenfeldt-Nielson et al. 2008; Mayra 2007; Newman 2002), many collections of essays by academics from all parts of the world where computer games are played and studied (Atkins and Krzywinska 2007; Wardrip-Fruin and Harrigan 2004; Wolf and Perron 2004) and at least two online journals (www.gamestudies.org; www.gamesandculture.com) devoted to the publication of new research. The new discipline has established itself in departments at many universities around the world, including the Game

Studies department at IT University in Copenhagen, where Taylor works, and is to some extent unified under a near global umbrella organization called the Digital Games Research Association (DiGRA). All these developments indicate that the computer game is securing recognition in academia as a cultural form that imposes its own demands on the would-be researcher.

Research in this period has shown that computer games are played by people of all ages and both sexes (Poole 2000) and are increasingly part of mainstream entertainment and media culture (Jenkins 2006). Moreover, computer games vary enormously in their content, from relatively crude 'fight' games to complex adventures with sophisticated plot lines (Wolf 2001). We even have educational games (Gee 2003), like *Palestine* – a game designed to teach young people about the Middle East conflict (Serious Games 2007). Given this, it is necessary to move critique of games forward from narrow-minded fixation on issues like violent content to more nuanced analysis and discussion of the sort formerly reserved for literature and artworks (Atkins 2003; Jones 2008) and towards sociological analysis of their wider significance (Burrill 2008). Works by Galloway (2006) and Bogost (2006) have begun to develop theoretical vocabularies with which to appraise computer games as a new form on the boundary of several established disciplines. This sea change in academic perceptions is by no means complete but, for younger scholars in particular, resistance to taking computer games seriously must seem increasingly anachronistic. The generation coming to sociological study in the second decade of this century will have no memory of a world where playing computer games was not a thoroughly normal part of growing up and of life. Controlling an avatar and having adventures in computer-generated environments are part of their cultural repertoire and it is entirely to be expected that the more sociologically inquisitive among them will want to question the significance of the activity and to study it properly.

The work just described has begun to make this possible, and it is in this context that Taylor's study should be understood. Indeed, referring to this newly emergent field, Taylor writes programmatically that 'in game studies … we would be well served to tease out specificities around not only different game genres but styles of play, forms of interaction/communication, and the various pleasures of gaming' (2006: 92). Taylor's work draws on ethnographic methods to reveal a complex social reality that is of the utmost significance to computer game studies and to sociology.

Play between Worlds

Play between Worlds is an exploration of how players of *EQ* make sense of their own activity and not an attempt to measure its 'impact' on their 'real lives'.

The central issue for Taylor is the avatar used by the player and the extent to which this carries or supports not an additional 'self' appended to the real one, but rather dimensions of self-hood within which symbolic projection, securing the recognition of others and experiencing personal development in a social setting are all factors. Her work is based on several years of participant observation as a player in *Norrath*, interviews with fellow players in both on- and offline settings and her participation at a 'Fan Faire' or player's convention hosted by Sony Online Entertainment in Boston. Drawing on these resources she is able to construct a rich portrait of the activities associated with game play, to explore the diverse motivations people have for playing and to examine the pleasures they derive from the activity. In this way, she provides a description of the world of play with *EQ* and conveys a sense of what playing the game means for its participants.

Taylor's key findings point us away from the idea that there is a dominant modality of experience that allows us to say what playing *EQ* means for 'most' players, or for the 'ideal type' of player. Rather, her explorations take us in the opposite direction towards a kind of decomposition of notions that we might take for granted as informing people's activities in a game environment. There are a number of senses in which this is so. First, the idea of the game as a bounded environment, within which we assume fantasy roles and 'play' (see, for example, Figure 2.1) and outside of which we cease doing these things and are restored to seriousness, turns out to be a misconception. Play does not occur within a 'magic circle' (Huizinga 1950) abstracted from society. Rather, 'the social aspects of the game drive its success and some of the pleasures derived from playing it' (Taylor 2006: 65). Taylor gives a striking illustration of how central communicative and collaborative practices are to play activities in *EQ* when she describes 'higher end areas [of *Norrath*] where a single monster can take upwards of 55 people to kill [it]' (ibid.: 30).

At the same time, elements of play and attitudes associated with it infuse conventional social space, providing a material basis for the development of social relationships and cultural life. Taylor describes how at the 'Fan Faire' in Boston, for example, participants wore badges proclaiming their in-game identities as elves or dwarves, which served as the basis for social connection. Similarly, friends and relatives who know each other offline come together in the game and help one another out with items and practical assistance. Helping people because you know them offline is referred to as 'twinking' within the game community. The evolution of a specific term within the game's informal lexicon is a sign of the frequency of the practice and Taylor writes that commonly 'families and friends bring social capital into the game space through pre-existing relationships' (ibid.: 53). She concludes that the boundary or distinction between the world of the game and that of social life generally is profoundly *porous*. Whatever novelty we find in terms of the configuration and organization of

Figure 2.1   Screenshot from *EverQuest*
Source: Sony Online Entertainment LLC.

social activity in the game cannot be assumed to be insulated from the rest of society but is almost certainly affected by and having effects on the world beyond the game.

Second, the game as technical artefact has developed in a way that reflects the importance of its social content to players and to the emergent culture that we find in *EverQuest*. This is particularly clear in the way that certain kinds of communication are catered for by the game program and in the mesh of these facilities with the emergent social and cultural practices of the game world. The clearest illustration of this is in 'player guilds'. Guilds are groups of players (the minimum number is ten (ibid.: 39)) who agree to combine for raids and other activities. Guilds form socially, through online encounters or because people have prior connections offline, and each one receives its own communications channel. Once a guild has been formed in this way, it has to conform to a hierarchical structure, with some players assuming a leadership role (ibid.: 43). Membership involves privileges in the form of improved gameplay – there are things you cannot achieve in the game as an isolated individual – but it also incurs obligations and responsibility to other guild members – you must provide assistance when asked, or risk expulsion (ibid.: 48–52). What we see here is that, just as social collaboration and coordination are essential to leverage certain parts of the functionality of the game program, so the program is a key factor shaping the kinds of social interaction that are possible in the game and the kinds of play that people can have with it. Technology and culture interact, reciprocally shaping one another.

Third, Taylor's investigation brings to light diverse social articulations of play, related to the diversity of players and their motivations. For some, *EQ* play is about strolling around in a fairly ineffectual way, perhaps enjoying the scenery and engaging with fighting and skills acquisition only to the extent necessary to maintain membership of one's guild (which is limited by the rule that the differences in skill level between highest and lowest ranking player cannot exceed a certain margin). In marked contrast to this variant of the play experience is that of the 'power gamer'. Power gamers, on Taylor's account, are involved in a profoundly instrumental relationship with the game program and its social world. Using special software called *ShowEQ*, many power gamers gain access to information about the current global state of the game world and use this perspective to their advantage. These kinds of strategies mean that they are often perceived by other gamers as a nuisance, or even as cheats, since they do not devote sufficient time to the niceties of social interaction and tend to convert game activities that should be pleasurable into repetitious tasks that are completed simply to improve one's ranking in connection with a given variable (e.g. strength, skill or magic). From a power gamer perspective, however, Taylor shows that more casual players are dilettantes who lack the ability or determination to really excel at the game. Power gamers see themselves as virtuosos.

Taylor's central research question is the issue of player embodiment through the avatar. She describes how her own initial choice of character type – she chose to be a gnome – had a number of consequences, only some of which could have been predicted. The aesthetics of her experience, for example, were different than if she had chosen a character type that lived above ground. When it came to teaming up with other players, it took longer for groups to recognize her particular contributions to collaborative projects because, unlike wizards for example, gnomes do not excel in any of the preassigned rankings. More subtly, Taylor reports that her choice to be a gnome inclined her to have a 'kind of instant playful bond with other gnomes' (ibid.: 54). Similarly, one of her respondents says that playing as a wood elf makes her want to be 'more cheery' and finds that other players treat her differently when she plays with this avatar than when she uses another kind (ibid.: 110). Just as in offline life, where the body is a 'cultural artifact ... through which our identities and social conventions are carried', so in 'shared virtual environments, how you choose to represent yourself has meaningful implications psychologically and socially' (ibid.: 117, 12).

Play Between Worlds advances a rich portrayal of *EQ*, which takes us across the fantasy landscapes of *Norrath* and into its emergent cultures, but also shows us computer-filled apartments of power gamers and hotel suites where guests play at being elves and gnomes. The overall effect of the book is to demonstrate that *EQ* is above all a social setting for play, within which people come together and find meaningful connection. This play is a deeply social activity and moreover it is fun largely because as players we are involved with other people and they are involved with us. At the same time, play works as a principle of exploration, of this social setting and of the game as a technical environment. It follows that the game and its pleasures are not hermetically sealed off from the rest of society. Rather, in practice, the boundary between them is profoundly porous and, Taylor argues, a central pleasure of gaming is precisely to play with it. This vision of what *EQ* is and why it appeals to people has important methodological implications. In particular, it raises the question of where we have to go in order to see and experience this world.

Achieving Authenticity

Ethnographic methods were first used by anthropologists who spent protracted periods as participant observers in the communities they were studying (Bryman 2004: 292). Ethnographic studies do not claim to generate factual truths that can be generated from a sample group onto the population as a whole, as in quantitative, survey-based sociology. Instead, they aim to provide an authentic account of a segment of social life in terms that disclose its meaning for the people who live it. This is only achieved if the author succeeds in convincing us that he or she has participated in the relevant symbolic processes, including securing the trust and confidence of the host population. In sociological uses of the method, the same effect is often produced by showing how boundaries that separate, or appear to separate, parts of the same society off from one another are actively produced and worked on by members of both the 'ingroup' and the broader society. The same principle of authenticity, therefore, is in play when Howard Becker (1963) describes the circle of marijuana-smoking jazz musicians in 1950s' America as when anthropologists describe life with an Amazonian tribe. In both cases, it works because the reader can appreciate the symbolic coherence of the alien environment for those whose lives are played out within it.

Two things are essential to achievement of this kind of authenticity. First, the researcher must convey a sense of the research site as a plausible social location. This means it must be coherent and bounded in such a way that we can understand how it is that people live there in the way described. Second, the characters in the study must be plausible human beings, recognizably like us apart from being members of an alien cultural situation. As we will see, these two aspects of authenticity are inseparable in practice but it is useful to distinguish them theoretically in terms of the question of the site of the investigation and of the reliability of respondents respectively. Both ideas face problems of implementation in online environments like *EQ*.

When planning an ethnography we would normally seek access to 'a social setting that is relevant to the research problem in which ... [we] are interested' (Bryman 2004: 294). It might seem as if this was a straightforward matter for Taylor: her site is the game world in *EQ*, the three-dimensional illusion on the gamers' computer screens. The emphasis on symbolic exchange and immersion seems to make online social environments highly conducive to this kind of meaning-oriented exploration. And indeed Taylor's work takes full advantage of the symbolic nature of the *EQ* game environment. This is clear, for example, in her analysis of avatar designs, which involves interpretation of colours and iconography as well as text. For example, she discusses gender-ambiguous avatars with girlish-sounding names like 'Mysticpurr', standing over slain dragons (Taylor 2006: 105) – scenes that combine overt femininity with signs of mastery and success in the game, which are commonly construed as masculine characteristics. Taylor uses this to question some of the dominant feminist criticisms of computer game design and culture. Here we see that the visual environment of *EQ* constitutes an invaluable symbolic resource for the researcher.

However, as Christine Hine points out, when it comes to virtual ethnography we are always dealing with two perspectives on the same set of activities. Virtual environments are spaces where people meet and interact and, as such, they resemble traditional sites of social interaction. But they are always also technical artefacts that people encounter in their broader, offline, cultural environments. What seems to be a convenient, technically delimited space is actually a potentially open-ended number of places in which it is being socially constructed as a plaything or a tool. As Hine puts it, virtual environments 'open up a space for thinking about ethnography as an experientially based way of knowing that need not aspire to produce a holistic study of a bounded culture' (Hine 2001: 10). In other words, when we are trying to make sense of players 'inside' *EQ* we are obliged to look at how they go about incorporating a technical system into their social lives.

Building on this methodological starting point, Taylor's work consistently demonstrates that the distinction or boundary between the real and virtual, the offline and online, worlds is not technologically determined but one that has to be worked at and produced by social actors. She writes that:

> While we sometimes imagine games as contained spaces and experiences in which a player sits down, examines the rules, and begins play, those like *EverQuest* seem to suggest a more complicated engagement. In large measure because of the multiplayer nature of the game, participants undergo a socialization process

and over time learn what it means to play far beyond what the manual or strict rules articulate.

(Taylor 2006: 32)

It follows that we want to know how people relate to *EQ* as an artefact as much as we want to see them playing in *Norrath*. In fact, each perspective will be integral to an adequate understanding of the issues raised by the other. Exploration of the culture of *EQ* shows that play with the game is indeed a *play between worlds*, as the title of Taylor's book emphasizes.

In conventional sites, resources like paper records and physical spaces, in which people are recognized and have publicly assigned roles, help us to create an authentic and credible context for the utterances, disclosures and reports of our respondents. But online environments provide other ways to achieve the same goal. These are both technical and social. As Taylor writes in an essay on methodology, having a good grasp of the online gaming research site entails some knowledge of technology:

Knowing how to log online interview sessions and take screen shots, as well as dealing with consent forms and more subtle issues of pacing/multi-threaded conversations is necessary. Staying abreast of the latest software your participants are using is also important. I make a point to always follow up and at least check out new software programs ... community members are using ... A researcher must be willing to try new techniques and work on learning the conventions and norms the worlds and software entails. Just as good note-taking is crucial in ethnographic work, online researchers must be adept with the software tools they use.

(Taylor 1999: 10)

Taylor uses email interviews, meetings in the game space, internet discussion boards and distinctively electronic resources like signature files appended to avatars to build a record of the game space and its culture. These methods do not merely mirror research practices in traditional settings, but actually offer potential advantages over them. For example, electronic logs clearly surpass the reliability of the ethnographer's handwritten diary. As well as technical skills, the virtual ethnographer also has to adapt practically to the environment. This involves cultivating habits – like always saving to a local machine in case the Web content gets deleted – and skills of memory relevant to retaining a mental picture of individuals who may appear on-screen in disparate visual representations. The upshot of these methods is what Taylor calls a 'multi-channeled' (ibid.: 9) system of data acquisition that results in a convincing, integrated picture of the *EQ* world.

The *EQ* research site now appears to be less a function of a technically delimited 'virtual space' and more a matter of the beliefs and orientations (to play, to socialize) of dispersed individuals. As Taylor puts it, '*EQ* is not one singular game but an artifact developed over time by many actors' (2006: 41). Clearly, this places extra strain on the second aspect of authenticity, namely the reliability of Taylor's respondents. In a sense, this is true for all ethnographic studies whose boundaries are not neatly coincident with some geographical location – Becker's musicians were 'on the road'. However, the problem of reliability becomes intensified when the central symbolic processes are online. As already mentioned, Sherry Turkle (1995) viewed online environments as inherently problematic to research because people used them to play with identity – to experiment with how others perceived them and with their own ability to assume different roles. If online roles are essentially experimental and these environments allow, even encourage, people to misrepresent themselves to one another then how are we to establish the real significance of their activities? We need reliable informants, participants in the field whom we can trust, and not inconstant characters who are toying with us and themselves.

Turkle's solution was to meet the people involved in her study in real life (RL), which she acknowledges is a 'real life bias' (ibid.: 324); but she justifies this by saying that her interest is primarily focused on the impact of C-M-C on how people really live. However, this approach seems a little outmoded since we are no longer habituated to thinking of C-M-C as something new, impacting on our real lives. The massive growth in the use of online environments, including game spaces, social networking sites, blogs, vlogs, and so on, since the mid-1990s, means that online social activity *is* a large part of real social life. As Anjali Puri (2007) puts it, 'cyberculture is increasingly a part of and overlaps with offline culture'. Taylor also questions whether the conditions of reliability and validity are intrinsically better in traditional, offline settings. She points out that 'there are many things that even in an off-line interview we must take at the interviewee's word', and, since ethnographers are particularly concerned with the subjective import of experience and activity, the relevant 'validity questions may be equally unverifiable off-line' (1999: 7, 8).

However, the unique anonymity conditions of life on the Web mean that we cannot see how to tell if, for example, several of Taylor's fellow gamers might all be the same person, or if the views they express are sincere. All online research faces the potential difficulty that respondent mendacity might undermine its validity. In her paper, Puri (2007) makes four recommendations that researchers can follow to improve the representativeness of data gathered online: (1) use online locations where people provide 'user profiles' (which rules out most chat rooms); (2) 'use content of individual posts to assess consistency over time, and also "fit" with stated profile' (ibid.: 11); (3) carry out the research in more than one online space to enable cross-referencing of findings; and (4) 'occasionally establish direct contact with the subjects of study' (ibid.). These recommendations are intended for people using the internet to collect market research data, but it is clear that they respond to issues that also arise in Taylor's research.

Taylor addresses the problem of reliability in ways that correspond to Puri's recommendations. First, while games might seem to resemble chat rooms, in that they are relatively open spaces in which 'real' identity is deliberately concealed, the player avatar is a point of constancy that has no parallel in other online environments. Gamers invest effort in designing them and, even if they do switch between them, it is possible to record the behaviours of an individual avatar over a series of encounters and thereby form an assessment of his or her character, including his or her motivations for playing. Taylor also analyses player posts on game discussion boards and, as we have seen, she checks reliability by identifying her respondents offline, in their homes and at the Fan Faires mentioned above. All of this facilitates cross-referencing that obviates the need to prioritize 'offline' aspects of *EQ* as being 'more real'.

By developing a file on each avatar included in her study, Taylor is able to establish consistency and pattern, as well as an evolving record of who associates with whom in the various *EQ* sites. Each file constitutes a kind of map of that avatar's life in the game and enables the researcher to move beyond a search for consistency towards a richer concern with pattern. As Taylor puts it, 'my file for an individual would list their offline information, as well as all their various avatars or textual bodies (often images or descriptions of them I could refer to were helpful as well)' (1999: 5). Indeed, on this basis, Taylor finds it possible to work out, with a fair degree of certainty, when multiple avatars trace back to the same individual player. Construction of a file on each player-character in the study enables her to situate her respondents in a broader web of social meanings and is a key device in assuring us of their reliability.

The Ethics of Playing with Disclosure

Taylor's innovative approach to the issue of authenticity and representativeness raises other difficult questions, especially concerning the ethics of this type of research. There are three related issues that need to be considered here: (1) when should a researcher disclose what he or she is doing to those around him or her? (2) Which online materials may be gathered as 'data' for social research? (3) Under what conditions is it necessary for a researcher to gain the consent of the people being researched?

In mapping the on- and offline lives of her subjects, Taylor explores the question of identity and, in particular, the ways in which being a player in *EQ* contributes to a person's sense of self and how others perceive him or her. Identity in this sense is a key concept for ethnography, since we are concerned with public symbolization processes whereby individuals are differentiated and integrated into society. People project different selves in different places – work that involves real bodies and (now) avatars – and they negotiate the variety of responses they encounter to produce and sustain a viable sense of themselves and their place(s) in society. How these multiple channels of selfhood are managed is part of the challenge of being a person in the modern world and it may be something that people are more aware of doing than they were in previous historical periods – a change sociologists have grasped in terms of increased reflexivity and risk (Beck 1992; Giddens 1990).

In this context, the online/offline distinction may vary in salience and significance for individuals. Indeed, Taylor says, part of the fun of playing a game like *EQ* lies precisely at this level of disclosure and sharing information with other players. Discussing the fact that players commonly use more than one avatar, she writes that

> rather than keeping identities secret from one another, it is not uncommon for players to know who their friends' alternate characters are. There are exceptions to this of course (sometimes people only share such information with a select group) but overall the terrain of identity play in *EQ* is something more akin to parallel or linked character threads than firm persona boundaries.
>
> (Taylor 2006: 96)

This highlights an important way in which social processes inform the play of *EQ*. Taylor makes the methodological decision to work with these processes of mutual disclosure, and in a sense they become her method as she participates, observes and records what goes on in *EQ*. Which name you choose and to whom you disclose it, which character you choose and with which players you want to play with it, are questions integral to playing the game. Identity here is multidimensional and part of the play. Revealing that you are a university professor to people who have only previously known you as an elf is not a straightforward revelation but potentially opens out onto a whole new set of perceptions, shared ideas, shattered prejudices, and so on.

In an important sense, what people are playing with is the social dimension of selfhood – the processes of disclosure and recognition that constitute us as selves in the first place. In other words, the fact that much of game play concerns the communicative dynamics of self-presentation and self-maintenance becomes a methodological resource that can be exploited by the sociologist. However, if the communicative dynamics of the game and the immersion of the researcher in a community in this way are strengths of Taylor's study, it is clear that these processes are also potentially problematic in other ways. Taylor does not say in *Play Between Worlds* when it was that she chose to disclose to people that she was a social researcher. It seems to have been a matter for judgement, based on the details of each specific relationship and situation. Moreover, for some time when she started playing the game Taylor says she wasn't actually researching but simply playing, so that this disclosure didn't present itself as an issue; but then, presumably, it actually became one once the decision was taken to use her experiences as the basis for a research project. Taylor seems to have negotiated this transition as one would in any social situation wherein one wants to affect a shift in the nature of one's association with colleagues or friends, namely by discussing it with them. If people were unhappy with the turn of events then presumably they were left out of the study.

However, this means that Taylor ran the risk of harming her respondents, in the very narrow sense that a person who did not want to be researched may have experienced the revelation that they were being so as a rupture in their social experience of the game. It is important to notice here that the many strengths of *Play Between Worlds* and especially the uniquely detailed and vivid portrait it provides of an online culture, would not have been possible without Taylor having been immersed in the game world and having a certain status as a player who was a member of a known guild and who clearly could hold her own in raids and other game activities. In this sense, her dilemmas are those of traditional covert participant observation, complicated by the multi-channelled nature of the online environment – the fact that Taylor and everyone else can assume different avatars, for example, and that you can discover things about people during in-game encounters, but also by reading their posts on game forums.

Generally, we assess the ethical justification of not telling people we are researching according to a principle of proportionality between the possibility of generating the knowledge we are seeking and its value on one side and the harm that might be done by deception on the other. It is, of course, important that even when covert strategies are used our unknowing participants have their anonymities protected, and Taylor points out that she changes both real names and avatar names of everyone who appears in the book, which ensures this. There is clearly a tension between the immersion that is essential to authenticity and the ethical principle that we should be open and honest about our activities. As we have seen, in online environments one has to move with the communicative dynamics of the environment we are in. To interrupt this process with disclosures that might result in people treating you differently would compromise the research. This is perhaps especially true when people are 'playing'.

There is currently little agreement on the ethical principles regulating the gathering of online data. In the early days of internet research it was argued that the public nature of cyberspace locations (chat rooms, bulletin boards) meant that anything people did online – all their data traces – were in principle useable, so long as researchers anonymized material before publication (Paccagnella 1997). However, this line of argument was questioned in connection with MUDs, as it became apparent that participants could be identified from descriptions of their characters and behaviours, regardless of name changes (Jankowski and van Selm 2007: 278). Moreover, it could not be plausibly applied to an online space like *EQ* because it is password protected and you have to pay to gain entry: *EQ* is private property. Some work on this issue has suggested a spectrum of types of discourse to be found online, with academic discussion lists considered thoroughly public and quotable, while support groups meeting online to discuss sensitive topics would be considered off-limits to researchers (ibid.). However, games and gamers do not feature in these discussions and it is difficult to see where ludic acts, like clubbing together with other elves to kill a dragon, might fall on this continuum of communicative acts and their contents. Although we might feel that *EQ* is private, it is still an entertainment medium and researchers would (rightly) bristle at the suggestion that we should not be permitted to analyse television shows, for example, because they are owned by entertainment corporations. Considerations like this lead one ethics committee to conclude that 'no definitive, single set of ethical guidelines is possible for a field as diverse as internet research' (cited in ibid.: 279).

Similar ambiguities concern the issue of consent as this arises in the special conditions of an online game. As Winnicott (1971) points out, play always takes place in a 'possibility space' for the self; it is inherently experimental and, as such, potentially sensitive as it concerns peoples' personal development. Playing a computer game involves a state of mind in which people allow exposure to parts of their characters that are normally repressed and concealed. Taylor's thesis, of course, is that play in *EQ* is not a separate, bounded space in this way, but she does not address other, psychological characterizations of play in the book. However, Sherry Turkle discerns discomfort in some of her role-playing MUD respondents, which she says can be both an integral part of why they are involved in the activity and a reason for not wanting other people, not themselves in play mode, to take an interest in it. There is, so to speak, an underside to Taylor's thesis that people are playing with disclosure and identity, which is that this activity is also linked to the dynamics of repression and personal development – themes that are much more foregrounded in Turkle's (1995) discussion. The methodological principle of playing with disclosure is perhaps inherently contentious from an ethical perspective.

On the other hand, it can equally be argued that traditional kinds of consent to be researched and to have one's actions reported or comments cited are unavailable to internet researchers, for the reason that we do not know anything about the people we meet in virtual worlds. As a report for the American

Society for the Advancement of Science points out, the equivalent to signing a consent form online 'would be a click to a statement such as "I agree to the above consent form". But how valid is such consent when the age, competency, or comprehension of the potential subject is unknown?' (cited in Jankowski and van Selm 2007: 278). Given that such issues can only be addressed in the course of playing the game, it makes sense to read Taylor's work as a case of 'emergent ethics' (Charmaz 2008).

Emergent ethics holds that rules of good conduct may be constructed in the course of a research process. They are generated out of the, albeit occasionally conflicting, goals of researchers and participants. According to Kathy Charmaz (2008), ethical questions arise in ambiguous situations, and they cannot be predicted or controlled for with reference to formalized principles brought to the situation from outside. The tension mentioned above between immersion and ethics is perhaps an instance of a more general one between the search for contextual understanding that drives qualitative research and the emphasis on general principles that define traditional ethics. 'Emergent ethics' allows us to overcome this by thinking of ethical conduct as something that is itself context-specific. This applies to Taylor's research particularly well because a central finding is that different aspects of the *EQ* experience are important to different kinds of players. Protecting the interests of the community of *EQ*, which, as Scharf (1999: 253) points out should be a primary concern of ethical research, cannot be defined in advance of discussions in the field. We see this most clearly in her discussion of power gamers and their use of the *ShowEQ* software, which might have been excluded from discussion from a less grounded perspective than Taylor's, on the grounds that it might promote 'cheating'. A more formalized ethical perspective would lead us to view forms of misbehaviour, like *ShowEQ* or sharing avatars (forbidden by the game's rules), with suspicion because they might form a threat to the game community – there is no a priori moral or ethical scheme in which cheating or rule breaking is viewed favourably! In fact the whole issue of cheating in computer games is one that is constantly being reworked and negotiated by players and designers (see Consalvo 2007), and the ramifications of this, including whether a researcher should do it or not, for *EQ* could only be understood through negotiation and discussion with other members of the community. Taylor's handling of this issue is a clear case of emergent ethics, on Charmaz's definition.

Conclusion

We have seen that Taylor's work addresses a number of important methodological issues for contemporary sociology. Her research practice highlights the availability, within computer-supported environments, of a new range of techniques and tools that, while not constructed with sociologists in mind, are certainly useful tools – email interviews, game logs and signature files are all examples of this. At the same time, these environments pose particular problems for the ethnographic researcher. Anonymity and a seeming lack of reliability attaching to the identity of respondents require us to think imaginatively about the places we are in and the people we are interacting with. Their identities and actions have to be assessed on somewhat different terms than if we encountered them in a traditional setting. Taylor gives us suggestive ideas about how to overcome these problems, working with the plays on identity and disclosure that are already part of the gameness of *EQ*, for instance, and the development of files that map player-character behaviours. Centrally, she invites us to give up the priority of 'real world' relations and to stop thinking of technology and artefacts as impacting on the latter and instead to favour a more nuanced approach that allows for a more dispersed sense of the social field. There are limitations to this line of argument, of course, and some questions remain to be answered.

Taylor's work stands as a pioneering, critical investigation of a relatively new field of social relations. It breaks down the common-sense idea of the online game or world as a bounded entity and shows how its reality is deeply meshed with the rest of social reality. At the same time Taylor describes novel technological affordances that are important in the contemporary context where communications technologies are constantly reconfiguring social and cultural practice. Finally, *Play Between Worlds* positions play as the central mediating category, enabling people to develop new social and cultural connections while at the same time testing technological limits. Taylor's work is a major contribution to contemporary sociology and to the burgeoning discipline of computer game studies, as well as to both our substantive understanding of computer games as social and cultural objects and to the development of methodological frameworks for social scientific enquiry appropriate to a world that is increasingly constituted out of technology.

Additional Reading

E. Castranova's *Synthetic Worlds: The Business and Culture of Online Games* (2005) is the best account of the political economy of online games like *EverQuest* and one of the best explorations of the economic significance of computer games generally. C. Hine's edited book, *Virtual Methods: Issues in Social Research on the Internet* (2005), updates her seminal investigation. This collection of important essays discusses a growing range of methodological issues faced by researchers working in online environments. S. Turkle's *Life on the Screen: Identity on the Internet* (1995) draws on ideas from psychoanalysis as well as sociology, and she opens to us a series of questions that remain central to this area of research. B. Wolf and B. Perron, in their collection, *The Video Game Theory Reader* (2004), present a range of mainly theoretical perspectives on the computer game as a social and cultural object.

Acknowledgements

I would like to thank T. L. Taylor, Fiona Devine and Sue Heath for helpful comments and suggestions on earlier drafts of this chapter.

References

Aarseth, E. (2001) 'Computer game studies: Year One', editorial in *Game Studies*, 1(1). Available at http://www.gamestudies.org.

Atkins, B. (2003) *More than a Game*, Manchester: Manchester University Press.

Atkins, B. and T. Krzywinska (2007) *Videogame, Player, Text*, Manchester: Manchester University Press.

Beck, U. (1992) *Risk Society*, London: Sage.

Becker, H. (1963) *Outsiders: Studies in the Sociology of Deviance*, New York: Free Press.

Bogost, I. (2006) *Unit Operations: Towards a Comparative Video Game Criticism*, London: MIT Press.

Bryman, A. (2004) *Social Research Methods*, Oxford: Oxford University Press.

Burrill, D. (2008) *Die Tryin' Videogames, Masculinity and Culture*, New York: Peter Lang.

Castronova, E. (2005) *Synthetic Worlds: The Business and Culture of Online Games*, Chicago: Chicago University Press.

Charmaz, K. (2008) 'Emergent ethics in qualitative research', presentation to ESRC Research Methods Festival, University of Oxford, June 2008.

Consalvo, M. (2007) *Cheating: Gaining Advantage in Videogames*, London: MIT Press.

Dibbell, J. (1999) *My Tiny Life: Life and Passion in a Virtual World*, London: Fourth Estate.

Egenfeldt-Nielsen, S., J.H. Smith and S.P. Tosca (2008) *Understanding Video Games: The Essential Introduction*, London: Routledge.

Galloway, A. (2006) *Gaming: Essays on Algorithmic Culture*, Minneapolis, University of Minnesota Press.

Gee, J.P. (2003) *What Video Games Have to Teach us about Learning and Literacy*, Basingstoke: Palgrave.

Gere, C. (2000) *Digital Culture*, London: Reaktion Books.

Giddens, A. (1990) *The Consequences of Modernity*, Cambridge: Polity.

Habermas, J. (1992) *The Theory of Communicative Action, vol. 2: The Critique of Functionalist Reason*, Cambridge: Polity Press.

Herring, S. (1994) 'Gender differences in computer-mediated communication: bringing familiar baggage to the new frontier', keynote talk, American Library Association, Miami. Available at http://www.cpsr.org/cpsr/gender/herring.txt.

Hine, C. (2001) *Virtual Ethnography*, London: Routledge.

Hine, C. (2005) *Virtual Methods: Issues in Social Research on the Internet*, Oxford: Berg.

Huizinga, J. (1950) *Homo Ludens: A study of the Play Element in Culture*, Boston: Beacon Press.

Jankowski, N.W. and M. van Selm (2007) 'Research ethics in a virtual world: guidelines and illustrations', in Carpentier, N. Pruulmann-Vengerfeldt, Nordenstreng, P., Hartmann, K., Vihaleman, M., Cammaerts, P. and Nieminem, H. (eds), *Media Technologies and Democracy in an Enlarged Europe: The Intellectual Work of the 2007 European Media and Communication Doctoral Summer School*, Tartu: Tartu University Press.

Jenkins, H. (2006) *Fans, Bloggers and Gamers: Essays on Participatory Culture*, New York: New York University Press.

Jones, S. (2008) *The Meaning of Video Games: Gaming and Textual Strategies*, London: Routledge.

Kirkpatrick, G. (2008) *Technology and Social Power*, Basingstoke: Palgrave Macmillan.

Klevjer, R. (2006) 'What is the avatar? Fiction and embodiment in avatar-based single player computer games', doctoral thesis, University of Bergen.

Levy, S. (1984) *Hackers: Heroes of the Computer Revolution*, Harmondsworth: Penguin.

Mayra, F. (2007) *An Introduction to Game Studies*, London: Sage.

McKenzie, D. and J. Wajcman (1999) *The Social Shaping of Technology*, Milton Keynes: Open University Press.

Mead, G.H. (1967 [1934]) *Mind, Self and Society*, Chicago: Chicago University Press.

Newman, J. (2002) *Videogames*, London: Routledge.

Paccagnella, L. (1997) 'Getting the seats of your pants dirty: strategies for ethnographic research in virtual communities', in *Journal of Computer Mediated Communication*, 3 (June).

Poole, S. (2000) *Trigger Happy: The Inner Life of Video Games*, London: Fourth Estate.

Puri, A. (2007) 'Web of insights: the art and practice of webnography', in *International Journal of Market Research*, 49(3).

Scharf (1999) 'Beyond netiquette: the ethics of doing naturalistic discourse analysis on the internet', in S. Jones (ed), *Doing Internet Research: Critical Issues and Methods for Examining the Internet*, Thousand Oaks, CA: Sage.

Stallabrass, J. (1996) *Gargantua*, London: Verso.

Taylor, T.L. (1999) 'Life in virtual worlds: plural existence, multimodalities, and other online research challenges', *American Behavioral Scientist*, 43(3), 436–49.

Taylor, T.L. (2006) *Play Between Worlds: Exploring Online Game Culture*, Cambridge, MA: MIT Press.

Turkle, S. (1995) *Life on the Screen: Identity on the Internet*, New York: Simon & Schuster.

Wardrip-Fruin, N. and P. Harrigan (eds) (2004) *First Person: New Media as Story, Performance and Game*, London: MIT Press.

Winnicott D.W. (1971) *Playing and Reality*, London: Tavistock.

Wolf, M. (2001) *The Medium of the Videogame*, Austin: University of Texas Press.

Wolf, M. and B. Perron (2004) *The Video Game Theory Reader*, London: Routledge.

CHAPTER 3

Crime:
Edgar et al.'s *Prison Violence*

ALICE MILLS

This chapter focuses on the study of violence in prisons as revealed by the research of Kimmett Edgar, Ian O'Donnell and Carol Martin. Conducting research in prison settings presents a variety of methodological challenges, some unique to the prison context, but others which are equally applicable to other research settings. Alice Mills first considers the use by Edgar et al. of a mixed method approach in their research, and whilst she highlights the strengths of such a research design she also notes the lack of a clearly stated rationale for adopting a mixed method design on the part of the research team. Mills's second theme relates to the methodological challenges of conducting victimization surveys, including some of the specific challenges of conducting surveys of this nature in prison settings. Finally, Mills draws attention to Edgar et al.'s innovative use of a research instrument called the 'escalator'. She concludes that, despite some missed opportunities along the way, Edgar et al. have made a valuable contribution to research on violence in prisons.

Introduction

For most of us, the prospect of being locked up in prison is a very frightening one. In addition to the obvious loss of freedom, imprisonment entails many hardships, including isolation from family, friends and other sources of support, the loss of personal autonomy and the deprivation of material goods. Being incarcerated also involves living at close quarters with many different individuals whom one does not know and whose behaviour one cannot predict, with little opportunity to escape their company. As one of the prisoners in Sykes's study of a New Jersey maximum security prison so deftly surmised, 'the worst thing about prison is you have to live with other prisoners' (Sykes 1958: 77). Despite the introduction of anti-bullying policies and institutional targets to reduce the number of serious assaults (HM Prison Service 2007), violence, albeit usually of a fairly mundane nature, remains an everyday occurrence in most prison establishments in England and Wales.

Prison Violence seeks to examine and explain the nature and extent of inter-personal violence between prisoners, such as assaults, threats, robbery and bullying. It is based upon two different studies carried out between 1992 and 2002 whilst the researchers – Kimmett Edgar, Ian O'Donnell and Carol Martin – were, at various periods, employed at the University of Oxford Centre for Criminological Research. The first study, known throughout the book as the 'victimization study', was funded by the Home Office. The second, the 'conflicts study', which grew out of the first, was funded by the Economic and Social Research Council (ESRC) as part of their Violence Research Programme. Numerous publications have been produced from this research, and in *Prison Violence* Edgar et al. aim to weave these two studies together in one text to provide a deeper understanding of how often and why violence occurs and to consider how violence in prisons might be prevented. To do this, they use a unique 'conflict-centred approach', which sets violence in the context of conflict to investigate the circumstances and processes out of which violent acts emerge, such as the tensions which might have driven prisoners into dispute. Guided by a symbolic interactionist perspective, which emphas-ises 'the subjective meanings individuals attribute to their activities and their environments' (Flick, 2006: 66), Edgar et al. explore the interpretations and intentions of the parties involved to ascertain the meanings of violence for them and how each person's actions influenced the reactions of the other party. Unlike previous studies of prison life and culture which have made lit-tle comment on how the ever-present risk of violence can structure social rel-ations between prisoners, Edgar et al. seek to understand violence not as an isolated act, but as a process with a history and a future.

In the next section, Edgar et al.'s work is located in the context of previous methodological approaches to the study of prisons and imprisonment and debates about prisoner behaviour and violence in prisons. The methods used by Edgar et al. are then discussed, along with a summary of their substantive findings. I then examine three relevant methodological issues: the use of a mixed method approach; the problems and pitfalls of using a victimization survey to measure violence; and Edgar et al.'s use of the 'escalator' tool to examine the development of conflicts. Within *Prison Violence* itself the authors employ a deliberate strategy of limiting discussion of methodological issues in order to free up as much as of the text as possible to concentrate on the per-spectives of prisoners so as to 'lower the barriers between the reader and the lived reality of prison violence' (Edgar et al. 2003a: 3). Other publications resulting from the two studies which provide valuable insights into various aspects of the research methodology will therefore also have to be drawn upon alongside *Prison Violence*, notably Edgar et al. (2003b).

Researching Prisons and Prison Violence

Within the sociology of crime and deviance, prison sociology is a relatively new field of study, with the first major study of imprisonment in the UK published in the 1960s (Morris et al. 1963). In a recent review of the sociology of imprisonment, Crewe argues that prisons have become the subject of much sociological enquiry, as they illustrate

> many of the discipline's primary concerns: power, inequality, order, conflict and socialization ... The prison's distinctive qualities ... are such that its inner world provides particularly striking illustrations of a range of social phenomena, from resistance and adaptation to exploitation and collective organization.
>
> (Crewe 2007: 123)

Many early studies of imprisonment were centred on particular institutions (Jacobs 1977; Mathieson 1965; Morris et al. 1963; Sykes 1958) and were studied through the 'sustained immersion' (Crewe 2005: 179) of the researcher in the field. Perhaps the most well-known classic study of imprisonment is Sykes's (1958) *The Society of Captives*, a US study which gave rise to a number of key debates about the nature of social life in prisons and determinants of prisoner behaviour. In this text, Sykes examines the psychological and organizational dynamics of life in a maximum security prison in New Jersey, including the composition and functions of the 'inmate code': the set of values and norms which were said to guide prisoners' behaviour. He also details five 'deprivations' or 'pains of imprisonment' – liberty, goods and services, heterosexual relations (although obviously not experienced as a deprivation by non-heterosexual prisoners), autonomy and personal security – and proposes that the internal prisoner subculture and prisoners' adaptive responses to their incarceration, including violence, could be explained by the prisoners' need to ameliorate these deprivations. Against this 'deprivation' model of prison adjustment (see also Goffman 1968), in the 'importation' model it is argued that prisoner subcultures and behaviours are influenced by the values and norms that prisoners import into prisons from the outside world (Irwin and Cressey 1962). Most commentators now acknowledge the need to use an integrative model which recognizes that some aspects of the prison culture and prisoner reactions to imprisonment are brought from outside, whilst others are unique to the conditions of confinement.

In the last 30 years the amount and range of research into prison life has grown alongside the ever expanding criminal justice system. Contemporary prison sociology in the UK has addressed a wide variety of different aspects of imprisonment and social groups within prison, such as suicide and self-harm (Liebling 1992), prisoner values and the inmate code (Crewe 2005), prison regimes (King and McDermott 1995), medical power and prison healthcare practitioners (Sim 1990, 2002), prison officers (Crawley 2004), prisoners' use of media (Jewkes 2002), order and social control in prisons (Sparks et al. 1996) and the social life and culture of particular establishments (Genders and Player 1995). These studies have used an assortment of different methods, often in combination, including large-scale surveys, qualitative interviews, focus groups and documentary analysis. Notably, almost all have also involved researchers attempting to emulate the early, classic studies of imprisonment by spending considerable amounts of time in the research establishments, often before other research methods are deployed, engaging in what DiIulio (1987) has termed 'soaking and poking': observing the day-to-day regime and talking and listening to prisoners and staff. This allows researchers to not only view the social phenomena and events under study, both in action and in context (Crewe 2005: 179), but also to build a full understanding of the dynamic of the prison's social life (Sparks et al. 1996: 113), the roles and expectations of the actors within the social setting and to learn the prison argot. Furthermore, 'doing time' in this way can allow researchers to become 'part of the furniture', to ensure that prisoners and staff feel able to act in their normal way in the researcher's presence, to build up trust and dispel any suspicions that respondents may have about the research.

Violence and victimization are widely acknowledged as being endemic in prisons and as such have attracted a significant amount of research interest, with recent studies examining the effects of different aspects of the prison regime and environment on violence (Cooke 1989, 1991; Sparks et al. 1996), fear and personal safety (Adler 1994), bullying amongst prisoners (Ireland 2005) and the influence of masculinity in sustaining a culture of violence in male prisons (Sim 1994). Traditionally, researchers measuring the extent of victimization in prison have relied upon official prison records of disciplinary offences, which report the number of times inmates have been found to have breached the prison disciplinary rules. However, these official data substantially understate 'the extent of violent victimization among inmates' (Bottoms 1999: 222), as they consist only of those offences that come to the attention of the authorities and are officially processed as disciplinary offences. Victimization surveys have therefore been used to attempt to uncover the 'dark figure' of victimization in prisons. The strengths and limitations of this method and its utilization by Edgar et al. will be discussed later in this chapter.

Explanations for violent behaviour in prison are customarily described as falling into one of two camps. Researchers from psychological backgrounds have sought to account for violence in prison with reference to the internal personal characteristics of individual aggressors, such as biological or psychological traits (Megargee 1982; Williams and Longley 1987). Those who take a more sociological perspective have emphasized the importance of social and situational factors, such as the deprivations and frustrations of prison life, whereby physical force may be used to obtain goods and services, and the dominant culture of masculinity in which prisoners are required to demonstrate their strength through aggression and toughness (Cooke 1991; Sykes 1958). However, whilst internal dispositions are rarely powerful enough to determine actions in all situations, no environment alone can ordain the action people take and produce identical responses from individuals (Zamble and Porporino 1988). It is thus now commonplace to seek to explain prison violence using an interactionist approach. This should consider both individual and environmental factors and recognize (i) that the environment's effect on behaviour is mediated by the way prisoners interpret and respond to their situation, which may be in turn influenced by their individual psychology, and (ii) that prisoners and staff themselves shape the nature of the prison setting (Bottoms 1999). Bottoms, however, argues that researchers following interactionist approaches have 'rarely addressed the minutiae of the average prison day, or considered in detail how violence can arise within this social order' (ibid.: 212). This challenge is taken up by Edgar et al. in *Prison Violence*, who not only take the unusual step of focusing on mundane, 'everyday' incidents of violence between prisoners, but also seek to examine the context of microrelations from which this violence emerges.

Prison Violence

In order to 'make the world of problematic lived experience of ordinary people directly available to the reader' (Denzin 1989: 7) and to capture the dynamic process of interaction between the individual and the prison setting, Edgar et al. use a combination of methodological techniques including surveys, interviews and documentary analysis. In both studies, they also spent hundreds of hours in the research prisons, simply observing life on the wings, learning about the day to day operation of the prison regime and the nuances of prison culture.

The victimization study took place in two prisons for adult males and two male young offender institutions and consisted of two stages. First, a large-scale survey was conducted with 1,566 prisoners to measure the extent of crime in custody. This asked prisoners' about their personal experiences, as victims and victimizers, of six types of victimization – assault, hurtful verbal abuse, exclusion, cell theft, robbery and threat of violence – in the previous month and whether they had witnessed any victimization of others. Feelings of personal safety and views of bullying and its prevention were also covered. All prisoners were approached as to whether they wished to participate and the survey achieved a high overall response rate of 90 per cent.

Second, 'structured' interviews were held with 61 prisoners who had been identified as having had experience of victimization in their current prison within the last month and with 31 others who had victimized others in the previous month in order to examine their motivations and techniques of exploitation. The majority of the perpetrators were identified as such by their residence on a unit for 'bullies', with a small number being recruited through personal contact with the researchers at the time of the questionnaire distribution or through being named by another victimizer. In addition, a broadly representative purposive sample of 111 staff was interviewed to discover how often they were informed about victimization and how they responded when such complaints were made. Although the interviews are described as 'structured' (Edgar et al. 2003a:16), participants appear to have had a considerable degree of flexibility in recounting their experiences, as demonstrated by the long quotes from the interviews presented in the text. Prisoners' accounts of their experiences were verified where possible by cross-checking them with reports from other prisoners and staff and from official sources such as wing observation logs and inmate files.

The conflicts study included several different prisoner populations, as it took place in four different institutions: three institutions for male prisoners – consisting of a high security prison, a local, multifunctional prison and a young offender institution – and a women's prison. A face to face survey was conducted with 590 prisoners, which aimed to determine the impact of violence in prison by asking respondents about their experiences and views of such violence. It was based on an opportunity sample, with some participants being recommended by staff and others being identified from records of disciplinary proceedings.

Prisoners identified by the survey as having been recently involved in conflicts were then invited to participate in an in-depth interview. This was carried out with 209 prisoners and covered 141 incidents. The interviews consisted of a combination of techniques which enabled Edgar et al. 'to interpret conflict situations from the perspective of those who were directly involved, and to recreate the context from which violence emerged' (ibid.: 20). Over 100 questions were asked about the incident to build a complete picture of what happened, including the circumstances under which the conflict arose and how this led to violence, or alternatively how violence was avoided. An analytic tool known as the 'escalator' (Alternatives to Violence Education

Committee 1996) was also used to gauge fully the sequence of events and to break the interaction into its component parts. Additionally, 51 witnesses were interviewed, primarily to clarify the sequence of events where there were discrepancies between the accounts of the two parties directly involved.

Far from violence being a break in the usual social order of a prison, Edgar et al. found that prisons seem to cope with a high rate of fights and assaults. Tables 3.1 and 3.2 indicate the prevalence of victimization among young offenders and adult prisoners, and the extent of self-reported victimizing behaviour, respectively.

From these tables it can be seen that neither victimization nor assault behaviour are limited to a small minority of prisoners. On the basis of these findings, Edgar et al. (2003a) argue that the experience of being insulted, assaulted or threatened is so frequent as to be a routine part of prison life and a formative aspect of the prison social structure. However, it is likely to have a destabilizing impact on the 'good order' of prison communities.

The victimization study also revealed the functions and purposes of the different forms of victimization and how these activities shape the world of

Table 3.1   Percentage of prisoners reporting experiencing victimization in the previous month

Type of victimization	All young offenders	All adults
Assault	30	19
Threat of violence	44	26
Robbery	10	4
Cell theft	27	34
Hurtful verbal abuse	56	26
Exclusion	18	7

Source: Adapted from Edgar et al. (2003a: 30).

Table 3.2   Percentage of prisoners reporting victimizing behaviour in the previous month

Type of victimization	All young offenders	All adults
Assault	32	16
Threat of violence	39	19
Robbery	11	5
Cell theft	8	3
Hurtful verbal abuse	43	16
Exclusion	13	3

Source: Adapted from Edgar et al. (2003a: 31).

the prisoner. For example, verbal abuse could be used to test a prisoner's strength of will, to gain dominance over weaker prisoners and to isolate the victim from a potential support base. Assaulting another prisoner might help the attacker to establish his status or toughness, could relieve tension between prisoners or function as a form of revenge (which was often linked with robbery). In such a dangerous environment, how prisoners respond to the ever-present risk of violence can determine how often they will be victimized – as to show weakness may make them vulnerable to sustained and systematic exploitation (Edgar et al. 2003a: 54).

Unlike previous portrayals of prison life, which have tended to assign prisoners to the status of either victim or victimizer, Edgar et al. (ibid.: 64) found that the roles of victim and perpetrator were transient and frequently overlapped. Forty-two per cent of young offenders and 36 per cent of adults who had experienced an assault in the past month had been both victims and perpetrators. Furthermore, in three-quarters of the cases they examined, the victim had made the attack more likely or even brought it about via their own actions. Prisoners' lifestyles and behaviour could increase their risk of being assaulted if, for instance, they dealt in goods or drugs or assaulted others, making them vulnerable to retaliatory attacks.

From their analysis of the conflict-study interview data, Edgar et al. constructed a 'conflict pyramid' (see Figure 3.1): an abstract model consisting of

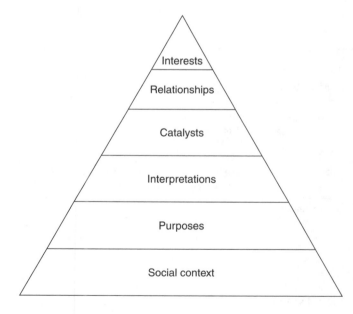

Figure 3.1   The conflict pyramid
Source: Edgar et al. (2003a: 102).

six basic but interrelated components which form their concept of a conflict. This tool can be applied to any dispute between two persons and Edgar et al. voice the hope that it will also prove useful to examine violent interactions in non-prison contexts.

Conflicts often arose over a clash of *interests* over what each party wanted out of a situation, such as when the ownership of material possessions was in dispute. The interests of each party also always included non-material needs and values such as respect, privacy or status. *Relationships* refer to the social distance between the parties involved. Violent encounters were slightly more likely between prisoners who did not know each other well and often resulted from misunderstandings, which were exacerbated by a lack of knowledge of the other party and therefore an inability to predict how they would react. A number of different *catalysts*, such as accusations, threats, insults, undermining behaviour and hostile physical gestures, seem to aggravate disputes, escalate tensions and move interactions towards violence. Such catalysts made violence almost inevitable and coerced prisoners into violent altercations by limiting the other options available to them.

Drawing on the work of Blumer (1969), Edgar et al. suggest that within social action 'interpretation functions on two different levels: understanding the meaning of specific actions and seeing the person's wider plan into which the particular action fits' (2003a: 129). The concept of *interpretation* considers how each person's understanding of the other party's actions and intentions can shape his or her own responses, leading to an intensification of tension and, ultimately, to violence. For example, threats could be interpreted as an attempt to gain dominance over the other party, leading to counter-threats and an escalation of the conflict as participants become involved in a stand-off over relative power.

The force used in conflicts was also designed to achieve a range of different *purposes*, which were heavily dependent on the social context of the prison. In adult male prisons, it was used to demonstrate the toughness of the individuals involved and dispel any suspicion of weakness so as to deter potential future victimizers. For young offenders, violence was viewed as the best method of resolving a dispute. Female prisoners generally disapproved of violence and tended to use it as a punishment against those who had wronged them.

The final element of the pyramid is the *social context* in which the conflict took place. Prisons are sites of intense emotional stress. The regime limits autonomy and resources, and enhances fear, thus increasing the likelihood of violence. In response to the lack of personal security, prisoners may use violence to restore their sense of control over their circumstances or to retaliate against those who have wronged them. Peer pressure from other prisoners encouraged participants to use force, and racial and ethnic differences between prisoners led to conflicts being sparked off by cultural misunderstandings and misinterpretations.

Edgar et al. conclude that violence and victimization are commonplace:

> Assaults and fights are tightly woven into the fabric of prison life. Prison violence occurs against the backdrop of a social context in which the risk of exploitation by others is endemic ... The prison's failure to meet basic human needs makes it a potentially high-conflict environment.
>
> (Edgar et al. 2003a: 185)

The ever-present threat of violence creates a social order in which each prisoner has good reason to suspect that others might be planning an assault. This can lead to a perverse cycle in which the individual prisoner, encouraged by the norms and values of the prisoner culture, perceives a need to use force to ward off potential and actual attackers. In short, in the tense, highly stressful environment of a prison, force and fear of violence begets force.

Prison Violence has been the subject of much interest amongst both academics and practitioners working with prisoners (Crewe 2003; Liebling 2003; *Prison Service News* 2003; Wilson 2003). The remainder of this chapter is concerned with three specific issues of method arising from the studies on which the book is based. First, I will focus on the use and implications of mixed method strategies and how such an approach fitted with Edgar et al.'s own theoretical inclinations. Second, I will consider the strengths and limitations of Edgar et al.'s victimization survey. Third, I will examine their use of the escalator tool to explore how conflicts develop into violence. Throughout this discussion, reference will be made not just to *Prison Violence* but to a range of other publications arising from the same research.

Mixing Methods, Mixing Studies

Mixed method approaches have grown in popularity since the 1980s and are clearly popular within prison sociology. Mixing quantitative and qualitative techniques is often seeing as 'having the best of both worlds' as their various strengths can be capitalized upon and their weaknesses counteracted. Traditionally, though, it has been argued that qualitative and quantitative methods cannot be meaningfully integrated because the epistemological positions that underpin the two approaches constitute irreconcilable positions concerning the nature of social reality and how it should be studied (Bryman 2008). In this view, quantitative and qualitative research methods cannot be meaningfully combined in the same research study due to the incompatibility of the paradigms underlying the methods (Teddlie and Tashakkori 2003: 7). Quantitative methods are often linked with positivism, which tends to be more concerned with explaining human behaviour and which advocates the use of the methods of the natural sciences in the study of social life. Qualitative approaches, on the other hand, are usually associated with interpretivism, which is focused on understanding human behaviour by uncovering the meanings that social phenomena and social action have for the individuals being studied, and argues that, to do this, distinctive social research methods are required (Bryman 2008). In recent years, however, it has been suggested that 'paradigm peace' has broken out (Bryman 2006), as more and more researchers take a pragmatic approach to research and let the research questions and practical constraints guide their choice of method.

Despite calls for researchers to be transparent about the aims of the methods employed in mixed method strategies and the techniques used to fuse together the qualitative and quantitative data (Brannen 1992; Bryman et al. 2007), and like many others who utilize mixed method strategies, Edgar et al. provide little discussion in *Prison Violence* and the associated publications of their rationale for doing so. Their actual justification for using a combination of methods can, in some respects, therefore only be speculated upon. In both the victimization and conflict studies, different methods were certainly used to facilitate other, later stages of the research. The participant observation undertaken by Edgar et al. in the research prisons allowed them to sound out general views on prison violence and build support for the research among prospective respondents. The quantitative surveys in both studies were then used to recruit potential interview respondents by identifying those who had recent experience of victimization and conflict.

Mixed method approaches are commonly used to perform 'methodological triangulation' (Denzin 1970), whereby the results from one method are cross-checked or corroborated with findings from another to enhance the validity of the data. However, some commentators have questioned the degree to which triangulation can take place when the different components of a strategy are focused on different aspects of a social phenomenon. The findings from mixed methods approaches are more likely to be complementary (Brannen 1992, 2005) rather than acting as a form of triangulation. Far from being a disadvantage, this represents a strength of using mixed method approaches, as the different methodological techniques enable a more robust picture of social phenomena to be produced, allowing for a richer understanding of human behaviour. In the victimization study, the datasets examined different aspects of victimization, but were integrated to form one overarching account of violence in prison. The survey measured the extent of victimization, reciprocal bullying and fear in prison. The interviews were then used to seek elaboration and enhancement of the findings from the survey by exploring the social relationships and situations within which victimization might flourish (O'Donnell and Edgar 1998a) and how the experience of victimization shapes the social world of the prisoner. For example, the survey data suggested that the prevalence of exclusion in prison was low, whilst the interview data implied the incidence could have been higher but that many of those who had been excluded tended to avoid situations where they could be further ostracized.

Qualitative techniques are often used in multimethod strategies to explore the relationships between different variables that are uncovered in the quantitative component. Unfortunately, in *Prison Violence*, Edgar et al. miss several opportunities to do this and thus to enhance the quality of their conclusions. Notably, they could have used the interviews in the victimization study as an opportunity to explore what Bottoms (1999) has since termed the 'safety paradox': the contradiction between the pervasive rule of force in prisons and the high levels of perceived safety among prisoners. The survey results revealed the existence of such a paradox within the research prisons, with a majority of prisoners reporting feeling safe from insults and attacks in prison, in spite of the high rates of violence. Those with recent direct experience of assault or verbal threats were much less likely to report feeling safe, but amongst young offenders a substantial number of those who had been victimized in this way said that they felt safe, and in one institution those who had witnessed assaults actually felt safer that those who had not (O'Donnell and Edgar 1999). Edgar et al. (2003a; see also O'Donnell and Edgar 1999) debate the possible reasons for this paradox, using the victimization survey data and the wider academic literature. For example, they suggest that as three-quarters of the adult prisoners surveyed felt that other prisoners would sometimes or always intervene to protect them, this may act as a protective factor and serve to diminish levels of fear. Furthermore, as most prisoners felt that the bullying of 'grasses' (informers) and sex offenders was legitimate, those prisoners who do not fall into these categories may not feel fearful even if they are at risk (Edgar et al. 2003a: 86; O'Donnell and Edgar 1999: 98). Edgar et al. also consider whether explanations for low levels of fear in high crime areas in the community can be applied to the prison setting, but the nature of the relationship between these potential mediating factors and self-reported feelings of safety was not routinely explored in the victimization study interviews. In a separate paper on fear in prison, the authors themselves admit the explanations they present can provide only a tentative and partial account of the dynamics of fear in prisons, and thus represent a series of hypotheses to be tested in future research (O'Donnell and Edgar 1999).

In the case of the victimization study, it is relatively easy to see how the quantitative and qualitative elements were integrated to examine the extent and nature of victimization. In the conflicts study, however, the data produced by the two methods are not fused together to provide a more robust picture of conflict in prisons, and the reasons for using a mixed method approach seem rather less clear. Despite surveying over 600 prisoners, Edgar et al. include few data from the conflicts survey in *Prison Violence* or in the final research report on which the book is based (Edgar and Martin 2001). One explanation for this lack of attention paid to the quantitative data may lie in Edgar et al.'s own epistemological preferences. In the introduction to *Prison Violence*, they firmly locate their work within a symbolic interactionist paradigm, and are therefore concerned with how individuals interpret the symbolic meanings of the social world and social action, and how such interpretations affect their own actions. The authors stress how the techniques of interpretive interactionism, such as open-ended, creative interviewing and personal experience and self-story construction, were part of their 'methodological tool kit' (Edgar et al. 2003a: 14). By contrast, the quantitative components are mentioned only briefly. Concerns have recently been expressed that multimethod approaches are being employed because they are favoured by funding bodies, rather than because they are appropriate to the research questions (Bryman 2006) and, at first glance, it is certainly questionable as to what degree the conflict survey contributed to Edgar et al.'s examination of conflict. It appears that it was used predominantly as part of the research process to provide background data for the research team by highlighting the areas of concern in each prison and to recruit participants for the interviews, rather than being a key source of data in itself (with the exception of data concerning the prevalence of sexual assault in prison).

It is also worth noting the potential dangers of integrating the data from two different research studies and two different samples. For the most part, the data produced by the victimization and conflict studies are discussed in separate chapters of *Prison Violence*. However, data from the conflicts study are occasionally used in the chapters based on the victimization study to highlight particular issues. Whilst this may contribute to a fuller explanation of the experience of victimization, the conflict study data has come from a non-probability sample (that is, a sample not based on random selection) and as a result 'the language of "representativeness" needs to be handled carefully, as the text switches from one to the other' (Brannen 1992: 17). At times, such as when discussing the conflict study data regarding the level of injuries sustained by prisoners, Edgar et al. do caution against extrapolating from these data. Yet elsewhere in the text, for example when discussing levels of sexual assault, this important caveat is not mentioned. Moreover, the conflict study was carried out with a different research population which included female prisoners, and consequently may be of only limited use in explaining the behaviour of both younger and older males.

Mixed method strategies have obvious benefits for sociological research as, among other uses, they can be used to produce a more complete understanding of the social phenomena under study and can facilitate different stages of the research process. However, researchers utilizing mixed methods 'frequently provide little explicit discussion of the rationale for using both approaches'

(Bryman 2006: 124) and *Prison Violence* would benefit from a more explicit discussion of why mixed method strategies were employed, particularly in the conflicts study.

Measuring Victimization

As noted above, previous studies of violence in prison have tended to rely upon official data which are likely to underestimate considerably the extent of victimization in prison. Edgar et al. (2003a) themselves found that less than one in five of those who had experienced victimization had reported this to a member of staff, and fear of being seen as an 'informer' – thus violating the inmate code – was the most common reason given for not wanting to do so. Furthermore, members of prison staff have a high degree of discretion in judging how to deal with incidents and may handle them informally so they do not end up in the official statistics. Victim surveys have been used in the community to reveal a significant proportion of the 'dark figure' of crime; that is, crime which is unreported and/or unrecorded by the authorities. Perhaps the most well-known victim survey in the UK, the British Crime Survey (BCS), was first conducted in 1982 and is now carried out annually with a sample of over 40,000 households. By asking participants to describe crimes that have been committed against them in the past 12 months, it has uncovered about three and a half times as many comparable crimes as appear in the police statistics (Maguire 2007). However, victimization surveys are rare in English prisons and have only been carried out as part of other studies such as the National Prison Survey in 1991 (Dodd and Hunter 1992) and King and McDermott's (1995) comparative study of prison regimes. Edgar et al.'s victimization study is the first large-scale survey solely dedicated to measuring the extent of victimization in English prisons.

Despite their advantages, victimization surveys have been subject to many criticisms. How such criticisms could be applied to Edgar et al.'s use of a victim survey will now be discussed, along with the measures they took to attempt to improve the quality of their data. For a variety of reasons, victimization surveys still only present a partial picture of crime. Respondents may not give accurate answers, and they may forget or deliberately conceal their experiences from researchers out of fear or embarrassment. Edgar et al. provide little critical discussion of whether the fear of being seen as an informer might have stopped prisoners reporting victimization to them, but they did try to improve the chances of receiving honest and complete responses, demonstrating their awareness of the difficulties that prisoners may have in discussing this issue. Anonymous self-completion questionnaires were used to encourage greater disclosure than might be possible within an interview.

The questionnaires were administered by visiting each prisoner whilst they were locked in their cells and explaining the research and its confidentiality to them. The researchers then returned half an hour later to collect the completed version. Edgar et al. do not comment on whether prisoners were alone when filling out the questionnaire and, if they were not, whether someone was looking over their shoulder, such as a cellmate (which might have inhibited their responses). As many prisoners suffer from literacy problems, it is also reasonable to assume that some will have needed help, either from a fellow inmate or from the researchers themselves, to fill the questionnaire in – and this too may have affected the answers they gave.

Victimization surveys have also been accused, particularly by feminist criminologists, of underreporting particular kinds of crime such as sexual offences, which are also the least likely to be reported to the authorities (Coleman and Moynihan 1996). The very first BCS in 1982 only uncovered one attempted rape, whilst other smaller studies focusing on sexual and domestic violence against women, such as Hamner and Saunders (1984) and Painter (1991), found a much higher prevalence of such offences. Edgar et al.'s victimization study did not even attempt to measure the extent of sexual assault in prison, and the researchers have been strongly criticized for this omission (Human Rights Watch 2001), based on the assumption that other jurisdictions may have rates of sexual violence as high as those found in US prison studies. According to the authors, sexual assault was not included because it 'had not emerged as a relevant issue during the pilot study, literature review or initial soundings with prisoners, staff and other academics' (2003a: 47). In a separate paper, one of the authors argues that previous research has revealed only very low levels of sexual assault in UK prisons and, unlike the US, there is no term in prison argot for participants in sexual violence, suggesting that it is uncommon (O'Donnell 2004). Nevertheless, specific questions on sexual assaults were included in the conflicts survey, with respondents being asked if they had ever been sexually assaulted while in custody. Less than 2 per cent reported personal experience of sexual assault and only 3 per cent reported being threatened with it, whilst 76 per cent of respondents claimed that sexual assault did not occur at all in prisons. Edgar et al. therefore conclude that sexual assault is rare in English prisons. This is supported by research into coercive sexual behaviour in prison conducted shortly after the victimization study, which found that 1 per cent of respondents had been raped and 4 per cent sexually assaulted (Banbury 2004). Nonetheless, both this and the conflicts study were based on opportunity samples rather than being representative of the prison population as a whole, and fear and shame may make victims of sexual violence reluctant to report it to researchers. Although the incidence of sexual victimization in UK prisons is clearly lower than the endemic levels reached in the US (Human Rights Watch 2001), as one of the authors themselves suggests, 'it may be, of course, that instances of sexual violence would be found more regularly in the UK if this issue were to be investigated more systematically' (O'Donnell 2004). Furthermore, in Banbury's (2004) study those prisoners who reported sexual victimization also reported being subject to multiple coercive incidents, suggesting that although overall rates may be low, for some prisoners, the threat of sexual victimization can pervade their daily lives and is worthy of further examination.

The definition of victimization or crime utilized in a study can also affect the validity and value of victimization survey findings. Surveys vary as to whether they accept the respondent's own definition of events as victimization or whether they ask respondents about particular incidents for researchers to then decide whether these should be counted (Coleman and Moynihan 1996). The first option has the advantage of acknowledging the meaning of the event to respondents, but it may lead to respondents excluding incidents, not seeing them as victimization. To avoid this, the questions in the victimization survey were posed in a way so as to define the six types of victimization under study; that is, assault, threats of violence, robbery, cell theft, hurtful verbal abuse and exclusion. For instance, to examine the extent of exclusion, Edgar et al. asked participants how many times over the past month other prisoners had 'tried to stop you joining in activities, for example not allow[ing] you to play pool or watch TV?' (Edgar et al. 2003a: 70). Differences in the way victimization is defined can also lead to wide variations in classification, making it difficult to compare the extent of crime/victimization revealed in one study with other sources. To gauge the level of assault in the prison population, Edgar et al. asked prisoners how many times in the last month they had been hit, kicked or in any other way assaulted by another prisoner, a much wider definition than that used in previous surveys. This may go some way to explaining why their survey uncovered high levels of assault (30 per cent of young offenders and 19 per cent of adults claimed to have been assaulted in the preceding month), compared to the National Prison Survey which found 9 per cent of prisoners had been physically assaulted in the preceding six months (Dodd and Hunter 1992). At first glance, it might be concluded that rates of assault in prison are rising, but the difference between the two figures could simply be accounted for by Edgar et al.'s wider definition.

The classification of victimization can also affect the manner in which multiple or serial victimization is recorded in victim surveys, if it is indeed recorded at all. Some victims experience victimization on a regular and ongoing basis, rather than as a one-off event, and simply counting the number of offences does not acknowledge the full extent of their torment. Perhaps the most well known critic on this matter is Hazel Genn (1988). She argues that, for some people, victimization may be a part of their everyday lives, particularly if it is perpetrated by someone with whom they are in a close relationship. She questions the whole notion of 'counting' certain crimes at all (Maguire 2007), arguing that for some victims 'violent victimisation may often be better conceptualized as a process rather than as a series of discrete events' (Genn 1988: 91). As a result of such criticisms, many quantitative studies of behaviour, such as domestic violence or sexual abuse, have presented their results in terms of its *prevalence* – the proportion of the population that have experienced it, rather than the *incidence* – the number of individual offences counted (Maguire 2007). Edgar et al. acknowledge that their figures are a minimum estimate, as some prisoners were repeatedly victimized, although such multiple victimization is not discussed in *Prison Violence*. A separate paper reporting the results of the victimization survey reveals that they did attempt to measure the incidence of victimization after all (O'Donnell and Edgar 1998b). This was 'done in an imprecise fashion' (Bottoms 1999: 220) but one which was likely to ensure respondent accuracy, as participants who said they had been victimized in the last month were simply asked whether this had happened 'once or twice' or more often. The percentage of prisoners reporting multiple victimization was small, but the proportion of young offenders claiming to have been robbed several times in the last month was particularly high (4 per cent amongst the 11 per cent who had been robbed in one establishment and 3 per cent amongst the 8 per cent robbed in the other), despite robbery having the lowest prevalence rates. Robbery victims were therefore proportionally the most likely to be repeatedly victimized.

There is no doubt that victimization surveys are likely to provide a more comprehensive picture of violence in prison than studies that rely on official prison records. Yet from this brief discussion it can be seen that they do have several pitfalls. Coleman and Moynihan warn that 'any data generated by a survey should be treated as a subjective measure of a social process' (1996: 82) and Edgar et al.'s findings are undoubtedly shaped to some extent by the way in which they chose to research and measure prison violence. Nevertheless, in a review of the literature on violence in prison, Bottoms (1999) strongly advocates the further development of victim survey methodology in the prison context in the future, but cautions that the methodological lessons from the use of community surveys should be noted in any such development. Certainly, Edgar et al. have taken on board some of the criticisms of previous surveys and taken several measures to try to improve the quality of their resulting data.

Use of Escalators

In order to investigate the circumstances from which violent incidents emerged, Edgar et al. used the escalator. Originally developed to assist in conflict resolution (Alternatives to Violence Education Committee 1996), the escalator is a schematic framework which is designed to break down conflict-ual interactions into their component parts. It logs accounts of violent inci-dents in a step by step sequence and thus, Edgar et al. maintain, it captures 'the dynamic process by which conflicts escalated into physical violence' (2003b: 72). Participants in the conflicts study were shown a blank diagram indicating a series of steps and were then asked about the first thing that happened between themselves and the other party. The response given was the first step of the escalator. Participants were then asked what happened next, until all steps in the sequence of the conflict were recorded and the escalator was com-pleted (see Figure 3.2).

Additional questions were then posed to elicit more detailed information about the distinctive steps of the interaction and further explore the development

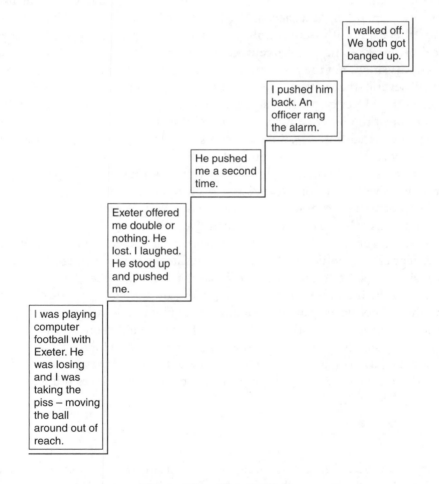

Figure 3.2   The escalator
Source: Edgar et al. (2003b: 211).

of the conflict into violence. Such questions covered respondents' interpretations of the other party's behaviour, the consequences of the actions taken and any steps that could have been taken to prevent the incident (Edgar et al. 2003b). Escalators were used to highlight how each party in the conflict pursued his or her own interests as prisoners were asked what they had hoped to achieve and what purpose they felt the actions of the other party were intended to serve. By asking participants to set out how exchanges were driven towards a violent outcome, escalators uncovered complex patterns of thinking. Essentially, they show how decisions are made about when and whether to use violence to resolve conflict on the basis of participants' interpretations of the actions and intentions of their counterpart. Escalators are key to Edgar et al.'s conflict-centred approach. Rather than reporting the facts independent of the circumstances that gave rise to the action, a charge which could be levelled at more quantitative studies of prison violence, they provide a more thorough understanding of why violence occurred by recreating the context from which it emerged. The act of organizing prisoners' personal accounts into a systematic and chronological framework also often sparked off recollection of further details about the circumstances leading to the violent event which had not emerged during the rest of the interview (Edgar et al. 2003b).

Where accounts were available from both parties in the conflict, these were juxtaposed by Edgar et al. to demonstrate the 'game-like' interplay by which each party decided on his or her next move in response to his or her interpretation of the other's behaviour (ibid.: 73). An example of such a two-sided escalator can be seen in Figure 3.3.

When two different accounts of the same incident could be compared, escalators allowed competing perspectives of how the conflict escalated into violence to be drawn out and demonstrated how misinterpretations of the other person's behaviour and intentions may aggravate conflict. They can also create a more complete and balanced understanding of the process, particularly as in the experience of Edgar et al. (2003b) where one party often provided information lacking in their opponent's account. At times, respondents used the interview to try to continue their conflict by vying to give the most authoritative version of events and to boost their self-esteem. Some prisoners claimed that they had inflicted more harm than they had in order to make themselves appear more powerful, whereas others appeared to play down the extent of the harm caused for fear of evoking disapproval from the interviewer. Personal accounts, such as those produced by escalators, may be used by respondents to justify the deployment of force (Edgar et al. 2003b), for example by portraying their actions as provoked or taken in self-defence, potentially producing an inaccurate description of events. Yet Edgar et al. suggest that the possible influence of such neutralizing techniques can be exaggerated. Respondent bias remains a risk as accounts of events are filtered through

Gregson	Wye
I'd had a share of a spliff, part of which was Wye's. But another girl smoked the rest of it and didn't pass it on.	
Wye must have thought I'd smoked it, she came back on the wing and asked for it. I told her that the other girl had got it but she had smoked it.	Gregson was given a joint for [another inmate], and Gregson smoked it. I found out. I went behind my door.
I heard that and went to Wye's door to say, 'Let's talk about it', and calm her down.	Gregson came to the door.
She told me to ✳✳✳✳ off and I said the same to her.	
I turned away and walked down the wing and I heard her running up behind me.	I told her, 'Fuck off!' Gregson replied: 'Why don't you fuck off?' She didn't know the door wasn't locked.
I said, 'Oh, so now I have to watch my back as well' and she swung at me.	I came out of my cell.
	Gregson said, 'Now do I have to watch my back?'
	Me: 'No. Watch me when I come from the front.' I slapped her on the face, a back hand punch that gave her a black eye.
I threw my hot coffee back over my shoulder and it went all up her arm.	I turned and walked away.
[Another prisoner] came towards us and we stopped.	Gregson threw her coffee on me.
We're mates – no hard feelings.	I carried on walking back to her cell.
	I felt my top was wet, but when I took it off it stuck to my arm.
	They filled out an accident – not a bully – form.

Figure 3.3   Gregson versus Wye

Source: Edgar et al. (2003b: 81).

interpretation (Edgar and Martin 2004), but the authors confidently maintain that comparing contrasting accounts of a conflict still produced clear explanations of how they escalated into physical violence in the vast majority of cases.

Completing an escalator as part of the research process also appeared to have some benefit for participants. According to Edgar et al., documenting the sequence of events helped participants to find a satisfying explanation of how their dispute had resulted in violence and enabled them to assert a sense of self-control over events by suggesting that they had caused something to happen (Edgar et al. 2003b: 78). This sentiment may be of particular value in the restrictive environment of a prison where prisoners suffer a loss of personal autonomy. Nevertheless, it is important to note that prisoners' options for choosing what action to take are likely to be extremely constrained by the confines of the prison environment, where due to living in such close proximity to other prisoners it may be difficult to avoid using violence as the opportunities to escape conflicts are so limited.

Notwithstanding their value in analysing interpersonal violence, escalators do have several limitations, some of which are acknowledged by the authors in a separate paper (Edgar et al. 2003b). Firstly, escalators may be of limited use in analysing conflict which results in anything other than interpersonal violence. Escalators are, for example, unlikely to be suitable for examining collective violence (ibid.), such as prison riots or gang warfare. In such cases, the interpersonal dynamics between the parties involved, their interpretations and intentions and the contribution of these to the violent consequence are likely to be considerably more complex and unsuitable for the simple escalator structure. Moreover, escalators are also inappropriate for specifically examining other aspects of prison violence discussed in the book, such as cell theft or robbery, where these arise not from mutual conflict but from the exploitation of one party by another and where the identity of the offender is not known.

If used on their own, escalators cannot examine the way a person is treated within or by a social structure, setting or organization. In reducing conflict to the microrelations between two parties, escalators are less able to account for the influence of the social structure on their situation, despite the fact that the prison environment may restrict the options and opportunities for action and non-action. As a method of exploring violence in prisons, it must therefore always be supplemented with other methods, as done by Edgar et al., in order to appreciate the impact of the prison culture and environment. The use of escalators in *Prison Violence* is also of limited value in examining the role of third parties in conflict. In several of the incidents in the study, the influence of third parties and of peer pressure in encouraging prisoners to use violence is noted. However, only witnesses to a limited number of violent incidents were interviewed and asked to complete escalators. Their perspectives may have contributed to the understanding of the development of the conflict into violence, but other third-party accounts of the escalation of conflicts and their interpretation of the interplay between themselves and the direct participants are left somewhat unexplored. The authors note that, in most cases, they lacked the perspectives of peers and thus much of their discussion about the role of peer pressure in conflicts is based upon the interpretations of the participants about the judgements and behaviour of third parties (Edgar et al. 2003a: 157).

Finally, Edgar et al. miss the opportunity to show how escalators could be used to demonstrate how conflicts can be managed and resolved. They themselves acknowledge that a more complete framework for analysing conflicts would have steps going down to show how parties might de-escalate the tension or open up opportunities for a resolution using non-violent means (Edgar et al. 2003b: 78). That the steps of the escalator diagram move upwards, representing the spiralling of conflict, may also lead to the impression that physical violence resolves the problem or, at the very least, brings the conflict to an end. Furthermore, any significant continuation of the conflict is not covered by the use of the escalator format in this way if they largely end with the violent act itself. Escalators appear more suited to examining the build-up to a violent incident, rather than for analysing how conflict might continue and affect social relations in the longer term.

Despite these limitations, when used with other methods as part of a symbolic interactionist approach which highly values people's interpretations of events as being crucial to understanding their decisions and actions, escalators remain a useful and innovative way to examine and explore the dynamics of interpersonal violence, and they could be applied in a range of different contexts in future research.

Conclusion

The research on which *Prison Violence* is based adopts a unique and inventive approach to the study of violence, which is likely to be of interest to criminologists and non-criminologists alike. Nevertheless, *Prison Violence* does contain a number of important limitations. The final chapter examines how prisoners avoided conflicts escalating into violence and suggests various violence prevention strategies, but the book lacks any summation of the main findings from the two studies or any real conclusion. Furthermore, although the studies took place in a range of different prison settings, allowing the nature and purposes of violence to be compared and contrasted, they did not include an open prison, which may have produced considerably divergent findings about the impact of the social setting on violence, as prisoners here experience better conditions and a higher degree of personal freedom.

Most significantly for the purposes of this review, Edgar et al.'s discussion of the methodologies used in the studies in *Prison Violence* itself is somewhat brief. They provide little commentary on the purpose of their multimethod strategies and almost no critically reflexive comment on the actual practice of doing the research and the quality of the resulting data. Although in the case of *Prison Violence* the lack of methodological discussion was a deliberate strategy, and methods are discussed in other publications (Edgar et al. 2003b), it is perhaps questionable whether readers will be prepared to seek out this additional material, and it would therefore be helpful for the methods to be discussed in greater detail in the book itself.

Prison Violence has certainly made a substantial contribution to our understanding of violence in prisons and has been well received by both academics and those working with prisoners. Edgar et al.'s victimization research reveals that violence is routine and endemic in prisons, a finding which should not surprise us considering the wider culture of masculinity that pervades life, at least in male prisons, which may act to sustain and legitimate violence (Sim 1994). The inclusion of a women's prison in the conflict study provides valuable insights into how the use and purpose of violence differs.

Some of the conclusions of *Prison Violence*, for example that the failure of prisons to fulfil basic human needs is likely to contribute to the development of violence, are notable, but not particularly new (see Toch 1992). What makes Edgar et al.'s contribution to the study of prison violence unique is their use of a conflict-centred approach for examining the social context in which violence emerges. This approach demonstrates not only how such conflicts might be influenced by features inherent in the prison setting, such as the competition for scarce resources and the expectations of the (largely male) prisoner culture that violence should be met with violence, but also how the ever-present risk of victimization and fear shape the social world of the prisoner. Key to this conflict-centred approach and the creation of the conflict pyramid is Edgar et al.'s use of escalators to examine the development of conflicts according to the accounts of the parties involved. In short, by focusing on mundane, everyday incidents of violence among prisoners and the micro-interactions from which they arise, Edgar et al. bring a new dimension to the study of violence in prison.

Additional Reading

For a concise and accessible overview of the sociology of imprisonment, see Crewe's chapter 'The sociology of imprisonment' in Jewkes's *Handbook on Prisons* (2007). Bottoms's 'Interpersonal Violence and Social Order in Prisons' (1999) remains the most comprehensive review of research on violence in prison. Coleman and Moynihan's *Understanding Crime Data* (1996) provides a humorous, if now slightly dated, discussion of victimization surveys. For more on the uses and implications of mixed methods, see the collection of papers edited by Brannen, *Mixing Methods: Qualitative and Quantitative Research* (1992) or the most recent version of Bryman's ever popular *Social Research Methods* (2008). For more information on the ESRC Violence Research Programme, see www.esrcsocietytoday.ac.uk/ESRCInfoCentre/research/research_programmes/violence.aspx.

Acknowledgements

I would like to thank Kimmett Edgar and Ian O'Donnell and the editors, Fiona Devine and Sue Heath, for helpful comments on earlier drafts of this chapter.

References

Adler, J. (1994) *Fear in Prisons: A Discussion Paper*, London: Prison Reform Trust.

Alternatives to Violence Education Committee (1996) *Alternatives to Violence Project: Supplement to the Basic and Second Level Manuals*, New York: Alternatives to Violence Education Committee.

Banbury, S. (2004) 'Coercive sexual behaviour in British prisons as reported by adult ex-prisoners', *Howard Journal of Criminal Justice*, 43(2): 113–30.

Blumer, H. (1969) *Symbolic Interactionism: Perspective and Method*, Englewood Cliffs, NJ: Prentice-Hall.

Bottoms, A.E. (1999) 'Interpersonal violence and social order in prisons', in M. Tonry and J. Petersilia (eds), *Crime and Justice: A Review of Research, vol. 26*, Chicago, IL: University of Chicago Press.

Brannen, J. (1992) 'Combining qualitative and quantitative approaches: an overview', in J. Brannen (ed.), *Mixing Methods: Qualitative and Quantitative Research*, Aldershot: Avebury/Ashgate Publishing.

Brannen, J. (2005) 'Mixing methods: the entry of qualitative and quantitative approaches into the research process', *International Journal of Social Research Methodology*, 8(3): 173–84.

Bryman, A. (2006) 'Paradigm peace and the implications for quality', *International Journal of Social Research Methodology*, 9(2): 111–26.

Bryman, A. (2008) *Social Research Methods*, 3rd edn, Oxford: Oxford University Press.

Bryman, A., S. Becker and J. Sempik (2007) 'Quality criteria for quantitative, qualitative and mixed methods research: a view from social policy', *International Journal of Social Research Methodology*, 11(4): 216–76.

Coleman, C. and J. Moynihan (1996) *Understanding Crime Data*, Buckingham: Open University Press.

Cooke, D.J. (1989) 'Containing violent prisoners: an analysis of the Barlinnie Special Unit', *British Journal of Criminology*, 29: 129–43.

Cooke, D.J. (1991) 'Violence in prisons: the influence of regime factors', *Howard Journal of Criminal Justice*, 30: 95–107.

Crawley, E. (2004) *Doing Prison Work: The Public and Private Lives of Prison Officers*, Cullompton: Willan Publishing.

Crewe, B. (2003) 'Review of *Prison Violence: The Dynamics of Conflict, Fear and Power*', *Howard Journal of Criminal Justice*, 42(5): 516–17.

Crewe, B. (2005) 'Codes and conventions: the terms and conditions of contemporary inmate values', in A. Liebling and S. Maruna (eds), *The Effects of Imprisonment*, Cullompton: Willan Publishing.

Crewe, B. (2007) 'The sociology of imprisonment', in Y. Jewkes (ed.), *Handbook on Prisons*, Cullompton: Willan Publishing.

Denzin, N.K. (1970) *The Research Act in Sociology*, London: Butterworth.

Denzin, N.K. (1989) *Interpretive Interactionism,* Applied Social Research Methods Series, vol. 16, London: Sage.

DiIulio, J. (1987) *Governing Prisons,* New York: The Free Press.

Dodd, T. and P. Hunter (1992) *The National Prison Survey 1991,* London: HM Stationery Office.

Edgar, K. and C. Martin (2001) *Conflicts and Violence in Prison,* Oxford: University of Oxford, Centre for Criminological Research.

Edgar, K. and C. Martin (2004) *Perceptions of Race and Conflict: Perspectives of Minority Ethnic Prisoners and of Prison Officers,* Home Office Online Report 11/04. Available at http://rds.homeoffice.gov.uk/rds/pdfs2/rdsolr1104.pdf.

Edgar, K., I. O'Donnell and C. Martin (2003a) *Prison Violence: The Dynamics of Conflict, Fear and Power,* Cullompton: Willan Publishing.

Edgar, K., I. O'Donnell and C. Martin (2003b) 'Tracking the pathways to violence in prison', in R.M. Lee and E.A. Stanko (eds), *Researching Violence: Essays on Methodology and Measurement,* London: Routledge.

Flick, U. (2006) *An Introduction to Qualitative Research,* 3rd edn, London: Sage.

Genders, E. and E. Player (1995) *Grendon: A Study of a Therapeutic Prison,* Oxford: Clarendon Press.

Genn, H. (1988) 'Multiple victimisation', in M. Maguire and J. Pointing (eds), *Victims of Crime: A New Deal?* Milton Keynes: Open University Press.

Goffman, E. (1968) *Asylums: Essays on the Social Situation of Mental Patients and Other Inmates,* Harmondsworth: Penguin.

Hamner, J. and S. Saunders (1984) *Well-founded Fear,* London: Hutchinson.

HM Prison Service (2007) *Annual Report and Accounts April 2006–March 2007,* London: HM Prison Service.

Human Rights Watch (2001) *No Escape: Male Rape in US Prisons.* Available at www.hrw.org/reports/2001/prison/report.html.

Ireland, J. (ed.) (2005) *Bullying among Prisoners: Innovations in Theory and Research,* Cullompton: Willan Publishing.

Irwin, J. and D.R. Cressey (1962) 'Thieves, convicts and the inmate culture', *Social Problems,* 10: 142–55.

Jacobs, J. (1977) *Stateville: The Penitentiary in Mass Society,* Chicago, IL: University of Chicago Press.

Jewkes, Y. (2002) *Captive Audience: Media, Masculinity and Power in Prisons,* Cullompton: Willan Publishing.

Jewkes, Y. (2007) *Handbook on Prisons,* Cullompton: Willan Publishing.

King, R.D. and K. McDermott (1995) *The State of Our Prisons,* Oxford: Clarendon Press.

Liebling, A. (1992) *Suicides in Prison,* London: Routledge.

Liebling, A. (2003) 'Review of *Prison Violence: The Dynamics of Conflict, Fear and Power*', *British Journal of Criminology,* 43(4): 820–2.

Maguire, M. (2007) 'Crime data and statistics', in M. Maguire, R. Morgan and R. Reiner (eds), *The Oxford Handbook of Criminology,* Oxford: Oxford University Press.

Mathieson, T. (1965) *The Defences of the Weak: A Sociological Study of a Norwegian Correctional Institution,* London: Tavistock.

Megargee, E.I. (1982) 'Psychological determinants and correlates of criminal violence', in M.E. Wolfgang and N.A. Weiner (eds), *Criminal Violence,* Beverley Hills, CA: Sage.

Morris, T., P. Morris and B. Barer (1963) *Pentonville: A Sociological Study of an English Prison,* London: Routledge and Kegan Paul.

O'Donnell, I. (2004) 'Prison rape in context', *British Journal of Criminology,* 44(2): 241–55.

O'Donnell, I. and K. Edgar (1998a) 'Routine victimisation in prisons', *Howard Journal of Criminal Justice*, 37(3): 266–79.

O'Donnell, I. and K. Edgar (1998b) 'Bullying in prisons', Occasional Paper 18, University of Oxford Centre for Criminological Research.

O'Donnell, I. and K. Edgar (1999) 'Fear in prison', *The Prison Journal*, 79(1): 90–9.

Painter, K. (1991) *Wife Rape, Marriage and the Law: Survey Report*, Manchester: Faculty of Economic and Social Science, University of Manchester.

Prison Service News (2003) 'In review: *Prison Violence: The Dynamics of Conflict, Fear and Power*', April.

Sim, J. (1990) *Medical Power in Prisons: The Prison Medical Service in England, 1774–1989*, Milton Keynes: Open University Press.

Sim, J. (1994) 'Tougher than the rest? Men in prison', in T. Newburn and E. Stanko (eds), *Just Boys Doing Business? Men, Masculinities and Crime*, London: Routledge.

Sim, J. (2002) 'The future of prison health care: a critical analysis', *Critical Social Policy*, 22(2): 300–23.

Sparks, R., A.E. Bottoms and W. Hay (1996) *Prisons and the Problem of Order*, Oxford: Clarendon Press.

Sykes, G.M. (1958) *The Society of Captives: The Study of a Maximum Security Prison*, Princeton, NJ: Princeton University Press.

Teddlie, C. and A. Tashakkori (2003) 'Major issues and controversies in the use of mixed methods in the social and behavioral sciences', in A. Tashakkori and C. Teddlie (eds), *Handbook of Mixed Methods in Social and Behavioral Research*, Thousand Oaks, CA: Sage.

Toch, H. (1992) *Living in Prison: The Ecology of Survival*, rev. edn, Washington, DC: American Psychological Association.

Williams, M. and D. Longley (1987) 'Identifying control problem prisoners in dispersal prisons', in A.E. Bottoms and R. Light (eds), *Problems of Long-Term Imprisonment*, Aldershot: Gower.

Wilson, D. (2003) 'Review of *Prison Violence: The Dynamics of Conflict, Fear and Power*', *Howard League Magazine*, July: 18.

Zamble E. and F.J. Porporino (1988) *Coping, Behaviour and Adaptation in Prison Inmates*, Secaucus, NJ: Springer-Verlag.

CHAPTER 4

Time:
Gershuny's *Changing Times*

DALE SOUTHERTON

This chapter looks at theories of post-industrial societies and research on time-use. Dale Southerton engages in a critical assessment of Jonathan Gershuny's book, *Changing Times* (2000), which is based on the analysis of time-diary surveys in 20 countries since the 1960s. Three issues of method are addressed. First, Soutnerton reflects on the difficulties of using time diaries and how they may be overcome. Second, the challenges of doing comparative data analysis are examined. Third, the extent to which the empirical data supports the key theoretical claims is considered. Southerton points to the limitations of time-diary surveys, although he contends they remain a rich source of empirical material. He also acknowledges the problems associated with comparative research that is good at capturing generic trends. However, he argues that variations in national experiences and the cultural significance of activities must not be ignored. Finally, he notes that Gershuny's empirical evidence is consistent with the post-industrial theories of socio-economic change but that it does not corroborate all of the claims.

Introduction

Nations of the (so-called) 'developed world' have enjoyed an exponential rise in affluence across all strata of society, often generically described in terms of a shift towards a post-industrial economy characterized by the growing significance of leisure and consumption, economic and cultural globalization, and the erosion of traditional (industrial) social divisions based around class and gender. Arguably, such economic changes have not led to corresponding social 'developments'. Inequalities persist. The relationship between work and consumption intensifies, creating new time pressures that compromise well-being. Economic growth and social status come to be increasingly centred on consumption rather than production, raising profound questions regarding how the resource of time is distributed across social groups. Jonathan Gershuny's *Changing Times* is a book which addresses such fundamental issues by providing a systematic comparative analysis of time-use across 20 countries since the 1960s.

Gershuny's research offers two major contributions to the social sciences. The first is to offer an innovative approach to the question of how to collect, collate and categorize national accounts of social and economic activity. Without effective tools for measuring socio-economic development, we cannot hope to understanding fully how societies change or the implications of that change. Conventionally, socio-economic change is measured through the circulation of money and 'productive' activity. Such accounts ignore the informal economy, voluntary work and domestic labour. The second contribution is to provide an overview of social and economic change during the last third of the twentieth century. Gershuny's key argument is that time-diary surveys offer a systematic data source capable of measuring production and consumption activity and of accounting for paid and unpaid work.

I start with a brief review of the core debates surrounding the changing relationship between work, leisure and the domestic economy. I then consider Gershuny's key findings and theoretical claims, before discussing time-diary collection, coding and the interpretation of temporal experiences, which will highlight the limitations of the methodology. This is followed by an exploration of the comparative analysis employed by Gershuny and a scrutiny of the empirical basis of his theoretical claims. In conclusion, I argue that despite critiques of the research methodology, time diaries remain a rich source of empirical data, with many theoretical and substantive applications. Gershuny's study represents a necessary platform for the development of detailed comparative analyses of changing social, economic and cultural practices, and for the further use of time diaries to explore the different temporal dimensions of everyday life. This is essential for advancing empirically informed theoretical accounts of the relationship between production and consumption.

Researching Work, Leisure and the Domestic Economy

The study of how time is used and experienced represents a particularly instructive way of empirically understanding the relationships between the domains of work, leisure and the domestic economy. This is because any change in one domain implies change in the others. More paid work reduces the time available for leisure and domestic activities, and this has implications for the ways in which those other domains are experienced. Despite agreement that studying time is an instructive subject for analysing social change, a division has emerged between quantitative and qualitative approaches; the former focussing on time-use and the latter on multiple experiences of time. As such, in reviewing debates surrounding the changing relationships between work, leisure and the domestic economy the tension between different research traditions becomes apparent.

Since the 1960s economic activity in advanced capitalist societies has moved away from manufacturing and towards the service sectors. This is often described as a shift towards a post-industrial economy (Bell 1979). Three key processes are widely identified: the opening-up of labour markets to women through the provision of service-related occupations; the growing significance of leisure and consumption as forms of social status and differentiation; and the emergence of time poverty. Each process has particular implications for the way in which time is distributed, allocated and experienced in everyday life; and they are at the heart of debates regarding gender inequality, how social groups relate to one another, and whether we work more to consume more at the expense of our interpersonal relationships.

The number of women in paid employment has increased significantly during the post-war period. This is partly because of changing ideologies surrounding gender 'roles' and partly because of shifts in the labour market towards service-related jobs. Technological innovations have facilitated greater flexibility in hours and location (e.g. homeworking) of employment. Such changes, argue Perrons et al. (2005), offer avenues through which the demands of work and family life can be reconciled and present further labour market opportunities for women. The central debate, however, rests on whether socio-economic change has produced greater gender equalities in paid and domestic work. Taking seriously Oakley's (1974) classic argument that domestic labour, predominantly performed by women, is underrepresented in accounts of socio-economic life, Gershuny et al. (1994) used time-diary data to explore the changing distributions of time devoted to paid and unpaid work between the sexes. They showed that while inequalities remain (with women doing more unpaid work and men more paid work) the difference has narrowed since the 1970s. This, they claimed, represents a 'lagged adaptation process' where women enter paid work and men slowly adjust to take on more unpaid work. Qualitative studies of time counter this argument. In their investigations of work and domestic life, Thompson (1996) and Hochschild (1997) demonstrated that women suffer a 'dual burden' of juggling paid and unpaid work. Time diaries, they suggested, may reveal greater equity in the amount of time devoted to domestic tasks, but they failed to capture experiences of obligation and responsibility felt by women when managing the competing temporal demands of activities. Resolution of the debate about gender inequality has come to depend largely on which methods – those that capture time-use or time experiences – are deemed most valid.

The second key process associated with post-industrial economies focuses around the rising importance of leisure and consumption as a source of social status. Social class, derived through the relationship of an individual to the 'means of production', was the principal source of social status within industrial societies. While work was a source of status for the majority, the very wealthy (who did not need to work) used leisure to display their social status. Veblen (1925 [1899]) described the urban elites of the late nineteenth century as a 'leisure class' because they used leisure as a means of social differentiation from less affluent groups. However, the shift to post-industrial economies allowed leisure (and consumption) to take on wider significance as a source of social status. The shift towards service sector occupations has rendered conventional distinctions between manual (working-class) and service (middle-class) occupations obsolete. Furthermore, the exporting of manufacturing has made consumer goods available and affordable to the significant majority of people in advanced capitalist societies. A post-industrial economy is accompanied by a 'leisure society', evidenced by time-diary data that reveals growing volumes of time available for leisure (Robinson and Godbey 1997). Despite this, debate has emerged around the quality of leisure time. For example, using economic modelling techniques, Linder (1970) argued that as leisure becomes increasingly available to everyone so the more affluent seek to differentiate themselves from other social groups by engaging in a high volume and variety of leisure pursuits. The middle classes become the 'harried leisure classes'. Again, the distinction between time-use (more leisure time) and experience (harried leisure) divides understandings of the implications of socio-economic change.

The third process follows the previous two. Schor (1992) argued that as consumption becomes more important to social status people 'work more' in order to gain the financial resources necessary to 'consume more'. Schor used time diary data to support her claims, although it is important to note that other time-diary studies do not reveal that people work more (e.g. Robinson and Godbey 1997). Schor's broad argument receives some support from qualitative research. Rubery et al. (2005) conducted qualitative research of six firms and demonstrated that flexible working arrangements produce new patterns of work which requires employees to work longer hours. Schor's conclusion is that working more results in a progressive degeneration of 'well-being' as time pressures come to dominate daily life. The rise of dual-income households adds to this time pressure as families juggle work, domestic responsibilities and leisure (Hochschild 1997). The net result is 'time poverty' where the time necessary to build relationships with family and friends and to engage in public life is squeezed out by the treadmill of working to consume in order to maintain a consumer lifestyle. By contrast, Southerton's (2003) household interviews revealed that experiences of 'harriedness' had little to do with working or consuming more but emerged from the difficulty of coordinating times of 'togetherness' amongst family and friends.

Studies of time and socio-economic change offer a range of insights into theoretical claims regarding the shift to post-industrial economies. Those studies are varied in the methodologies employed, and the division between quantitative and qualitative approaches are entrenched within different research traditions. The former is associated with measuring the changing distributions of time allocated across domains of activity, providing clear indications of processes and patterns, but they are limited in their capacity to capture temporal experiences and meanings – which is the strength of the latter. The consequence is that the empirical groundings of key debates are contentious, particularly in terms of how trends in time-use are interpreted as representative of how different social groups experience and make sense of time in their everyday lives. Gershuny's *Changing Times* takes a quantitative approach to time-use in order to provide the first systematic empirical study of the changing relationship between work, leisure and the domestic economy across different social groups. It makes no claims of capturing temporal experiences, but provides an exhaustive account of how time-use has changed and what those patterns mean for our understandings of socio-economic development.

Time-Use and Socio-Economic Change

Gershuny advances a 'recursive theory' of the relationship between socio-economic change and time. The theory rests on the interactions between three levels of conceptualizing time-use. The first is the micro-sequential level, which refers to the range and sequencing of activities that any individual may conduct in a 24-hour period. The second is the micro-aggregate level: individuals understand their time-use by aggregating activities within categories of, say, work, household chores and leisure. The third is the macrolevel, which accounts for the aggregate time-use of different social groups. Each conceptual level cannot be understood without reference to another: 'the micro-sequential is summarized within the micro-aggregate, which is in turn encapsulated within the macro' (Gershuny 2000: 80). By taking this recursive approach, Gershuny creates a theoretical framework in which socio-economic change can be understood through the balancing out of activities in time – a balancing act that occurs at the level of the individual, who adjusts his or her activities in light of their aggregate time-use, and at the societal level, as any change in consumption (leisure) affects production (work).

Gershuny analysed 35 time-use studies (comprising a sample of 120,000 respondents) conducted in 20 different countries between 1961 and the early 1990s. The time-diary data was harmonized by Gershuny and colleagues through the Multinational Time Use Study (MTUS) and weighted to control for differences between weekday and weekend, in order to produce representative samples of each national population at the date of survey. The key socio-demographic variables analysed were age, sex, civic status, employment status, educational achievement, household composition and income. Given the variations in the data collection method and the need to measure change against the standard of 24 hours, only primary activities were analysed (some diary surveys record secondary or even multiple activities that occur simultaneously). The activities that make up the 24-hour day can be divided into four generic categories – paid work, unpaid work (including domestic chores, shopping, care for dependents, etc.), leisure and consumption, and sleep. As the amount of time spent sleeping remained relatively constant across societies and over historical time, this was excluded from the analysis.

Analysis of the data produced some striking results. Most significant was identification of what Gershuny calls 'the three convergences'. First, there has been convergence across nations in their distributions of paid and unpaid work, such that a common norm of 55 per cent of total work-time devoted to paid work and 45 per cent to unpaid work has emerged. Over the same period, all countries show an increase in time devoted to consumption. At a macrolevel, the way that nations distribute time has converged towards a common norm. The second convergence relates to gender. In all countries, women do more unpaid and less paid work than men. Over the period studied, the two balanced out such that the total amount of work (paid and unpaid) done by men and women remained relatively stable. However, this balance changes over time. By the 1990s, men had increased their amount of unpaid work and their time spent in paid work had declined, while women experienced the reverse. This demonstrates a convergence between the sexes with respect to the distribution of paid and unpaid work. The third convergence was between socio-economic status groups. In the 1960s, those with lower socio-economic status had less leisure time than did those with higher status. By 1990 this situation had reversed, although the difference between the groups had diminished.

Gershuny posits four possible explanations for this convergence. The first is a 'leisure preference': that our wants are saturated and, with growing economic productivity, we need to work less. This, in essence, is the logic behind claims of a 'leisure society'. It does, however, contradict the trend for convergence between socio-economic status groups – for if 'wants' have become saturated why would the highest income groups have increased their time in paid work relative to low income groups? Rather, Gershuny (2000: 8) suggests, the increase in leisure time is better understood as a 'consumption-time require-ment: a society may need more leisure time to consume its growing product'. For any economy to grow in real terms, not only do new goods need to be pro-duced and sold, but they also need to be consumed.

The second explanation is 'pressure for gender equality'. As the data reveals, women conducted a significantly larger proportion of society's unpaid work in the 1960s. The shift towards post-industrial economies and the impact of femi-nist movements have produced a 'strain to fairness', where women demand more from their partners and men no longer see their role as primarily based in the paid economy. This supports the 'lagged adaptation' theory, although Gershuny is quick to note that this is only a tendency and full gender conver-gence is not inevitable.

The third posited explanation relates to 'the end of the leisure class'. Veblen's theory of the leisure class is based on the claim that leisure and consumption signifies social status. To the contrary, Gershuny suggests that what we may now be witnessing is a shift so that those occupations which are better rewarded are also the jobs that are the most demanding, challenging and interesting. Those with higher socio-economic status may find their occupations more rewarding – and a more clearly defined source of social distinction – than they do their con-sumption.

The fourth explanation refers to a 'global model of time allocation'. Technological globalization means that the same products are available (almost) everywhere. Cultural globalization has the effect of homogenizing cul-tural modes of consumption across the developed world. The penetration of global media, especially films and television from the United States, leads to the development of global cultural norms: norms that are reflected in the strik-ing similarities of growth rates in leisure and consumption time across nations. Furthermore, economic globalization undermines the capacity of national governments to determine their own economic, social and welfare policies. In the 1960s and 1970s, national differences of time-use were identifiable; by 1990 they had disappeared. During the same period, 'free-market' ideologies had come to dominate politico-economic regimes.

Having explained the three convergences, Gershuny turns his attention to the key features of socio-economic change in the UK since the 1960s. He takes the 'great day' of society (the total population minutes per day divided by the population size) to examine the changing allocation of mean minutes per day devoted to different societal 'wants' and 'needs' (such as food pro-duction and consumption, transport and travel, and shelter). Three trends are identified. First, greater technological efficiencies have increased the product-ivity of basic needs (e.g. food and shelter), reducing time devoted to paid work in those sectors. Second, he identifies a trend towards 'self-servicing' and uses time spent on shopping, which increased from 40 to 70 minutes per day between 1961 and 1984, to illustrate this. In the 1960s, the movement of goods was largely done by firms through transportation to many neighbour-hood shops. By the 1980s, the system had changed to bulk transportation to larger more centralized stores (supermarkets) to which the consumer travels in order to buy goods. In the activity of shopping there has been a transfer of time from the 'paid work' of the transport employee to the unpaid self-servic-ing work of the consumer. Third, he identifies an increase of time spent con-suming and producing 'luxury services' (out-of-home leisure, education and medicine) by 30 and 8 minutes respectively. This signals a shift from basic to more sophisticated wants and a corresponding growth of high-skilled labour (necessary to produce luxury services) relative to low-skilled.

For Gershuny, these three trends, together with the three convergences, point to a critical moment in the socio-economic development of advanced capitalist societies. This moment rests on the balance between the production and consumption of low-value-added and high-value-added goods and services. Low-value-added services are those of mass production/consumption where comparatively small workforces produce a large volume of commodities that are sold at relatively low prices. High-value-added services are niche forms of pro-duction/consumption characterized by a large number of people relative to the volume of commodities produced, and which are sold at higher prices. Crucially, high-value-added services typically require more total leisure time in which to be consumed because they are services added on top of the consumption time required for 'basic needs' (we still need to buy mass produced foods from the supermarket even if we eat out at restaurants more frequently). The last 40 years have seen a saturation of low-value-added goods and services to the extent that the basic needs (for the vast majority) of the population are catered for.

Time as well as monetary constraints represent significant limits to further socio-economic development. This is captured by the three convergences. Convergence across socio-economic groups reveals that those with high socio-economic status (high-value-added service workers) have increased time in paid work relative to low socio-economic status groups (the low-value-added service workers). Higher socio-economic status groups therefore have the money but not necessarily the time to consume high-value-added products. Convergence between the sexes and the rise of time devoted to self-servicing suggests that while households (as measured by the combined work time of all adults within a household unit) spend less time in paid work than they did in the 1960s, this does not amount to the volume of leisure time needed for the mass consumption of high-value-added services. Finally, the changing 'great day' of UK society is likely to be repeated across other advanced capitalist soci-eties because of national convergences in time-use.

For socio-economic development to continue and progress, more time for consumption of high-value-added services and a redistribution of the occupational structure is necessary. To achieve this, Gershuny proposes a set of welfare policies that he describes as 'humane modernization'. These include a reduction across hours of paid work without decreases in rates of net pay, to be paid for out of changes to the general taxation system. The logic is that shorter durations of paid work without a decline of income would produce the time necessary for individuals to engage in high-value-added consumption. In turn, this would create more high-skilled occupations, produce income growth and, therefore, the tax yield would remain stable. At the microlevel, policies are required to provide the material and technological conditions necessary to facilitate 'extra' leisure time. And, at the macrolevel, societal shifts in the distribution of time from paid work to leisure and consumption will benefit all social groups by maintaining trajectories of convergence, thus reducing social inequalities.

The Limitations of the Time-Diary Methodology

There are a number of limitations to time-diary methodology and the data it produces. In the case of Gershuny's research, the most pressing concerns relate to the reliability of time-diary samples, the recording and coding of activities, and the accounting for multiple experiences of time. Each of these will be discussed in turn.

Reliability of Time-Diary Samples

Time-use studies provide respondents with a diary in which they record what activities they engaged in for intervals of 5, 15 or 30 minutes (depending on the survey) throughout the course of a 24-hour day (see Figure 4.1). This makes time diaries onerous to complete, and as a result they have a high non-response rate when compared to other survey instruments. This raises questions as to who is missing from the sample, whether there is any systematic data bias from high non-response rates and, ultimately, whether the data is reliable.

Like most national surveys, time-diary studies routinely exclude segments of the population: members of the armed forces on active duty, hospital patients and prisoners. However, for practical reasons related to the challenge of comparative data analysis (see below) Gershuny also excludes groups below the age of 20 and above the age of 59. While the samples were weighted to take account of socio-demographic changes, the exclusion of the elderly and young adults is problematic. As has been well-documented, a major social trend of the period studied is the growing number of elderly people. This is a group of active consumers who use retirement to engage in a range of leisure pursuits (Higgs et al. 2007) and provide an important source of unpaid work (especially childcare). Likewise, the period studied has witnessed the growth of Further and, subsequently, Higher Education as the likely destination of those leaving compulsory education, and the emergence of youth-based consumer lifestyles (Miles 2000). Despite Gershuny's claims of providing a comprehensive account of socio-economic change, his analysis is then undermined by the exclusion of two social groups who are symbolic of some of the major transformations of the period studied.

A second issue is whether any systematic bias results from high non-response rates. It could be expected that those who are particularly busy or lazy may not complete diaries, and that those not involved in productive activity (the retired, ill and unemployed) may regard their time as not relevant to the objective of time-use studies. To test for such systematic non-response Gershuny takes the 1987 UK time-diary survey, which included both a diary and a questionnaire that asked for self-reported estimations of time-use. Since non-response is largely a case of respondents not completing the diary (in this case 50 per cent of respondents), Gershuny was able to compare the answers to the questionnaires of those who completed diaries with those who did not (the 'non-diarists'). First, the general pattern of self-reported activities for non-diarists was consistent with that of diarists – leading Gershuny to conclude that non-response is not likely to reflect any degree of busyness or laziness on behalf of the respondent. Second, there was no discernible socio-demographic variation between those who completed and those who did not complete the diaries. Of course, there were those who did not complete any component of the survey (diary or questionnaire), but the rate of such non-response was similar to that found in conventional surveys. Gershuny therefore demonstrates that while time diaries have a high non-response rate, this is because of the onerous nature of diary completion and does not significantly bias the sample. Time diaries are reliable sources of data but the omission of the elderly and young adults restricts the capacity to claim that the findings can be generalized across, or are comprehensive accounts of, the populations of the countries studied.

The Recording and Coding of Activities

Time-diary formats vary from 'free text' (illustrated in Figure 4.1), where respondents simply write next to a time slot what it was that they were doing (e.g. 8.00–8.15 a.m.: ate breakfast and supervised children), to precoded diaries in which respondents select from a standardized list of activities. Each approach has its different implications for the way in which time diaries are

Time	What were you doing		Who was involved with you in the main activity?	Where were you during the main activity?	Time
	Main activity in each quarter hour				
12noon	Working		People at work	✓	12noon
.15					.15
.30					.30
.45					.45
1pm	Ate lunch			✓	1pm
.15		read paper		✓	.15
.30	Working	Talked with for eman		✓	.30
.45					.45
2pm					2pm
.15					.15
.30					.30
.45	Travelling (car)		✓	✓	.45
3pm	At dentist	Chat with receptionist	Dentist etc	✓	3pm
.15				✓	.15
.30				✓	.30
.45	Picking up child from school		✓	✓	.45
4pm	Relaxing at home	Get children's tea		✓	4pm
.15	Mowing lawn				.15
.30					.30
.45	Mending fence				.45
5pm	Prepar ed evening meal				5pm
.15					.15
.30					.30
.45	Helped child with homework		✓		.45
6pm	Watched television		✓		6pm
.15	Visiting friends (neighbours)		Neighbours	✓	.15
.30				✓	.30
.45	Ate evening meal		✓ ✓	✓	.45
7pm	Entertained neighbours	Clear ed away	✓ ✓ Neighbours	✓	7pm
.15	Travel (bus)			✓	.15
.30	Drink in pub				.30
.45				✓	.45
8pm	Cinema-to watch film	XXXXXX		✓	8pm

Figure 4.1   A sample time diary
Source: Gershuny (2000: 257).

administered and activities recorded. Free-text diaries provide greater scope for respondents to record the details of their activities, but they can also produce vague accounts. Consider for example the phrase 'get ready for work', which may refer to getting dressed and a range of personal care activities, but which could also include taking care of children, eating or collecting together work files. The free-text approach creates more work for the researcher who must decode respondents' stated activities, and this can lead to inaccuracies when coding. The precoded approach removes such problems by restricting the range of activities from which a respondent can select when filling in the diary. However, this simply transfers the burden of categorizing activities onto the respondent. It is this last factor that has made the free-text collection method the most popular, and was the most common method employed in the 35 time-use studies included in Gershuny's analysis.

1. Paid work	21. Walks
2. Paid work at home	22. Religious activities
3. Second job	23. Civic duties
4. School/classes	24. Cinema, theatre
5. Travel to/from work	25. Dances, parties
6. Cooking, washing up	26. Social club
7. Housework	27. Pub
8. Odd jobs	28. Restaurant
9. Gardening, pets	29. Visiting friends
10. Shopping	30. Listening to radio
11. Childcare	31. Television, video
12. Domestic travel	32. Listening to tapes, etc.
13. Dressing toilet	33. Study
14. Personal services	34. Reading books
15. Meals, snacks	35. Reading papers, magazines
16. Sleep	36. Relaxing
17. Leisure travel	37. Conversation
18. Excursions	38. Entertaining friends
19. Active sport	39. Knitting, sewing, etc.
20. Passive sport	40. Other hobbies and pastimes

Figure 4.2   Forty-category activity classification
Source: Adapted from Gershuny (2000: 279).

How activities are recorded belies a deeper problem with the coding of activities. For Gershuny's analysis, a 40-category activity classification was used (see Figure 4.2), and this formed the basis of Gershuny's broad categories of paid work, unpaid work and leisure and consumption. This is the standard classification devised by the MTUS, and it represents a comprehensive range of activities that more or less have meaning across cultural contexts. Yet difficulties of interpretation remain. Activities that involve eating could be coded as 'pub', 'social club', 'dances and parties', 'restaurant', 'visiting friends', 'entertaining friends' or, of course, 'meals and snacks'. Even where categories of activity appear non-contentious, it remains a matter of subjective opinion as to whether that activity should be classified within broader categories of unpaid work or leisure. Take gardening for example: for one person, mowing the lawn and tending the flowerbeds may be a blissful pastime (leisure); for another, the same activity may constitute a chore to be completed with the utmost haste (unpaid work). While these cases point to the potential for misrepresentation of activities in the coding and categorizing process, diaries also miss some activities altogether. Diaries cannot anticipate fast emerging activities, such as the internet and other computer-mediated activities. Because of these coding difficulties, time diaries can only be seen as crude instruments for capturing the allocation of activities in time; any detailed analysis of specific activities (such as eating and drinking) is subject to much slippage across categories. What is captured by diaries is, at least partially, the implicit social construction of categories by researchers as they attempt to order and organize activities into a coherent and analysable dataset.

The interpretation of activity categories is further complicated by the conduct of simultaneous activities. Most diary formats allow for the recording of at least two activities by respondents. This is important as rarely do people consider themselves to be doing only one activity. Even driving to work often involves more than one activity – travelling to work and, perhaps, listening to the radio. While analysis of simultaneous activities provides important detail, it is difficult systematically to analyse them across several surveys. For the data to be comparable, aggregate analysis of the 24-hour day is necessary. If more than one activity per time slot is accounted for then some members of the population will have more than 24 hours worth of activities! The solution for Gershuny, and the common approach across time-use studies, is to look at primary activities only. In most surveys, what counts as the primary activity is decided by the respondent as the diary is set out with columns for primary and secondary activities (see Figure 4.1).

What gets recorded as a primary activity is subject to normative gender bias. Bonke (2005) and Robinson (1985), writing respectively about Dutch and US time-diary surveys, demonstrate that people who work full-time tend to overstate the actual number of minutes when recording paid work as a primary activity, while those who report working part-time hours tended to underestimate. Interpretations of what counts as a primary or secondary activity also varies across gender. Nock and Kingston (1988) reveal that when fathers watch television with their children, they record childcare (unpaid work) as the primary activity and television (leisure) as the secondary activity. Women record the reverse (childcare becomes the secondary activity). They argue that there is a systematic under-reporting of unpaid work by women when 'primary activities' only are included in diary analysis (as was the case with Gershuny's study). In addition to revealing systematic bias in the coding of activities this suggests more serious flaws in Gershuny's analysis of gender convergence. As men are still more likely to work full-time and women part-time, it is reasonable to suggest that the diaries overestimate the amount of paid and unpaid work that men do and underestimate the amount of paid and unpaid work performed by women. Gershuny's gender convergence may be exaggerated.

Accounting for Differential Experiences of Time

Time-diary methods are limited in the temporal experiences that they capture. As Roberts (2002) states, time-diary data tend to be sex and crime free, and the surveys are constrained by the diary format in their capacity to record information about meanings, motivations and feelings. Many argue that attempting to treat time like money condemns the analysis to a rationalized, scientific account of daily life in which time is nothing more than a commodity to be exchanged (Adam 1995; Paolucci 1993). Missing are accounts of temporal experiences beyond the duration of an activity. For one person the experience of shopping may be slow, boring and repetitive, for another that experience passes quickly, is fun and exhilarating, but both may spend 70 minutes a day in that activity.

While Gershuny's analysis does not capture differential experiences of time, it is wrong to suggest that the methodology is incapable of doing so. Sullivan's (1997) analysis of domestic tasks performed jointly between couples was able to demonstrate convincingly that the sexes take responsibility for the organization of particular domestic tasks and therefore experience those tasks differently. Bittman and Wajcman (2000) also captured differential temporal experiences in relation to leisure time. They took time-diary data for all OECD countries (broadly similar to the countries included in Gershuny's study) and showed that while men and women reported having the same amount of leisure time, the quality of that time was very different. Men's leisure time was uninterrupted by secondary activities. Women's leisure time was punctuated with interruptions, and a much greater proportion of it was done simultaneously with secondary activities like childcare. This is important with respect to Gershuny's substantive finding regarding gendered time-use. Even if there has been convergence in work and leisure between the sexes, it does not necessarily produce equality of experience of that time. More significantly, these studies demonstrate that when secondary, as well as primary, activities are analysed, time diaries have the capacity to capture differential experiences of time.

Gershuny is fully aware of the weaknesses of time-diary methodologies and provides a robust defence of them. He rightly points out that no survey data is perfect, and that over- and underestimates are part and parcel of any research methodology. A reflexive sociology requires that the researcher recognizes the limitations of the data, but that does not render empirical evidence flawed or worthless. Gershuny is correct to reiterate that time-diary data can only indicate tendencies, and that no data source can provide *actual* measures of time spent working or in other activities (unless based on real-time recordings). Further, it is important to recognize that time diaries have consistently been shown to measure the changing distribution of activities within time and across social groups in more accurate ways than any other data source (see also Andorka 1987; Bonke 2005; Chenu and Lesnard 2006; Robinson and Godbey 1997). Despite its flaws, the time-diary methodology has value as an instrument for indicating 'broad-brush' patterns of socio-economic change.

The Challenge of Comparative Data Analysis

One of the great attractions of time-diary data is that the surveys have a degree of comparability. Because many activities are universal (everyone must eat, in most developed societies people go shopping, watch television, and so on) it is possible to compare activities on a 'like-with-like' basis. A deeper look at the data does, however, raise further questions about the degree to which it can capture the detail of change across societies.

The first problem emerges when comparing the time intervals used by different surveys to record respondents' activities. Chenu and Lesnard (2006) demonstrate that changes between surveys in the time intervals recorded have a significant impact on comparative analyses. To illustrate this they explore the French time-diary surveys of 1986 and 1998. The former used time intervals of five minutes while the latter employed ten minute intervals. The impact of this change in survey design was significant. The surveys showed an increase of mealtime duration, which contradicted the trend revealed in other countries where fast foods had the effect of reducing the length of meal times. Chenu and Lesnard (2006: 346) explain this apparent contradiction not as a result of the particularities of French culinary tradition, but because the 1998 diaries with longer intervals included 'small' unpaid work tasks, such as 'laying the table, doing the dishes, and taking a mid-meal break'. The implications are twofold: (i) comparing diaries that use different time intervals produces misrepresentations of comparative rates of change; (ii) surveys with shorter time intervals capture in more detail those activities that tend to be least memorable and most mundane – unpaid work. At the 'broad' level of activity analysis conducted by Gershuny it is unlikely that variable intervals between surveys undermine the general patterns identified, but the accuracy of more specific observations related to comparative change of singular activities is brought into question.

A second issue relates to the difficulty of harmonizing variables used in different surveys. Because the data need be comparable, coding must be done to the lowest common denominator. This was the practical reason why only those aged between 20 and 59 were included in the sample: some studies did not contain data for respondents outside of this age bracket. A similar problem occurs with the analysis of social class, which was omitted or classified differently across the studies and rendered non-comparable. To address this,

Gershuny was forced to construct a 'socio-economic status' variable using educational achievement and income. This is difficult given that educational systems and income levels vary from country to country such that what constitutes high or low educational achievement or a generous salary is difficult to compare. Gershuny's solution is to analyse respondents' levels of income and education relative to others within the same survey (and therefore the same society). To some extent this overcomes the problem of accounting for variable systems of classifying education and income within surveys, but it leaves the analysis of change over time to be largely a construct of relative measures imposed on the data to render it comparable (since those with high socio-economic status will always be a set percentage of the highest earners with high educational achievement). What constitutes 'high' or 'low' socio-economic status is based on sets of assumptions regarding variable classifications of education and income across a wide range of studies.

The final weakness of Gershuny's comparative analysis is the interpretation of what constitutes 'trajectories' of change. Critical to his account is the empirical identification of 'three convergences'. In producing these results the focus is on the trajectories of broad activity categories (paid work, unpaid work, and leisure and consumption) rather than the relative rates of change across the activities that make up those categories. This results in the masking of much national variation. The following example illustrates the point. Gershuny's data reveals a general decline in time spent reading for men but a moderate increase for women. The accuracy of this finding is not in dispute, but the implication of a common international trajectory is. Using the same data, Southerton et al. (2007) reveal that between the 1970s and 2000 the Netherlands and the USA have both seen a significant decline of time spent reading. However, for the latter years of the study, 87 per cent of the Dutch population took part in this activity, devoting on average 42 minutes per day, while in the USA only 19 per cent of the population read on the days of survey and the average for the population was 22 minutes per day. Both countries share a trajectory of declining time spent reading, but in the Netherlands this is a decline from a situation where almost everyone read, while in the USA it represents the decline of a minority activity. Southerton et al. (2007) also reveal different patterns for other countries. Book reading has increased in France but is masked by a decline of time spent reading magazines and newspapers, whereas in the UK and Norway time spent reading has increased since 1975. When particular activities are examined in detail, comparative trajectories of change are revealed to be far more complex and contradictory than Gershuny's 'broad category' data can allow for.

Even when trajectories of change in social practices are revealed as consistent, caution is still required before identifying convergence. Again, using the same data as Gershuny, Warde et al. (2007) reveal similarities of trajectory in changing time-use allocated to food consumption across France, the Netherlands, Norway, the UK and the USA. The dominant trend is for a decline in time spent eating at home and a rise of time spent eating out (corroborated by Gershuny's data). However, in France and the UK the practice of eating out remains strongly differentiated by social class, indicating this to be an activity symbolic of social status and a source of distinction. This was not the case in the other countries. Similarity of trajectory does not equate to similarity of experience, and, despite the generic trends, eating out clearly means something very different across these nations.

Comparative research is hugely problematic because different activities can mean something different across societies. In Gershuny's case, the data at his disposal is so vast that to provide any more detailed analysis than he already does would produce several volumes of results and render any general patterns indecipherable. His study does provide more detail beyond the 'three convergences', but variability of time intervals used by different studies, assumptions required to construct the variable of socio-economic status, and a focus only on the trajectory of broad activity categories lead the general empirical conclusions to be little more than tendencies. When those tendencies are subjected to detailed scrutiny the comparative picture becomes far more complex. However, and building from Gershuny's starting point, more systematic and detailed comparative accounts of change in relation to specific social practices is necessary. Such analyses would provide the basis for a synthetic account of the complexities of socio-economic change across societies. For now, Gershuny's tendencies must be taken for exactly that and not assumed to be evidence of globalization towards some common norm: variations in national experiences and the cultural significance of activities must not be dismissed on the basis of generic trends.

Theory and Time-Diary Data Capacity

Gershuny's empirical evidence is consistent with the theory advanced, but it does not corroborate all of the claims. The acid test of any research is the extent to which the empirical data supports the key theoretical claims. As Roberts (2002) points out, a significant claim is that there has been a shift from low- to high-skilled work, but time diaries provide no evidence or measure of the amount of 'skill' required in conducting paid work. Gershuny takes income levels as an indication of the increased 'value-added' of an individual or group of workers, and hence to support the notion that they are 'higher' skilled. This is a dubious assumption: higher earnings do not necessarily equate with higher skill; and, as already discussed, income was measured in relative terms within each study and does not necessarily reflect a growth of 'high-skilled' workers. Regardless of measurement, the claim that increased consumption of high-value-added services will produce more high-value-added jobs is problematic. Many such services are located in the food, drink, tourism and entertainment sectors – leisure industries that comprise a large number of low-skilled workers. Even in the most exclusive restaurants low-value-added jobs (cleaners and waiting staff) outnumber the high-value-added jobs (the head chef). Occupations are far more varied within the service sector than Gershuny's theory allows for.

A second and related difficulty is that even if we do see a shift towards high-value-added production (jobs) and consumption (leisure), it is difficult to sustain the argument that this represents socio-economic development. The underlying assumption is that such production and consumption activities bring greater intrinsic rewards to the individual. Many low-skilled production activities provide for senses of accomplishment. There is undoubted drudgery involved in washing dishes and preparing meals, but such labour also brings some emotional satisfactions (Hochschild 1997). There is also a growing weight of evidence to suggest that consumption plays a significant role in the generation of contemporary time pressures. This evidence is not the same as Schor's (1992) 'work-spend cycles' where people work more to consume more: a theory refuted by Gershuny's data which does not show more time in paid work. Rather, the growing varieties of goods and services available for consumption, coupled with greater individual flexibility in the scheduling of consumer practices, leads to problems of coordination across social groups. It is not that people lack time, it is that the time they have available for leisure is not aligned with the people whom they would like to spend that time with (Southerton 2003). If this is the case, more time for consumption will not necessarily reduce 'time pressures', improve well-being or represent 'social progress', even if it would encourage economic growth.

The third and final weakness of Gershuny's theoretical account is that it treats time in 'zero sum' terms, where the addition of, say, ten minutes in one activity must result in the loss of ten minutes allocated to another. Time is far more elastic than this. Gershuny's data takes no account of the rhythms of daily life, that consumption activities have temporal constraints not only related to how much leisure time one has available or whether one can afford to engage in the activity. Many consumption activities require the co-participation of others, such as eating a family meal and playing sport (Southerton 2006). Changes in time-use may, therefore, be better explained by processes such as geographical mobility (where people live and work increasingly further away from family and friends), flexible working hours (people work at different times from family and friends) and the changing materialities of daily life (technologies not only save but shift the sequencing and timing of practices (Shove and Southerton 2000)). By focusing his data analysis on explaining his key theoretical claims Gershuny does not fully explore alternative, and not necessarily contradictory, accounts of the changing ways in which time is organized and experienced.

Conclusion

Gershuny succeeds with his primary objective: he convincingly demonstrates the rich and wide application of time-diary data to an enormous range of fields within the social sciences. The consumption and production of goods and services, urban planning and infrastructures, social inequalities, the informal economy, globalization, sustainability, technological and organization innovations, indicators of well-being, and health are just some of the fields of enquiry in which time diaries could offer fresh insights. Gershuny takes the lead by using the data to good effect and by producing a sophisticated and largely persuasive account of socio-economic change.

There are limitations to the time-diary methodology. High non-response rates, the omission of certain groups, normative bias in the recording of activities and interpretation of coding categories, and the use only of primary activities raise questions as to the detailed accuracy of the data. This is problematic as one of Gershuny's key findings is gender convergence, a finding undermined by other time-diary evidence which shows systematic bias in the recording of paid and unpaid work and differential experiences of time across the sexes. The need to render the data comparable, results in the construction of a relative variable of socio-economic status that makes comparison between status groups problematic and leads to the omission of important age groups. Further, the broad categories of activity (paid work, unpaid work and leisure) used to identify trajectories across nations mask the complexities of comparing changing time-use across cultures. Looked at this way, the 'three convergences' identified by Gershuny must be subjected to empirical caution.

Gershuny's theory, which essentially explains socio-economic change through the shifting balance of time devoted to production and consumption, rests on a zero sum empirical interpretation of time. This interpretation discounts alternative explanations that focus more on the rhythm and coordination of practices. This does not have to be the case, as other time-use studies demonstrate the methodology's capacity to capture differential experiences of time, to analyse simultaneous activities and produce detailed comparative examination of how practices change over time and space. Despite their limitations, time-diary methodologies do provide an essential tool for systematic comparative analysis of the changing organization of social, economic and cultural life, and this is demonstrated in *Changing Times*. While Gershuny's account can only be read as generic, that was always his intention. As he rightly states, his analysis 'is undoubtedly, as yet, thin evidence on which to base a picture of the way the world is changing. But ... we have to start somewhere' (Gershuny 2000: 15).

On final reflection, the theory advanced from the data analysis is honourable in its intentions, but the call for humane modernization is based on generalized claims about 'high-skilled' labour, 'high-value-added services' and the assumption that more time for consumption would benefit society. This does not undermine the importance of the research. This is a study that represents a crucial start, an exemplar of and call for the comparative analysis of time-diary evidence necessary to understand fully the relationships between time and socio-economic change. Gershuny succeeds in this objective and, most important of all, demonstrates the necessity of advancing methodologies, such as time-diary data, that measure national accounts by taking full consideration of social as well as economic forms of development.

Additional Reading

Robinson and Godbey's (1997) *Time for Life* is an excellent account of the changing patterns of time-use in the USA and is an authoritative book on time-diary methodologies, while Schor's *The Overworked American* (1992) presents an influential account of socio-economic change and welfare with the aid of evidence from time diaries. For a more general overview of theories of time and a critique of time-diary data see Adam's book *Timewatch* (1995). To find out more about quantitative methods and comparative research, Rose and Sullivan's *Introducing Data Analysis for Social Scientists*, 2nd edn (1996) is a good place to start.

Acknowledgements

I'd like to thank Jonathan Gershuny, for his comments on a draft of this chapter, and the editors, Fiona Devine and Sue Heath, for their highly constructive comments during the writing process.

References

Adam, B. (1995) *Timewatch*, Cambridge: Polity.
Andorka, R. (1987) 'Time budgets and their uses', *Annual Review of Sociology*, 13: 149–64.
Bell, D. (1979) *The Cultural Contradictions of Capitalism*, London: Heinemann.
Bittman, M. and J. Wajcman (2000) 'The rush hour: the character of leisure time and gender equity', *Social Forces*, 79(1): 165–89.
Bonke, J. (2005) 'Paid work and unpaid work: diary information versus questionnaire information', *Social Indicators Research*, 70: 349–68.
Chenu, A. and L. Lesnard (2006) 'Time-use surveys: a review of their aims, methods, and results', *European Journal of Sociology*, 47(3): 335–59.

Gershuny, J. (2000) *Changing Times: Work and Leisure in Postindustrial Society*, Oxford: Oxford University Press.

Gershuny, J., M. Godwin and S. Jones (1994) 'The domestic labour revolution: a process of lagged adaptation', in M. Anderson, F. Bechhofer and J. Gershuny (eds), *The Social and Political Economy of the Household*, Oxford: Oxford University Press.

Higgs, P., M. Evandrou, C. Gilleard, M. Hyde, I.R. Jones, C. Victor and D. Wiggins (2007) 'Ageing and consumption patterns in Britain 1968–2001', *Generations Review*, 17: . Accessed at http://www.britishgerontology.org/newsletter2/research14.asp.

Hochschild, A. (1997) *The Time Bind: When Work becomes Home and Home Becomes Work*, New York: Metropolitan Books.

Linder, S.B. (1970) *The Harried Leisure Class*, Columbia: Columbia University Press.

Miles, S. (2000) *Youth Lifestyles in a Changing World*, Buckingham: Open University Press.

Nock, S. and P. Kingston (1988) 'Time with children: the impact of couples' work time commitments', *Journal of Statistics*, 67: 59–85.

Oakley, A. (1974) *The Sociology of Housework*, London: Martin Robertson.

Paolucci, N. (1993) *Tempi Postmoderni*, Franco Angeli: Milan.

Perrons, D., C. Fagan, L. McDowell, K. Ray and K. Ward (2005) 'Work, life and time in the new economy: an introduction', *Time & Society*, 14(1): 51–64.

Roberts, K. (2002) 'Review of changing times: work and leisure in postindustrial society', *Sociology*, 36(2): 465–67.

Robinson, J. (1985) 'The validity and reliability of diaries versus alternative time-use measures', in F. Juster and P. Stafford (eds), *Time, Goods, and Well Being*, Ann Arbor: University of Michigan Press.

Robinson, J. and G. Godbey (1997) *Time for Life: The Surprising Ways that Americans Use their Time*, University Park, PA: Pennsylvania State Press.

Rose, D. and O. Sullivan (1996) *Introducing Data Analysis for Social Scientists*, 2nd edn, Buckingham: Open University Press.

Rubery, J., K. Ward, D. Grimshaw and H. Beynon (2005) 'Working time, industrial relations and the employment relationship, *Time & Society*, 14(1): 89–111.

Schor, J. (1992) *The Overworked American: The Unexpected Decline of Leisure*, New York: Basic Books.

Shove, E. and D. Southerton (2000) 'Defrosting the freezer: from novelty to convenience: a story of normalization', *Journal of Material Culture*, 5(3): 301–19 .

Southerton, D. (2003) 'Squeezing time: allocating practices, co-ordinating networks and scheduling society', *Time & Society*, 12(1): 5–25.

Southerton, D. (2006) 'Analysing the temporal organisation of daily life: social constraints, practices and their allocation', *Sociology*, 40(3): 435–54.

Southerton, D., A. Warde, S.-L. Cheng and W. Olsen (2007) 'Trajectories of time spent reading as a primary activity: a comparison of the Netherlands, Norway, France, UK and USA since the 1970s', CRESC Working Paper 29.

Sullivan, O. (1997) 'Time waits for no (wo)men: an investigation of the gendered experience of domestic time', *Sociology*, 31(2): 221–40.

Thompson, C. (1996) 'Caring consumers: gendered consumption meanings and the juggling lifestyle', *Journal of Consumer Research*, 22: 388–407.

Veblen, T. (1925 [1899]) *The Theory of the Leisure Class: An Economic Study of Institutions*, London: Allen & Unwin.

Warde, A., S.-L. Cheng, W. Olsen and D. Southerton (2007) 'Changes in the practice of eating: a comparative analysis of time-use', *Acta Sociologica*, 50(4): 365–87.

CHAPTER 5

Place: Savage et al.'s *Globalization and Belonging*

WENDY BOTTERO

This chapter focuses on some of the methodological challenges involved in a large-scale qualitative study of 'attachment to place' conducted in Manchester by Mike Savage and his colleagues, based on 182 in-depth interviews with residents in four middle-class neighbourhoods of the city. Wendy Bottero explores a number of questions that are raised by this research. First, she considers some of the challenges of analysing qualitative data on such a large scale, and the attendant risk that the sample might be regarded as too large for qualitative researchers, yet too small for quantitative researchers. Second, Bottero explores the related issue concerning the degree to which narrative accounts generated in interviews can be used to develop macrolevel theorizing of the kind engaged in by Savage et al. Third, she considers the analytical affordance of interview data and the extent to which the patterns of response generated by the research team might be an artefact of the method as much as a reflection of the participants' own concerns and silences. Fourth, Bottero notes the investigators' shifting research aims as the project unfolded, before considering the implications of these shifts for the project's research design.

Introduction

Globalization and Belonging is about 'the nature of local belonging in a global world' (Savage et al. 2005: ix). An ambitious large-scale qualitative study of the relationship between locale, lifestyles and social identities, Savage et al.'s book examines the formation of 'attachment to place' in Manchester, a large city in the north-west of England. Arguments of globalization have put such 'local' attachments under theoretical scrutiny, but they remain empirically under-researched. The book addresses this gap by researching 'elective belonging' in four Manchester neighbourhoods, drawing on in-depth interviews with 182 local residents, exploring issues of cultural identity, lifestyles, neighbourhood milieu and social networks. The research subject of the book – attachment to place – straddles several distinct areas of sociological analysis: community studies, globalization debates, class analysis and urban sociology, which all pursue quite different research agendas and methodologies. The book links these debates, but also moves beyond them, placing them in a different theoretical and methodological framework. The authors adopt a critical approach to conventional understandings of 'class', 'community' and 'globalization', and their own preconceptions of some of these concepts changed radically during the course of the research. The project also shifted its theoretical and research aims midway through the research, with interesting implications as to how we view the research process and its findings. By interviewing such a large number of respondents the study also combines quantitative and qualitative methods.

The study concludes that local identities remain important, but are not generated through face-to-face interaction or long residence in a 'neighbourhood'; instead they emerge through 'mediated' means and a symbolic 'sense' of place. People feel 'at home' not according to whether they are 'born and bred' in a neighbourhood, but rather according to whether their locale 'feels right for someone like them'. So 'belonging is not that of an individual to a fixed community rooted in place, but rather, one in which the place becomes valuable to the individual' (ibid.: 80). Rejecting older views of 'community', the study argues that we must recognize new kinds of 'elective belonging', in which (many) people actively *choose* a place to live that suits their sense of self, using media and other signifiers to help them to do this, and so linking their personal identification with that of place. But more advantaged groups have greater control over this process and are better able to search out how to live with 'people like us'. The project raises a host of methodological questions: in this chapter, I focus on four, interrelated, issues. First, what problems arise from using qualitative methods on a very large sample? Second, can interview narratives reveal broader social processes or patterns? Third, what is the impact of using interview material to explore questions of embodiment and the tacit practices of the habitus? Fourth, did the project's shifting research aims and theoretical focus influence the effectiveness of its methodological strategy? Before considering these issues, I turn to the broader background to Savage et al.'s research.

The Shifting Theoretical Context and Project Aims

This study changed its theoretical direction midway. Arising from a 1996 project entitled 'Lifestyles and Social Integration: A Study of Middle-class

Culture in Manchester', the original intention was to explore the significance of *class* for consumption, leisure and lifestyle. At that time, there had been considerable research in Britain on the impact of (occupational) class on life-chances and educational achievement, but much less work on the impact of class on *lifestyles*. The authors wanted to explore this angle, with a particular focus on *middle-class* lifestyles. However, between the course of the research (conducted between 1997 and 1999) and the bulk of the analysis (conducted between 2002 and 2003) the authors became increasingly disillusioned with the 'employment-aggregate' style of class analysis (whereby social class status is derived from one's occupational status) and doubtful whether 'employment class' was a major influence on identity and lifestyles. One of the first project publications was an article indicating the relative weakness of (occupational) class identities (Savage et al. 2001). So when they came to write the book, the authors' 'framing concerns' had shifted from occupational class to under-standing the *locales* in which they had conducted the interviews and the impact of such locales on lifestyle and identity. Could class cultures and lifestyles be seen as the result of residential processes?

This shift reflects the 'cultural turn' in class analysis, and one of the authors, Mike Savage, has been a major figure in this theoretical move. A response to the increasing awareness of the significance of consumption and lifestyle in social life, the cultural turn reworks how 'class' is understood (Savage 2000). In the older employment-aggregate mode of class analysis, 'classes' – identified as groupings of occupations with similar employment rela-tions – were investigated, using large-scale quantitative analysis, for their impact on life-chances (Crompton 1996: 59). However, for 'cultural class analysts', cultural practices and lifestyles are not simply a *consequence* of employment relations, but are a central mechanism by which class inequalities are *constituted* (Devine and Savage 2000). Such accounts draw inspiration from the French theorist Pierre Bourdieu (1984). For Bourdieu, our position in the social hierarchy depends on the *combination* of the 'capitals' available to us – as it is not just our economic resources, but also our social networks and symbolic and cultural resources, which maintain and advance our social pos-itions. This expanded understanding of 'class' provides the key interpretative framework of the book.

The authors' shifting understanding of class redirected their attention from issues of work and employment to, instead, an exploring of the local contexts in which consumption and lifestyle takes place. In doing so, the authors had to engage with another set of debates about the impact of *globalization* on local communities and attachment to place. Older debates in community studies, using case-study research, had already questioned the idea that a 'community' comprised a discrete, relatively homogeneous grouping, engaged in face-to-face interaction within a clearly defined locality; later work in urban sociology further fragmented the notion of 'community' by establishing the considerable geographical mobility and fluidity of local social relations (Bulmer 1985; Crow and Allan 1994; Crow 2002; Savage et al. 2003). This questioning of the significance of 'community as locality' has been exacerbated by theoretical debates on the impact of globalization, which argue that 'in a world characterised by virtual communication, institutional deregulation, and the movement of capital, information, objects and people at great speed across large distances, social life cannot be seen as firmly located in particular places with clear boundaries' (Savage et al. 2005: 1). Could the project legitimately explore how locality affects class processes, if globalization means that locality is no longer really important? The problem was that 'it was not clear what the-oretical warrant there was for emphasising local processes when, in a global-ized world, people and objects were held to be mobile' (ibid.: ix).

Authors rarely raise such problems unless they feel they can solve them, and these authors were sceptical of grand theoretical suggestions that globalization has eroded the impact of locale on social life. Long-running debates on this topic have indicated the lack of empirical evidence to support such claims, with critics suggesting that globalization does not destroy the 'local', but simply refashions it, producing new forms of '"home", "community" and "locality"' (Robertson 1992: 30). However, the authors were cautious of these arguments too, because they felt that it was not clear what the 'local' now meant in such accounts, for 'given the general acceptance that neighbourhoods are not now (even if they ever were) face-to-face communities, how could we understand the salience of place?' (Savage et al. 2005: ix).

The authors had to come up with new theoretical tools to analyse their data; data which they felt showed the continuing importance of territoriality for social relationships. They looked for alternative frameworks for under-standing 'the stakes that fixed sites bring', arguing that 'global flows do not eclipse embodiment and property' (ibid.: 8). A theory of embodiment was needed to recognize the 'relative immobility of humans vis-à-vis flows of goods and symbols' and the significance of territory, whilst a theory of property was needed to examine how territory 'defines landed property and capital ... elaborated through the idea of a spatial fix' (ibid.: 7). The project explored how the 'spatial fixity' of certain social practices (such as the relative availability and affordability of different types of housing, or the significance of educational provision for parenting and schooling in different areas) affects people's relations to their physical locale. The project was also concerned to explore how some practices (such as media use) are less spatially fixed than others, and so needed to address the symbolic nature of understandings of 'place' and the impact of the (global) media in such processes. To do so, the authors drew upon 'network and relational conceptions to suggest the need for an account of the "local" which is not contrasted with the "global", but which situates the local against *other locals* in an environment where comparisons and references are multiple and complex' (ibid.). Finally, there was a need to explore the *embodied* nature of social life. For this the authors again looked to Bourdieu (1984) and his emphasis on the relations between habitus and field, which sees people's dispositions as embodied and so 'necessarily territorially located'.

Bourdieu argues that our tastes and ambitions are shaped by the people and social conditions around us and become bodily incorporated into our habitus. This approach was used to focus on 'attachment to place' in terms of embodied, territorial feelings of 'comfort'. In Bourdieu's framework, the habitus is our 'practical knowledge' or 'sense' of how to move in the social world, which operates in implicit, taken-for-granted ways, as a sort of 'social instinct'. The key issue is how well our habitus – our bodily know-how and social dispositions – fits the social circumstances and places in which we operate. For the social world is also divided into different social *fields*, relatively discrete social arenas (such as the field of education or of housing), which have their own distinct 'rules of the game'. When our habitus is adapted to the field in which we operate then we have an instinctive 'feel for the game' and we feel at ease. If our habitus is less well adapted, then we are uncertain as to how to 'play the game' and we can feel like a 'fish out of water'. For Savage et al., this theoretical framework is crucial for understanding attachment to place, since such attachments depend on how well the individual's sense of self fits his or her sense of the social milieu, affecting the 'bodily comfort that people experience in different social situations – *which are also physical situations*' (Savage et al. 2005: 9).

Research Strategy, Design and Findings

Reflecting the original intention to investigate *middle-class* consumption and leisure practices and lifestyles, the project design compared four middle-class neighbourhoods (see Figure 5.1), drawing on in-depth qualitative interviews with local residents, to explore issues of cultural identity, lifestyles, neighbourhood milieu and social networks. The strategy was deliberately selective: though the areas were chosen to 'exemplify different kinds of social mix', this was within a range of loosely middle-class neighbourhoods with a conscious avoidance of working-class or poorer areas. The neighbourhoods were chosen on the basis of their different combinations of economic and cultural capital, with the aim of exploring diversity within the city 'without sacrificing detailed knowledge of the particularity of each area' (ibid.: 15). Rather than attempt to explore Manchester as a whole, the team chose varied neighbourhoods which would allow them to explore the 'interplay between global processes and the formation of distinct local milieux' (ibid.).

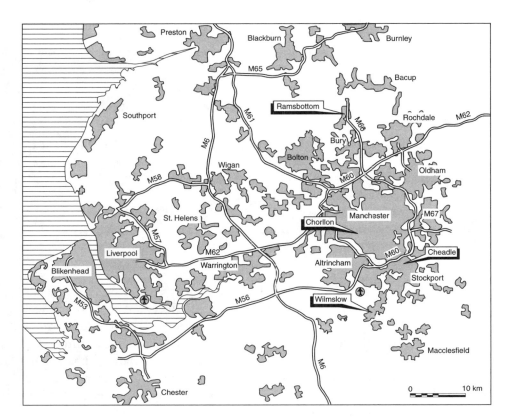

Figure 5.1   Location of case study areas
Source: Savage et al. 2005: 18.

The areas used were: *Wilmslow*, in the desirable north Cheshire suburban belt, an area whose inhabitants had high levels of economic capital but more moderate levels of cultural capital; *Chorlton*, a district of urban gentrification with new cafes, wine bars and restaurants, whose inhabitants had high levels of cultural capital but more moderate levels of economic capital; *Ramsbottom*, a commuter zone of rural gentrification with relatively affluent households but fewer highly educated respondents; and *Cheadle*, an 'ordinary' suburban estate whose inhabitants had lower levels of economic and cultural capital. The team used data from the Census Small Area Statistics to establish neighbourhood variation and to identify target areas to study; and they confirmed that the areas they selected did indeed have very different profiles of economic and cultural capital, according to their combination of ACORN postcode categories (a geodemographic information system which categorizes UK postcodes into various types based upon census data and lifestyle surveys). However, the selection criteria and the rationale behind this strategy are only very briefly outlined. Beyond mentioning their desire for contrasting middle-class neighbourhoods, the authors do not indicate how or why these neighbourhoods, rather than others, were chosen.

Table 5.1   Statistics of achieved sample

Dimensions	Cheadle	Chorlton	Ramsbottom	Wilmslow
Mean household income (£)	23,000	30,000	36,000	70,000
Graduates (%)	14	60	19	45
Upper service class (%)	3	18	26	42
Service class (%)	24	60	62	63
Female (%)	35	53	45	62
Mean age	46	40	45	54
Ethnic minority (%)	2	2	4	4
No. of interviews	43	47	47	45
Response rates (%)	29	39	30	41

Source: Savage et al. 2005: 21.

Manchester is a revealing case study because, as well as containing neighbourhoods which are economically and culturally diverse, it has experienced many of the processes of globalization that have been alleged to undermine local attachments and identities. A leading European population centre, with over 4 million inhabitants, it was the first 'industrial city', and it has experienced both urban decline, as a result of deindustrialism, and urban regeneration, with the city having been 'rebranded' to attract capital, professionals and visitors (Devine et al. 2000; Britton et al. 2004). The city is now known for its football, its arts and music scene, and for the city centre redevelopment which has encouraged affluent residents back into urban living – in warehouse conversions and the 'gay village'.

To select their sample of respondents within each neighbourhood, the project used the electoral register as a sampling frame. In each area, the researchers took a one-in-three sample of particular streets, arranging interviews by letter, telephone and by knocking on doors, to generate around 45 interviews in each location (182 in total), with a response rate of 34 per cent. Although the study was of middle-class neighbourhoods, like all areas they varied in their social composition, and this is reflected in the sample, with some respondents working in manual (working-class) occupations. However, reflecting the initial project aim of exploring middle-class lifestyles, overall the research was based upon a predominantly middle-class (and overwhelmingly 'white') sample (see Table 5.1).

The methodological strategy was to conduct large-scale qualitative research, in order to look at social and cultural practices *in context*, relating people's narratives to the sites of their work, residence and leisure. The interview schedules were designed to ask people about their daily routines at work, at leisure, at home, and with friends and kin, so as to explore the 'spatial range' of these practices, but also to explore how people's narratives 'spontaneously invoked any other kinds of issue as they talked' (Longhurst et al. 2004: 108). The semi-structured interviews covered a range of topics: neighbourhood and the local milieu; leisure activities; household relations; work and work histories; as well as specific questions on class and ethnicity. The 182 interviews lasted around 75 minutes and, when the recordings were transcribed, resulted in over 1.5 million words of transcription on a wide range of topics.

The use of qualitative methods on such a large-scale is unusual, particularly in the British context (although see Buck et al. 2002; Butler and Robson 2003). Most qualitative studies are based on much smaller sample sizes. The authors drew on the example of two American studies, Bellah et al. (1996) and Wolfe (1998), both of which involved large-scale in-depth interviews to explore changing middle-class American culture. The idea behind conducting so many interviews was partly to use qualitative research to address 'macro' issues of global change, attempting to link agency and structure, the subjective and the objective.

Findings

Have global connections and flows affected local attachments and identities? Many local areas are now characterized by considerable diversity and fluidity (perhaps they always were), and the authors found that, in all but one of the neighbourhoods studied, 'local' people were a minority of their sample, with 'incomers' the dominant group. The authors conclude that such geographical mobility, and the role of the media in breaking down barriers of space, do undermine any notion of the 'local' as a fixed and bounded attachment to place, such that 'local social relations' are not 'defined by the activities, values and cultures of those "born and bred" in an area' (Savage et al. 2005: 29). But this does not undermine 'attachment to place' or the impact of local milieu. The authors stress three main issues here: (a) the importance of 'elective belonging', based on the fit between people's 'sense of self' and their 'sense of place'; (b) that 'belonging' must be 'worked at'; and (c) that 'belonging' is also about how people place themselves within an 'imaginary' landscape.

Elective Belonging

While 'born and bred' locals in the study did report a sense of *familiarity* with their area, they did not necessarily convey a sense of *belonging*. It was the 'perceptions and values of incoming migrant groups' who established 'dominant place identities and attachments' (Savage et al. 2004: 28) for 'those who have an account of why they live in a place, and can relate their residence to their choices and circumstances, are the most "at home"' (Savage et al. 2005: 45). 'Elective belonging' emerges when places are 'sites for performing identities. Individuals attach their own biography to their "chosen" residential location, so that they tell stories that indicate how their arrival and subsequent settlement is appropriate to their sense of themselves' (ibid.: 29).

It is the 'fit' between a group's *sense of self* and their *sense of the place they live in* that results in a feeling of 'elective belonging' to that area. For example, in Chorlton, the liberal urban professional residents felt most 'at home', as their 'cosmopolitan' outlook meshed well with their neighbourhood's good 'social mix', and its gentrified provision of trendy cafes and shops supported their preferred style of life. Such findings mean the authors reject a view popular in post-war community studies, the idea that neighbourhoods are characterized by tensions between 'locals' and 'incomers'. In the areas studied, it was not 'incomers' but rather transients, like students, who were met with disapproval. This disapproval was related to the issue of 'elective belonging'. Such transients were merely 'passing through' and had not made a commitment to 'place', compared to those who felt 'at home', who had made a 'choice to live somewhere and make "a go of it"'.

Working at Belonging

Making 'a go' of living in an area, and developing feelings of belonging, are dependent on the ability to engage in specific sorts of activities, for 'having a sense of community, or feeling that you belong are not inherent qualities of living in a particular locality, but rather have to be worked at, have to be achieved' (ibid.: 62). Children – and schooling – were important in the 'work' of 'locating' families (particularly for women), with the process of choosing schools, and of forming (weak) ties at the school gate or in the Parent Teacher Association, a means for 'performing' belonging. The nature of educational provision was important for whether 'people feel more or less comfortable in place', which the authors connect to 'the extent to which educational options [e.g. state or private schooling] are more or less congruent with the habitus of the respondents and/or their cultural values and imaginary construction of place' (ibid.: 71–2). The key question is whether people are able to perform such activities in a manner that 'fits' their sense of their values and biography. The 'comforts of place' generated by such activities varied enormously between the respondents, depending on how their cultural and economic capital and values matched with the local facilities, and with that of their neighbours. The sense of 'fit' – between respondents' senses of self and the 'feel' they had of their neighbourhood – was crucial. However, this *sense* of locale was not just dependent upon the activities and social connections managed within it. The study also looked at the nature of people's social ties, and found that 'situational ties' (arising from daily routines, at work and from neighbouring and schooling activities) were relatively 'weak' and limited forms of connection, clearly demarcated from closer ties with friends and family. Ties with neighbours were weak, with 'good' neighbouring partly about keeping a 'proper distance'. So whilst 'elective belonging' was partly about being able to 'identify one's neighbours as "people like us"', this was less a concern about the 'quality and nature of local ties and personal relationships' than about the ability 'to place oneself in an imaginary landscape which is central to people's sense of belonging' (ibid.: 90).

The Imaginary Landscape

The 'aura of place' emerged relationally, through the contrasts respondents made between their neighbourhood and other locations, with a 'mediatised imagination' used to mark affinities between local and far away places. Many individuals in the study had a well-developed sense of regional and 'northern' identity, partly established through their discussions of favourite TV programmes like *Coronation Street* (a soap opera set in a fictional location in Greater Manchester). 'Arrival' stories of how residents had come to decide upon their area as the 'appropriate' place to live, and to have chosen it over others, were full of these symbolic contrasts and identifications, which helped people construct a 'sense' of their location. In Ramsbottom, residents spoke of how they had been attracted to its 'hilly landscapes' and to a particular vision of (suburban) 'rural' living; whilst in Chorlton, respondents valued the area's 'diversity of lifestyles ... especially with respect to sexuality, occupation, and leisure pursuits' (ibid.: 42). The *choice* of Chorlton was also a *rejection*: of staid suburbs, for example, with the area seen as having affinities to London, imagined as a cosmopolitan space. In fact, the authors argue, 'bohemian' Chorlton was marked by a 'liberal, academic homogeneity', with the area dominated by well-educated professionals, espousing 'a particular set of urban professional values' (ibid.: 43). But choosing to live in Chorlton was a form of *symbolic* identification, a way of affirming one's liberal celebration of diversity, even if that actually meant living amongst people with the same well-educated liberal values. People had a 'highly charged senses of the symbolic importance of place to them', but this sense was relational, defined in terms of 'imaginary connections with other symbolically powerful sites' (ibid.: 78–9). The connections drawn were very particular, as respondents did not demonstrate a general 'global awareness' but instead made specific connections between places. Connections to places outside of England were shaped primarily by a 'white, English speaking, diaspora' (to Australia or Canada) and 'enhanced local identities through allowing respondents to understand the specificity of their local with a wider range of reference points' (ibid.: 202). A small number of more 'globally reflexive' respondents had a more 'cosmopolitan' outlook, but these respondents were unusual in having 'turbulent life histories' marked by living in a number of different nations.

In concluding, the authors acknowledge their book is 'an empirical elaboration of the familiar argument that globalization constructs local identities, attachments and belonging' (ibid.: 203), but their research rejects many of the conventional theories of this. The 'local' was not constructed as a defensive response to globalizing forces, since respondents did not contrast the local with the global, but instead counterposed specific localities to other local places, in terms of how they supported preferred ways of life. Nor was there much evidence of global reflexivity as a general 'awareness of the world' or of a cosmopolitan global elite, since the most likely candidates (the Wilmslow global corporate elite) had tastes 'considerably more parochial and "national" than those found in the other areas'. The authors debunk the notion of a clear-cut distinction between 'locals' and 'cosmopolitans', since the self-professed 'cosmopolitans', the Chorlton professionals, in fact moved in homogeneous social circles, had 'little engagement with cultures outside the English speaking metropolises' and had the strongest ties to, and knowledge of, their local area. Finally, the book argues that 'place' is of overriding significance for social identity with residence 'possibly *the* crucial identifier of who you are' (ibid.: 207). However, this process is profoundly class-based, supporting Bourdieu's argument that it is the relative distribution of capitals that produces a 'sense of place', with the *alignment* of habitus and field generating social 'comfort'. Fields *vary* in their degree of spatial fixity, as the various chapters of the book – on education, neighbourhood and work ties, media use and the symbolic imagination of place – indicate: the authors use the concept of 'elective belonging' to address, and draw together, the uneven spatialization and territoriality of these different practices.

Arguments and Evidence

I have reported the book's conclusions at length, partly to indicate the sheer scale of the study. The book makes some sophisticated theoretical arguments, derived from a large and complex dataset. The rigorous nature of the analysis and the detailed presentation of the findings is striking. One problem in assessing the arguments of the book lies in the difficulty of properly comprehending the detail and complexity of the evidence on which it is based. The project generated over 1.5 million words of transcription, from 182 taped interviews, covering topics from what the participants watched on TV to their radio listening, their interests in music, cinema, concert and gig attendance, their social networks and leisure associations, their neighbourly and work connections, and their views on class and ethnicity. The book has eight densely written chapters, each with very distinct themes and theoretical arguments, yet it only mines a portion of the yielded data. The research team published a series of journal articles on themes not addressed or only partly covered in the book, such as 'local habitus' (Savage et al. 2004a, 2004b), class identities (Savage et al. 2001), social capital (Bagnall et al. 2003; Savage et al. 2005), radio listening (Longhurst et al. 2004) and museum use (ibid.). The manner in which the study's findings are reported in *Globalization and Belonging* is similarly detailed and extensive. The book itself is crammed with 24 tables, three maps, uses interview quotes from 159 of the 182 respondents (87 per cent), with many quoted several times; and a further 29 (16 per cent) of the respondents are treated as extended individual 'box' case studies, reported in greater detail 'so that readers can see how our account of key processes are instantiated in the narratives and life histories of respondents'. The Appendix lists all the interviewees (anonymized), including their occupation and income, and indicates the pages of the book where they are quoted or referred to so the reader 'can see how we have not "cherry picked" but have drawn on the wide array of material from across most of the sample' (Savage et al. 2005: 17).

Nonetheless, any research project, however carefully conceived and executed, raises questions of interpretation and evidence. In its ambitious theoretical framework, and its unusual combination of large-scale qualitative methods and a case-study approach, this study raises some methodological questions. The first question relates to the difficulties that arise from using qualitative methods on a very large sample and how to satisfy, or adjudicate between, the competing claims of different methodological approaches. The second question is concerned with how to relate 'micro' experiences to 'macro' structures and whether we can draw together the narratives that people generate (whether in interviews or in everyday situations) to reveal broader social processes or patterns. The third question is about how people perceive, and articulate, their own experiences, which is also a question about the use of interview material for exploring questions of embodiment and the tacit practices of the habitus. The fourth question relates to whether the project's shifting research aims and theoretical focus influenced the effectiveness of its methodological strategy.

The Difficulties of Large-Scale Qualitative Analysis

One practical problem of large-scale qualitative studies is the sheer amount of data they generate. The intensive transcript analysis necessitated by qualitative interviews must be endlessly repeated and, to avoid losing sight of key themes or patterns in the data, the authors combined their qualitative analysis with more quantitative analyses. The authors acknowledge the difficulties of coding and analysing such a large dataset, even when using a software package (QSR-Nudist) and coding interviews using Excel spreadsheets. Their analysis involved looking at 'the range of answers across the case, as well as the way that answers were related to other parts of the narratives within cases' (ibid.: 16). Given the scale of the evidence collected, it is not surprising that the results are reported in such detail and at such length. A similar large-scale qualitative study, Butler and Robson's analysis of middle-class London neighbourhoods (2003), shares the same densely detailed manner of presentation. However, in this exhaustive reporting we can also see the authors' methodological anxiety to do justice to both the amount and the different types of data that they collected.

The reporting style of the book is part of the authors' strategy to circumvent any potential methodological criticisms that they might encounter, recognizing that their research strategy might 'displease both quantitative and qualitative researchers' (ibid.). Because of the large number of interviewees, the research team used 'mixed methods', employing both quantitative and qualitative forms of analysis. In addition to their interpretative analysis, the team also wanted to identify any general patterns in the four areas, and so they also reported 'simple frequencies' for 'the practices and values of interest to us'. The authors emphasize that these more quantitative analyses are not meant to imply that the information derived from the neighbourhood samples is generalizable to the broader populations from which the respondents were drawn, 'given our sampling strategy which is not on a random basis' (ibid.). Instead, the quantitative summaries reported in the book are part of their *descriptive* research strategy, summarizing patterns in the sample and locating 'quoted' material within it. The team's analyses were aimed at showing 'how particular individuals exemplify certain core processes', developing typologies 'around which individuals could be meaningfully linked', with the quantitative summaries allowing the reader to 'check' how the qualitative material in the book reflected the range of cases.

The authors acknowledge their study could 'fall between two stools', that is, be dismissed as too large by qualitative researchers (since qualitative research 'does not depend on generating a large sample or trying to generalise' but rather on doing justice to the complexity of particular cases) and too small by quantitative researchers (who 'may worry that 182 cases are not enough to allow any kind of statistical analysis') (ibid.). Clearly, the authors' careful and extensive use of quotes and cautious use of descriptive statistics are strategies to forestall such potential criticisms. They are cautious too about overgeneralization, arguing that their theoretical conclusions are all 'anchored in the empirical findings' of the book, though they clearly think that their findings *are* more generally applicable, since they suggest that they are offering an approach which 'might have application elsewhere':

> we think it is useful to generalise about broad differences, and similarities, between our four areas, by reporting frequencies and patterns, even though such generalisations need to come with a 'health warning' that they might not be sustained by more statistically representative survey analysis.
>
> (Ibid.)

The authors acknowledge that their study may be dismissed as too large by qualitative researchers and too small by quantitative researchers, but there is also the question of whether the study falls awkwardly between conflicting epistemological and methodological principles. Surprisingly, this is not something the authors address in any detail.

Using 'Micro' Data to Reveal Macroprocesses

The authors used qualitative research to address 'macro' issues of global change, trying to capture the intersection of 'structure and agency' and 'society and individual' by using 'people's own narratives of connectivity and global ties' as these emerged from their accounts of their work, leisure and residential routines. But despite the researchers' caution, there remains a question about the extent to which interview narratives can, or should, be relied on to reveal social structures or broader patterns. In one sense, case studies are revealing because they *illustrate* broader processes, and this is something the project attempts: exploring how – for *these* people in *these* localities – global forces affect the experience of local living. The authors are careful to indicate the limits to the generalizability of their findings, but, despite these 'health warnings', the project authors do make broader claims about the areas they studied, and the reader develops quite a vivid picture of life in Chorlton or Wilmslow, for example. But how is this bigger picture shaped by the particular nature of the sample? And how strongly should we distinguish between, say, the broader Chorlton and the 'Chorlton' conjured by the voices of the sample?

In the book, there is an extensive discussion of the varying construction of different 'fields' and their articulation across the neighbourhoods studied. For example, the educational field in Chorlton is described as being very different to the one in Wilmslow, with important consequences for residents' 'feelings' of elective belonging. However, it appears that much of *our* sense of the fields in which agents are located comes from *their* 'sense' of them, as articulated in their interview narratives. Of course, there are a large number of these narratives, so the characterization of fields extends beyond any individual's perception. But is it enough to point out that such aggregations come with a health warning, if the *effect* of aggregation is to give us a sense of underlying patterns within the neighbourhoods? Although we can use interviews with an unrepresentative sample to explore the impact of the macro on the micro, with a very large sample there is a danger of slipping into a more risky strategy: by using the many interviews of micro experience to derive accounts of macro patterns. The authors draw on small area statistics and ACORN profiles of cultural and economic capital and lifestyles to provide more 'objective' measures of the fields within neighbourhoods, but these are essentially 'summary' measures of the neighbourhoods themselves, rather than a detailed mapping of the interconnection of resources and relations between the people in those neighbourhoods. Here we might wonder whether an analysis of the neighbourhoods' social relations that was not based solely on the qualitative interviews would strengthen the claims in the book.

This concern is part of a broader question, of whether agents' accounts (however we draw the sample) always miss crucial aspects of their situation, because social location shapes our perceptions but is not reducible to them. For some analysts, the aim of qualitative research is to investigate the agent's viewpoint, so that the research exploration stops at indicating the different 'versions' of events, an account of multiple perspectives rather than an attempt to generate a broader picture of some underlying 'reality'. Such analysts use interviews to explore how people see their world, not to question their perspective. However, this is not the approach adopted in this book, which at a number of points picks out discrepancies: between how people perceive (and represent) their situation and how it might be viewed by the analyst. For example, the authors note that the Chorlton professionals, the group who most self-consciously claimed a 'cosmopolitan' identity with a liberal celebration of diversity, in fact moved in homogeneous social circles. Here the authors use discrepancies *within* their respondents' accounts (between their *characterization* of their lives as 'cosmopolitan' and their *descriptions* of their concrete social ties) to suggest that people's grasp of their social situation is selective. This, again, suggests the partial nature of agents' perspectives. But this raises a question about the study's reliance on the interview method, since our understanding of respondent's social situations ultimately derives only from their account of it.

Take, for example, the lengthy discussion of social ties in the book. This is based on the respondents' *perceptions* of their social ties, as they revealed them in the interviews, rather than being derived from any more formal measurement of their social networks. Formal network analysis maps out the web of ties between individuals, examining how people may be connected directly, but also indirectly (as in, for example, the 'friends of friends' who we may not meet or be aware of) (Scott 2000). In fact, the team did collect detailed network data for part of the sample (the local membership of two groups, the Labour Party and a Conservation association, in one neighbourhood). However, this is not discussed in the book. Such analysis is unwieldy (it takes a long time to collect and analyse the data), and the decision not to adopt it generally for the sample is understandable, considering the sheer scale of the data that was collected. But people's *perceptions* of their social ties are inevitably partial and local, as their networks extend well beyond their immediate knowledge of them. And some of the most interesting impacts of networks on behaviour occur through such indirect connections and through network patterns of which the participants are, at best, only dimly aware. For example, people in 'dense' social networks (in which a person's contacts are also connected with each other) tend to develop shared world views and shared narratives because the same information, ideas and viewpoints reach agents via different contacts, reinforcing a sense of their importance (Crossley 1998). Such network patterns might help to explain the cohesive values in some of the neighbourhoods (the 'cosmopolitanism' of the Chorlton professionals or the Wilmslow elite's view of private schooling as the local norm) and their difference from the more diffuse viewpoints espoused in others (Cheadle and Ramsbottom). The authors sometimes seem to imply this, but their choice of methodology makes this impossible to confirm since the study can only pick up the 'direct' impact of social connections.

This is also an issue of how we understand the *reflexivity* of social agents, of how people perceive and articulate their own experiences. What is the authors' view of this and how does it relate to their methodological approach? There is a Bourdieusian influence on the book's theoretical framework, but Bourdieu himself sees agents' reflective awareness as being very limited. Most people, he argues, are largely unaware of their social predispositions at a self-conscious level, with much of their practice based on pre-reflective routines, 'social instincts' and a 'feel for the game'. This suggests that people's experiences cannot be uncovered simply by asking them about it. Bourdieu (1991: 235) insists that 'the essential part of one's experience of the social world … takes place in practice, without reaching the level of explicit representation and verbal expression'. But if, as he suggests, such practice is 'beyond the grasp of consciousness, and hence cannot be touched by voluntary, deliberate transformation, cannot even be made explicit' (Bourdieu 1977: 94), then can the interview method access it?

Relatedly, there is a question about the use of the interview method to conduct field analysis. Conventional field analysis relies on an analysis of 'objective' relational positions which may be hidden from the agents who occupy them. Bourdieu's field analysis stresses that there are 'objective relations which exist "independent of individual consciousness and will"' (Bourdieu and Wacquant 1992: 97), so that to undertake field analysis we must go beyond the 'subjectivism' of simply focusing on agents' representations in order to explore the 'structure of objective relations which determines the possible form of interactions and of the representations the interactors can have of them' (Bourdieu 1984: 244). Bourdieu believes that agents' subjective understandings of their situation are always distorted and so can only tell us so much about field relations. Bourdieu sees his own approach as uniting 'both actor perceptions of objective reality and objective measures of aggregate behaviour' (Swartz 1997: 146). In his early empirical work, Bourdieu combined interview-generated narratives with a more structural analysis of the 'objective relations' (generally the distributions of economic and cultural capital) within fields (although see Bourdieu 1999).

Again, this is a question of how the authors' reliance on interviews sits within their theoretical framework. A strict field analysis would *locate* the subjective perceptions and accounts of agents within an objective mapping of the relations between positions; yet, as we have seen, the study only generates limited aggregate summaries of broader social patterns. Now, again, it is unfair to criticize a study, which generated such an immense amount of data, for not collecting even more. And, in fact, the study's interview-based methods cover the core research question – what makes people feel attached to place? – rather well. But the research strategy of the project does not cover all the angles raised by the theoretical architecture of the project, angles that the authors clearly thought were important.

Reflexivity and the Interview Method

It is unclear how far the authors follow Bourdieu on questions of reflexivity; and their methodological discussion would be stronger for addressing it. The authors are aware of such issues, indeed their discussion of class identities has an extensive discussion of the more implicit forms of identity that may not feature strongly in people's reflexive accounts (Savage et al. 2001). This also raises questions about how much investigators read into the answers their respondents give them.

How should we view the answers that people give in interview situations? The authors justify their approach to interviewing, arguing that 'we do not seek to extrapolate issues which are not germane to respondents themselves: rather, our account organises narratives which are salient and meaningful to respondents' (Savage et al. 2005: 17). The basis of this claim is the use of 'indirect' methods of inquiry. Rather than posing direct or loaded questions about people's attachment to place the researchers instead used indirect questions, asking for general information about people's daily routines of work, residence and leisure to see whether issues of place and global connectivity would 'spontaneously arise' in respondents' narratives.

> We are not persuaded that it is a useful exercise to ask people directly about global issues, their sense of global belonging, and so forth ... Here we support Silverman's (2001) invocation to use naturally occurring data wherever possible, which in the context of our research involved looking at how the local and the global was articulated in the various questions on aspects of everyday life and identity.
>
> (Ibid.: 15–16)

Their idea was to draw upon respondents' *own* frameworks rather than to impose the investigators' concerns and categories. However, as Payne and Grew (2005: 906) note, 'interviews are not a common occurrence for respondents, so that any spoken responses cannot be seen as strictly "naturally occurring" and therefore unstimulated in some sense'. They also argue that 'silence on a topic does not mean it is not salient (or conversely that non-silence necessarily indicates salience'. On this basis, Payne and Grew criticize the paper (Savage et al. 2001) on class identities that arose out of the project. That paper used the sample's failure to invoke spontaneously questions of class, and its ambivalent response to direct questions, as evidence of the relative weakness of (occupational) class identities. But how are we to interpret this silence? In fact, at a number of points (particularly in relation to issues of 'whiteness') the book refers to significant 'silences', but it is always hard to know how to interpret these or to guess at what other silences might have been unnoticed in the data.

There is some theoretical discussion and extension of Bourdieu's account of how reflexivity arises within practice in the book. Bourdieu argues that as people move between different fields, with different structuring assumptions to that of their own habitus, their 'social instinct' may fail them and they are forced to become more reflexive (and strategic) about how to proceed. The authors argue that there has been an increase in these reflexive disjunctures, through field differentiation, suggesting that 'we use an increasing variety of spaces in our lives as we move between fields, such as those of work, different leisure pursuits ... [and] thus no one space where we feel at home all the time'. The implication is that people have become more reflexive about such issues, with 'field crossing' meaning that residential fields become subject to 'more strategic reflection, and are less interpreted as "where one happens to live", or "where one was brought up"' (Savage et al. 2005: 10). This claim might be used to justify the interview method of investigation (on the grounds that people have become more reflexive about their spatial situation so we can use their narratives to explore it). However, the authors do not do so. Their discussion of reflexivity is only a passing theoretical comment that is never addressed in methodological terms.

There is also a question of whether some respondents were more reflexive than others and whether this affects the study's conclusions. Is it possible that the highly educated professionals in the sample were better able to articulate their experiences than their less educated neighbours? Do their voices speak more loudly than others in the study? As a reader, I developed a much stronger sense of the 'Chorlton' liberal professionals and the 'Wilmslow' elites than I did of their co-residents or any of the 'Cheadle' or 'Ramsbottom' respondents. This, no doubt, reflects the quantitative patterns the team identified in their subsamples, with some viewpoints legitimately more prominent than others, but the suspicion remains that, with different sampling, a different narrative based on different voices might have emerged. Could it be that the concept of elective belonging emerges primarily from the accounts of certain elements of the sample, members of 'dense' networks in which a common narrative of belonging might have emerged? The fact that the sample may have had varying degrees of reflexivity is a crucial concern, given the study's concluding emphasis on elective belonging as the main form of attachment to place. The more affluent, educated and more mobile members in the sample are likely to be more reflexive about attachment to place and to have heightened feelings of belonging because their greater freedom of choice over where to live means they have had to work at establishing themselves in new locales in ways that the immobile do not have to do. This is something the authors' acknowledge, but as a theoretical conclusion rather than as a methodological discussion.

Shifting Research Aims

Some of these concerns are about the links between the theoretical framework of the project and its methodological strategy, and may reflect the way that the project shifted its theoretical direction and research aims midway. The Bourdieusian influence on the research seems to have grown over time. If the researchers' interest in embodiment and tacit feelings of the comforts of place had been as strong at the *outset* of their project they might have used a different range of research instruments. Such changes in emphasis routinely emerge in research and the researchers in this case have been remarkably open about their shifting focus. More troubling is the fact that whilst they *outline* the changes in some detail, they spend less time *reflecting* upon the consequences of the shifts: for the fit between theory and methods, or for the sorts of claims that they can make for their data. Whilst we learn a great deal about *how* the study was conducted, the reflexive methodological discussion of the *consequences* of that conduct is less well developed, and perhaps the weakest element of the book.

We might also wonder how well a project designed to look at middle-class residential lifestyles can explore questions of globalization and attachment to place. Of course, the changed theoretical question emerged from the research itself, as the researchers came to see that their data raised different sorts of theoretical questions about place than they had originally envisaged. Whilst a study of middle-class neighbourhoods inevitably throws up a predominantly middle-class sample, such a sample still has much to tell us about processes of globalization and attachment to place. Manchester has experienced many of the globalizing processes alleged to undermine local communities, and many of these processes are said to apply particularly to more privileged groups, seen as more spatially mobile and culturally eclectic. The study's predominantly middle-class sample, of the economically and/or culturally advantaged, therefore offers a reasonable test of whether or not globalization 'disembeds' such individuals from local contexts. If these privileged groups fail to experience disembedding, then globalizing claims look much weaker. The study also looks at the impact of these more transient privileged groups on their less privileged neighbours, with whom they share (middle-class) locales. So again, the study offers a good test of how the movement of different groups, and the redefinition of local areas, affects attachment to place.

However, there are significant omissions from the study, particularly other ethnic groups, who might tell us even more about processes of globalization and attachment to place. As the authors note, 'our sample is definitely not a representative sample of Mancunians, many of whom are members of ethnic minority groups, such as the large Jewish communities in both south and north Manchester, or Pakistani immigrants' (Savage et al. 2005: 182). The researchers attempt to turn the 'ethnic exclusiveness' of their sample to their advantage 'by considering how the "whiteness" of our sample is articulated in our respondents' own narratives' (ibid.) and by showing the limited, post-colonial, global connections of this group. But we miss the story of Mancunians who might have very different connections and sense of place. Finally, the concept of elective belonging, and the process of choice that it implies, sits well with a sample of middle-class homeowners, but the question arises as to whether an alternative terminology would be required for working-class tenants in the comparative study that is invited by Savage and his colleagues' concluding question requiring the broader applicability of their approach.

Conclusion

I have questioned some of the methodological decisions made in this study; but it is worth noting that all research projects involve pragmatic choices as to how to research a topic, and such decisions *always* have limiting consequences for the sorts of information we can gather. Any study raises questions of method, analysis and interpretation. The team could have done things differently: they could have used quantitative survey research or network analysis techniques for the areas they studied, and this might have given us a different angle on the questions they considered and, perhaps, different answers to some of those questions. But if they had done so, other methodological concerns would have arisen. It is unlikely that the team would have had enough time or resources to gather the same scale or depth of qualitative material, and so could not have explored questions of the *sense* of self and of attachment to place in such richly detailed fashion. As it is, the study's qualitative methods cover the core research question – how do (certain) people feel attached to place? – extremely well. The interview-based methods used provide a wealth of vivid data which makes questions of locality leap off the page.

It is also worth noting that any single study sits within a wider community of research findings and so must be assessed within this broader context. One strength of *Globalisation and Belonging* lies in the sophistication and complexity of its theoretical arguments, which provocatively challenge and reframe previous research understandings of 'community', 'class' and 'globalization'. A further strength is the richness of the study's data, which offers a fascinating glimpse of how people view their local neighbourhoods and their place within them. The authors interpret this as a question of elective belonging and, whilst we might query some elements in the research process which gave rise to this interpretation, the core strength of *Globalisation and Belonging* lies in how its fresh perspective on locality and territoriality opens up a whole new series of questions for future research.

Additional Reading

For a further discussion of some of the issues that arise when combining methods of quantitative and qualitative analysis, see Spicer's chapter, 'Combining Qualitative and Quantitative Methods', in the edited collection, *Researching Society and Culture* by C. Seale (2004). For an introduction to social network analysis, see Scott's *Social Network Analysis: A Handbook* (2000). For another large-scale qualitative study of middle-class neighbourhoods, this time in London, see Butler and Robson's (2003) *London Calling: The Middle Classes and the Remaking of Inner London*. Finally, for a study by Savage, again based on research on neighbourhoods in Greater Manchester, but this time directly exploring social networks and their impact on trust, social activism and people's engagement with their environment and urban space, see Savage et al.'s contribution, 'Political Participation, Social Networks and the City', in Blokland and Savage's collection, *Networked Urbanism: Social Capital in the City* (2008).

Acknowledgements

I would like to thank Mike Savage, Gaynor Bagnall and Brian Longhurst, and the editors, Fiona Devine and Sue Heath, for their very helpful comments and advice during the writing of this chapter.

References

Bagnall, G., B. Longhurst, and M. Savage (2003) 'Children, belonging and social capital: the PTA and middle class narratives of social involvement in the north-west of England', *Sociological Research Online*, 8(4).

Bellah, R., R. Madsen, W. Sullivan, and S. Tipton (1996) *Habits of the Heart*, Berkeley, CA: University of California Press.

Blokland, T. and M. Savage (2008) *Networked Urbanism: Social Capital in the City*, Aldershot: Ashgate.

Bourdieu, P. (1977) *Outline of a Theory of Practice*, Cambridge: Cambridge University Press.

Bourdieu, P. (1984) *Distinction: A Social Critique of the Judgement of Taste*, London: Routledge & Kegan Paul.

Bourdieu, P. (1991) *Language and Symbolic Power*, Cambridge: Polity.

Bourdieu, P. and L. Wacquant (1992) *An Invitation to Reflexive Sociology*, Oxford: Polity.

Bourdieu, P. (1999) *The Weight of the World*, Cambridge: Polity.

Britton, N.J., P. Halfpenny, F. Devine, and R. Mellor (2004) 'The future of regional cities in the information age: the impact of information technology on Manchester's financial and business services sector', *Sociology*, 38: 795–814.

Buck, N., I. Gordon, P. Hall, M. Harloe, and M. Kleinman (2002) *Working Capital: Life and Labour in Contemporary London*, London: Routledge.

Bulmer, M. (1985) 'The rejuvenation of community studies? Neighbours, networks and policy', *Sociological Review*, 33: 430–48.

Butler, T. and G. Robson (2003) *London Calling: The Middle Classes and the Remaking of Inner London*: London: Berg.

Crompton, R. (1996) 'The fragmentation of class', *British Journal of Sociology*, 47 (1): 56–67.

Crossley, N. (2008) 'Pretty connected: the social network of the early UK Punk movement', *Theory, Culture & Society*, 25(6): 89–116.

Crow, G. (2002) 'Community studies: fifty years of theorization', in *Sociological Research Online*, 7 (3). Available at http://www.socresonline.org.uk/7/3/crow.html.

Crow, G. and G. Allan (1994) *Community Life: An Introduction to Local Social Relations*, Hemel Hempstead: Harvester Wheatsheaf.

Devine, F., J. Britton, R. Mellor and P. Halfpenny (2000) 'Professional work and professional careers in Manchester's business and financial sector', *Work, Employment and Society*, 14: 521–40.

Devine, F. and M. Savage (2000) 'Conclusion: renewing class analysis', in R. Crompton, F. Devine, M. Savage and J. Scott (eds) *Renewing Class Analysis*, Oxford: Blackwell.

Longhurst, B., G. Bagnall and M. Savage (2004) 'Audiences, museums and the English middle class', *Museum and Society*, 2: 104–24.

Payne, G. and C. Grew (2005) 'Unpacking "class ambivalence": some conceptual and methodological issues in accessing class cultures', *Sociology*, 39: 893–910.

Robertson, R. (1992) *Globalisation: Social Theory and Global Culture*, London: Sage.

Savage, M. (2000) *Class Analysis and Social Transformation*, Milton Keynes: Open University Press.

Savage, M., G. Bagnall and B. Longhurst (2001) 'Ordinary, ambivalent and defensive: class identities in the north-west of England', *Sociology*, 35: 875–92.

Savage, M., G. Bagnall and B. Longhurst (2004a) 'The comforts of place: belonging and identity in the north-west of England', in T. Bennett and E. Silva (eds) *Everyday Cultures*, London: Sociology Press.

Savage, M., G. Bagnall and B. Longhurst (2004b) 'Local habitus and working class culture', in F. Devine, M. Savage, R. Crompton and J. Scott (eds) *Rethinking Class*, Basingstoke: Palgrave.

Savage, M., G. Bagnall and B. Longhurst (2005) *Globalization and Belonging*, London: Sage.

Savage, M., G.Tampubulon and A.Warde (2008) 'Political participation, social networks and the city', in T. Blokland and M.Savage (eds), *Networked Urbanism: Social Capital in the City*, Aldershot: Ashgate.

Savage, M., A. Warde and K. Ward (2003) *Urban Sociology, Capitalism and Modernity*, 2nd edn, Basingstoke: Palgrave.

Scott, J. (2000) *Social Network Analysis: A Handbook*. London: Sage.

Seale, C. (ed.) (2004) *Researching Culture and Society*, 2nd edn, London: Sage.

Silverman, J. (2001) *Interpreting Qualitative Data*, London: Sage.

Spicer, N. (2004) 'Combining qualitative and quantitative methods', in C. Seale (ed.) *Researching Society and Culture*, 2nd edn, London: Sage.

Swartz, D. (1997) *Culture and Power*, Chicago, IL: University of Chicago Press.

Wolfe, A. (1998) *One Nation After All*, New York: Viking.

CHAPTER 6

Subculture: Hodkinson's *Goth*

Paul Sweetman

> It is often argued that researching a subculture to which a researcher belongs can confer considerable advantages: facilitating privileged access to research settings, for example, or allowing researchers to bring their own insider knowledge to bear on the process of interpretation and analysis. In this chapter, Paul Sweetman considers some of these issues in relation to Paul Hodkinson's ethnographic study of the UK goth scene, a subculture in which Hodkinson is an active participant. Sweetman focuses on three key themes. First, he considers the degree to which Hodkinson considers his insider status to be advantageous, highlighting some of the pros and cons which come with researching a topic with which he is so familiar. Second, Sweetman considers the balance in Hodkinson's work between the theoretical treatment of goth subculture and detailed description of 'what goths do', and he questions whether Hodkinson's interpretations are sufficiently 'distanced' given his insider status. Third, Sweetman explores the significance of Hodkinson's work in relation to current debates within 'the new subcultural studies', which has sought to reconceptualize established definitions of 'subculture'.

Introduction

This chapter focuses on Paul Hodkinson's recent research on the UK goth scene, and, in particular, on his book of 2002, *Goth: Identity, Style and Subculture*. Like other recent work in this area, Hodkinson's research can be seen in part as a response to, and critique of, earlier work on subcultures conducted or informed by writers associated with the Birmingham Centre for Contemporary Cultural Studies (CCCS) during the 1970s and 1980s. As is true of other recent studies, Hodkinson's research is critical of the theoretical framework employed within this earlier body of work (which is discussed below) and attempts to redress some of these perceived difficulties in substantive terms by offering a more sustained examination of what it is that those involved with youth and/or subculture actually do. Unlike much of this more recent work, however, Hodkinson is keen to retain the term 'subculture'. He suggests it can be used to refer to relatively distinctive and autonomous lifestyle groupings which are important to their members' sense of identity and to which their members exhibit a significant level of commitment. He argues that the concept is still relevant and applicable even if it does need to be divorced from many of its previous connotations.

Hodkinson's work is notable, then, for its contribution to wider debates about youth and/or subculture (and to debates about the internet, too), as well as for offering a detailed account of a particular subculture and the way that it actually works. Like other recent work it moves beyond some of the more theoretical accounts associated with the CCCS in that it is based upon careful ethnographic inquiry rather than simply a reading-off of the meaning and significance of subculture from a predominantly textual analysis of selected aspects of practice and style: unlike certain earlier subcultural theorists (see below), Hodkinson actually went out and conducted significant amounts of fieldwork, his 'multi-method ethnographic approach' involving 'participant observation, in-depth interviews, media analysis and even a questionnaire' (Hodkinson 2002: 4).

At the same time, Hodkinson's work also attempts to demonstrate the continuing relevance of the concept of subculture itself. He suggests that, whatever the difficulties associated with earlier understandings of the term, and however far its applicability has been tested by recent developments, we should still avoid throwing the conceptual baby out with the theoretical bathwater where this particular term is concerned. His work is also interesting in methodological terms thanks to his status as a goth himself – and thus as an 'insider researcher' – and because of the way in which his study made use of the internet as both an area of inquiry and a significant research tool (as well as using online resources for data, Hodkinson also focuses considerable attention on the ways in which the internet was used by his participants and helped to facilitate the day-to-day workings of the subculture).

I first look at the background to Hodkinson's work, outlining some of the key features of the CCCS approach and some of the criticisms which have been levelled against it, before exploring the more recent body of work that has attempted to reconceptualize the area, of which Hodkinson's work forms a part. As has been indicated, whilst sharing a critical stance vis-à-vis the classical work on subcultures associated with the CCCS, Hodkinson's approach also differs from other recent work in arguing for a retention of the concept of subculture rather than its abandonment in favour of terms such as 'scene' or 'neo-tribe'. I then move on to focus on Hodkinson's own study, looking first at his methods and results, before concentrating on three key areas: his position as an insider researcher, his methodological position vis-à-vis the interpretation of his data, and his continued use of key concepts – notably 'subculture' itself – despite his rejection of the overall theoretical framework with which the concept has tended most recently to be associated.

From 'Imaginary Solutions' to Contemporary Tribes

Like other recent work on youth and/or subculture, Hodkinson's research should be viewed in part as a response to the earlier approach developed by writers associated with the CCCS during the 1970s and beyond. This work was not homogeneous so the following is necessarily somewhat caricatured, but it does describe what has come to be regarded as the core CCCS approach, even if certain writers associated with the Centre diverged from – and were critical of – the broad template described. The CCCS was established by Richard Hoggart at the University of Birmingham in 1964, but really came into its own under the directorship of Stuart Hall during the 1970s, when a variety of soon to be key figures – such as Dick Hebdige, Angela McRobbie and Paul Willis (each of whom were initially associated with the centre as postgraduate students) – began to research and publish on subcultures, moral panics and related issues (Turner 1990).

Resistance through Rituals (Hall and Jefferson 1976), *the* seminal text on post-war youth subcultures, collected together papers on mods, Teds, skinheads and other groups, alongside a number of more exclusively theoretical or methodological pieces of work, the bulk of which adopted a neo-Marxist approach which suggested that subcultures represented a creative response by groups of working-class youths to difficulties and contradictions experienced by the 'parent-class' as a whole (Clarke et al. 1976). The skinhead subculture, which had developed at the end of the 1960s, for example, represented a response to the loss of traditional working-class communities in places like London's East End and an attempt to resolve magically the tensions and contradictions experienced as a result through the re-creation of what had been lost in a symbolic form. According to John Clarke (1976a) and Phil Cohen (1997), the skinheads' emphasis on territory and adoption of an exaggerated version of working-class masculinity were to be viewed in this regard, but such solutions were necessarily 'imaginary' because they only operated on a symbolic level and could not hope to arrest the community's actual decline.

That is not to say that they were insignificant. On a symbolic level, skinhead style and aspects of skinhead practice were subversive, resistant and counter-hegemonic even if they were, ultimately, futile. They were also creative: like the Teds before them and their immediate precursors, the mods, skinheads took everyday items such as 'AirWair' boots, Levi jeans, Fred Perry and Ben Sherman shirts, and various aspects of young West Indian style, and combined them in a distinctive overall ensemble which assigned new or subtly inflected meanings to the items thus assembled. The mods had done the same, albeit in a more subtle way, combining smart suits and other signs of 'bourgeois respectability' with signifiers of European and US 'cool' and a love of soul and R&B, alongside an amphetamine-fuelled, all-night lifestyle (Hebdige 1976).

However innovative and creative the mods and skinheads were, it was the punks who took subcultural bricolage to its extremes, appropriating items from a variety of likely and unlikely sources in a subcultural smash-and-grab raid which made previous styles look tame in comparison and which Dick Hebdige (1979: 105) described as 'semiotic guerrilla warfare'. For a while, punk was all but unreadable. As with the mods, punk dress also linked up with, and was only 'meaningful' in relation to, other aspects of punk lifestyle, with appearance, behaviour and choice of music, for example, all related as particular aspects of a subcultural whole (ibid.: 113).

Like the mods and skinheads before them, but arguably on another level, the punks were also creative and subversive, playing around with meanings in a significant way. Where previous approaches to youth culture had been largely pessimistic, bemoaning mass or popular culture as trivial, superficial and degrading – predigested pap for an undiscriminating audience who grew steadily less discriminating the more they consumed – CCCS writers were motivated, in part, by a wish to rescue young working-class consumers from accusations of passivity and vacuity. Where theories of mass and popular culture had implied that teenagers and others were becoming more stupid and more disengaged by the day from both politics and either 'authentic working-class culture' or 'uplifting high culture', the CCCS approach instead emphasized their agency and creativity, even if the focus on spectacular sub-cultures implicitly condemned the remainder of their contemporaries to the same set of accusations as had been levelled at them previously (Clarke 1990).

And from the CCCS writers' neo-Marxist perspective, all of this was import-ant because culture was regarded as a site of struggle and contestation. Where previous Marxisms had frequently regarded culture as a largely uncompli-cated reflection of the economic base, the Gramscian approach adopted by Stuart Hall and his contemporaries instead emphasized its relative autonomy and the need for 'consent' to be won rather than assumed (Clarke et al. 1976). Hegemony could not simply be taken for granted, and in this context 'semi-otic guerrilla warfare' took on greater significance than might otherwise have been implied. That is not to say that the subversive effects of subcultures could be assumed to last. Reserving their celebratory stance for subcultures in their 'authentic' or originary moments (Muggleton 2000: 20–1), the CCCS framework also suggested that as subcultures became popularized, mediatized and commodified they lost their subversive power and were then sold back to the masses in a neutered form.

Early criticisms of the core CCCS approach – including from within the centre itself – focused in part on the masculinist bias of the original studies (McRobbie and Garber 1976; McRobbie 1990) and on their elitist concentration on spectacular subcultures in their original incarnations (Clarke 1990). More recently, engagement with the CCCS framework has tended to focus on two issues. First, the plausibility of the approach per se has been considered, including the extent to which it was ever appropriate, and whether it painted an accurate or distorted picture of the subcultures examined at the time. Second, its current utility has been assessed: whether it is still applicable, or whether recent developments have rendered the framework redundant and outdated, unable to capture the complexity of contemporary conditions and the fragmentation of the subcultural scene. Over the last decade, work within what might loosely be termed 'post-subcultural studies' has attempted to address perceived difficulties with the CCCS approach and provide new ways of making sense of the subcultural terrain (see Muggleton 2000; Muggleton and Weinzierl 2003; Bennett and Kahn-Harris 2004).

Criticisms of the CCCS approach per se include the idea that it focused too much on class and painted an overly rigid, committed and homogeneous picture of the subcultures it explored, downplaying movement, flexibility and heterogeneity in terms of subcultural membership or composition, including in class terms (Muggleton 2000). In more directly methodological terms, the CCCS approach has also been criticized for privileging the structural or semiotic aspects of subculture and for conspicuously neglecting what it is that 'subcultures actually *do*' (Clarke 1990: 90). This is despite Phil Cohen's early insistence that there are *three* levels to subcultural analysis: historical; structural or semiotic; and 'the phenomenological analysis of the way the subculture is actually "lived out" by those who are its bearers and supports' (P. Cohen 1997: 95).

Semiotics involves the study of signs, so to adopt a semiotic approach is to focus on a particular phenomenon as a cultural *text*, asking what it means or doesn't mean (and how its constituent parts may come to mean different things) in a particular cultural context (see Storey 1993). In relation to subcultures, then, a semiotic approach would involve focusing on aspects of subcultural style and associated paraphernalia, asking what these things say to us as readers of these particular texts and whether, for example, their meanings have been altered – or subverted – through being combined with other aspects of the subculture's overall ensemble in new and innovative ways. In relation to punk, for example, this might involve asking what the use of everyday items such as bin-liners and safety-pins (as forms of 'clothing' and 'jewellery' respectively) *means*, and whether the use of such items in ways for which they were not apparently intended plays around with dominant meanings or understandings. Does it undermine common-sense understandings of the world, themselves a reflection of (and supportive of) particular ideologies? What such an approach *wouldn't* involve is asking punks for their own opinions, or trying to find out why they enjoy being punks or what they do with their time, and it is this privileging of theoretical interpretation over the views or opinions of subcultural participants themselves for which the CCCS approach has been (rightly) criticized (S. Cohen 1997; Muggleton 2000; Sweetman 2001). Recent work has, then, attempted to redress this difficulty by foregrounding the experiences of 'subculturalists' (Muggleton 2000; Macdonald 2001). It has also emphasized the importance of embodiment and 'affect' (a focus on feelings and emotions) in this regard and has sought to reappraise the relationship between subcultures, media and commerce, questioning the distinction between 'authentic' subcultures, on the one hand, and their mediatized, commodified and sanitized offspring on the other, in CCCS and related accounts (Thornton 1995).

While recent work in this area has partly been concerned with critiquing and attempting to redress difficulties with the CCCS approach per se, it has also attempted to address the changing nature of the relevant terrain. Even if the CCCS framework was appropriate at the time, it is argued, this is no longer so, and the increasing complexity and fragmentation of youth and/or subculture over recent years has meant that new ways of conceptualizing these areas have had to be found. Numerous contributions to this exercise have drawn on Michel Maffesoli's (1996) work on contemporary sociality. Where simple or organized modernity was characterized by fairly straightforward sociological groupings (organized around class and other key variables), postmodernity, according to Maffesoli, has seen a rejection of ascriptive forms of identity in favour of multiple, diffuse and temporary forms of identification with contemporary 'tribes'. Neo-tribes are characterized by their emphasis on tactility, proxemics, based on 'a succession of "we's"', which constitute the very essence of all sociality' (ibid.:139) and on 'being-together for being-together's sake'. Based around shared lifestyles and tastes, they are elective groupings that reject modern forms of association (and concomitant expectations of ideological commitment) in favour of non-instrumental gatherings characterized by an emphasis on experience and affect.

This framework has been adopted by a number of commentators because it is regarded as a helpful way of conceptualizing contemporary subcultures, which are themselves regarded as unstable, fragmented and heterogeneous. It has been argued that the emphasis within the original CCCS framework on relatively stable, distinct and homogeneous groups no longer makes sense in relation to contemporary subcultural formations. With its connotations of

class-based solidarity, ideological commitment, and relative stability, autonomy and homogeneity, and its emphasis on 'resistance through rituals', it has
also been argued that the concept of 'subculture' itself is out of date and
should be replaced with a looser, less weighted, term, conceptually more in
keeping with the nature of contemporary groupings of this type. Despite quali-
fications, the term 'neo-tribe' has been argued to capture the ephemeral, multiple and fragmented nature of contemporary youth culture, and to tie in well
with existing accounts of developments such as dance music or rave (Bennett
1999; Malbon 1999; St John 2003; Sweetman 2004). That is not to say that
this is the only term that has been put forward – other suggestions include
the concept of the 'scene', which again is felt to capture more accurately (or
allow for) the looser nature of contemporary youth and music-based culture
than the more rigid, restrictive and 'over-theorized' notion of 'subculture',
with all that this implies (Bennett and Kahn-Harris 2004).

Hodkinson's research, then, should be placed in the context of a wider
body of work that has attempted to address perceived difficulties with the
framework associated with the CCCS and to provide new ways of conceptualizing subcultural formations in keeping with the shifting nature of the groups
and practices in question. He is critical of what he regards as the CCCS
understanding of subcultures as distinct from (or prior to) media and commerce and, building on Sarah Thornton's (1995) work on 'club culture',
shows that such interests are actually crucial to the establishment and maintenance of the goth scene. Whilst questioning the CCCS framework in this
and other ways, however, Hodkinson is keen to retain the notion of subculture, albeit reformulated specifically in relation to issues of '(sub)cultural substance' (Hodkinson 2002: 28). In this sense, whilst part of the new subcultural
studies, Hodkinson's work is also a response to other work in this area which
suggests that the concept itself is outdated and should be replaced by terms
such as 'neo-tribe'. Suggesting that the concept should now be understood
in terms of 'four indicative criteria ... *identity, commitment, consistent distinctiveness* and *autonomy*' (ibid.: 29), he argues that in relation to these criteria
'goth' can be firmly characterized as a subculture, and in this sense is also
indicative of the continuing relevance of the term. What Hodkinson's book
offers, then (in conjunction with a number of related articles and book chapters), is a careful and detailed study of a contemporary subculture which can
also be read as a significant contribution to the debates and issues identified.

Researching Goth Subculture

Hodkinson's research employed a range of qualitative methods – or what he
refers to as 'a multi-methods ethnographic approach' – including participant

observation, in-depth interviews, media analysis and a self-completion questionnaire, all of which were carried out from the position of a 'critical insider' (ibid. 2002: 4–6), as will be discussed below. Although the research was centred on three English cities – Birmingham in the West Midlands, Plymouth in the South-West, and Leeds in west Yorkshire – participant observation took place 'at clubs, gigs and festivals across Britain' (ibid.: 5). Indeed, the research increasingly came to emphasize the 'translocal' nature of the scene: in other words, it transcended particular regions or locations, and instead operated as a relatively consistent and strongly interconnected network across the UK as a whole and, in certain respects, beyond. Fifty-six interviews were conducted with 72 different participants, including 'DJs ... promoters, fanzine editors, bands, record label proprietors ... specialist retailers' and 'general participants' in the scene. Although most interviews were conducted face-to-face, four were conducted by post and five via email (ibid.: 6).

As well as observing a variety of 'real-life' events, Hodkinson also focused on the internet as a subcultural space in its own right and used quotes from mailing lists and discussion groups as a way of supplementing his interview data and other material. The traditional – as opposed to online – media that were investigated included fanzines, posters and flyers, each of which was considered in relation to its practical uses and implications rather than in semiotic or other terms. The various events Hodkinson attended included the biannual Whitby Gothic Weekend, with an account of the October 1998 event opening the book as a whole. This event is also where his questionnaire was distributed 12 months previously. At the October 1997 event, 112 questionnaires were completed by participants and a summary of the results is included in the book's appendix. This includes data on the 'social profile of respondents' as well as a question-by-question summary of the results obtained, which focused on the attractions of the weekend itself, respondents' attendance at other 'non-local' events, the most important factors contributing to respondents' participation in the goth scene, and their sources of music, clothes and other accessories.

Aside from this summary questionnaire data, however, very little additional information of a systematic sort is provided about Hodkinson's sample as a whole – including his interviewees and his survey respondents – making it difficult to assess the nature of his sample in anything more than anecdotal terms, and also raising certain questions about the particularity of his findings. Despite Hodkinson's (2002: 198) claim that 'the specificity of [his] case study does not somehow render the levels of affiliation, commitment, consistent distinctiveness and autonomy which characterized the late 1990s British goth scene entirely peculiar to it', he does seem at times to have focused on more committed participants, with all of his questionnaire respondents being those with sufficient levels of interest and commitment to attend the Whitby weekend.

Other gaps in the information provided about methods include the decision to concentrate particularly on three main cities – Birmingham, Plymouth and Leeds. We learn in an accompanying book chapter that this was to allow for a 'comparative focus', that Birmingham was Hodkinson's 'base during the ... project', that Plymouth is a 'small and rather isolated port' and that Leeds is 'associated with several well known 1980s goth bands' (Hodkinson 2004a: 132); but, aside from these limited hints, no real explanation is provided for this particular aspect of his research design. It may have been that this was essentially pragmatic, but there may also have been another, more significant, rationale. In the absence of a clear statement one way or another, however, it is not possible to say.

As well as telling us something (albeit not as much as we might wish) about his methodological approach, the first part of Hodkinson's book also contextualizes the study. He establishes his distance from both classical work on subcultures – with its focus on elite subcultures in their 'pre-commodified' forms – and recent discussions of tribes and scenes – which fail, respectively, to allow for groups that display 'cultural substance' and for the 'translocal' aspects of subcultural formations. He then suggests a revised version of 'subculture' which dispenses with the theoretical connotations of the CCCS understanding of the term (pre-commodified, subversive, resistant, and so on), and which also differs from alternative concepts such as 'tribe' or 'scene' in that it not only allows for, but is specifically conceptualized in relation to, four key indicators of '(sub)cultural substance': *'identity, commitment, consistent distinctiveness* and *autonomy'* (Hodkinson 2002: 29). One can then distinguish between subcultures and 'more fluid elective collectivities' to the extent that they satisfy these criteria in relative terms. The substantive chapters of the book then go on to illustrate how goth does display these characteristics and is therefore best conceptualized as a subculture, and is itself indicative of the continuing applicability of the concept when recast in these terms.

The first of the more substantive chapters then provides a descriptive account of the key aspects of goth style, rejecting CCCS-style semiotic analysis in favour of a more straightforward run-through of the style's three main themes: 'the sombre and the macabre'; 'femininity and ambiguity'; and the appropriation of 'fragments of related styles' (ibid.: 41). In line with his refusal of a semiotic approach, Hodkinson also refuses to link these different aspects of goth style together in homological terms (that is, assuming that these different aspects share a structural affinity) or to 'over-interpret' these themes in relation to some sort of assumed political or subversive intention or effect in a way that would privilege theoretical interpretation over the views and opinions of his participants. As Hodkinson points out, his own experience as an insider had convinced him 'that there was no underlying shared structural, psychological or political meaning to be discerned from the style', and a key point 'that came across, from both interviews and general ethnographic experience, was that style was held to be significant in and of itself as a set of … preferences located within, and not beyond, the sphere of the aesthetic' (ibid.: 62).

Hodkinson's substantive account then goes on to focus on goths' strong sense of subcultural identity and collective distinction. Noting how everyone he interviewed indicated a strong sense of group affiliation, to the extent that factors such as class and ethnicity took a backseat to participants' sense of subcultural identification, he also points out how this alone problematizes attempts to reframe 'subculture' in solely tribal terms. He then proceeds to focus specifically on the attendance of goths at local and 'translocal' events, noting their importance for learning about goth, accumulating and displaying subcultural capital, forming contacts and friendships, and as sources of practical information in a self-reinforcing, virtuous circle which also solidified the 'translocal consistency of the scene' (ibid.: 108).

The book then elaborates on the part played by media and commercial interests in 'the facilitation and construction of the subculture' (ibid.: 119), looking first at the importance of 'external' or non-subcultural producers in the early years of the scene, before considering the increasing importance of smaller-scale, subcultural entrepreneurs during the 1990s. Noting the importance of magazines such as the NME in helping to establish the subculture in the 1980s, Hodkinson notes that this is illustrative of 'Thornton's point that the music press specifically seek to report on, and hence construct … new genres or subcultures', while the increasingly important part played by 'an internal network of … subcultural institutions' (ibid.: 109–11) from the 1990s onwards also serves to indicate that the subculture should not be considered 'as occupying an authentic position outside or in opposition to consumerism' (ibid.: 121). Rather than being seen as antithetical, the part played by commercial interests as a whole – internal and external – demonstrates how 'commerce and subculture must [instead] be regarded as highly compatible' (ibid.: 122).

This is also illustrated, from the other side of the counter, by the way in which the 'selection, purchase and consumption of … music, clothing and accessories, was a key element in participants' experience of the … scene' (ibid.: 131). Rejecting the idea that goth style was 'somehow resistant to hegemony … symbolically or otherwise' (ibid.: 133), Hodkinson still argues that CCCS-style accounts of the appropriation of non-subcultural commodities are of some relevance, in that goths' consumption practices 'involved the selective, creative appropriation of goods from non-specialist sources alongside the … less active … use of more pre-packaged, subcultural items' (ibid.: 132). Regardless of the degree of agency or creativity involved, however, the consumption of specialist and non-specialist commodities was a key part of what being a goth entailed and 'shopping was … a fulfilling subcultural activity in its own right' (ibid.: 149). Specialist shops were places to hang out and chat, and shopping trips reinforced friendships and identities, as well as allowing participants to enhance and display their subcultural capital.

Where retail played a key role, so too did traditional and online media. Reiterating Thornton's point that 'the media do not just represent but participate in the assembly, demarcation and development' of subcultures (Thornton, quoted in ibid.: 154), Hodkinson distinguishes between 'non-subcultural' and 'subcultural' media and notes the importance of the former 'in the initial construction of the ... scene' (ibid.: 155). This was followed by declining mass and niche media coverage in the 1990s, however, when specialist or subcultural media acquired increased significance. Fanzines, posters and flyers all acted as important sources of information, and formed one of the key ways in which participants contributed to 'the general survival of their subculture' (ibid.: 173), with fanzines, in particular, also helping to reinforce a 'sense of shared identity' (ibid.: 169) throughout the scene as a whole. Their restricted availability meant that rather than 'being conducive to movement or flow between groupings, as emphasized in notions of neo-tribalism', fanzines instead acted as gatekeepers, reinforcing 'the substantive, bounded form taken by the goth scene' (ibid.: 165).

Internet-based resources played a similar (and increasingly significant) part in the day-to-day workings of the subculture, acting as an important source of practical information and playing a key role in the construction of shared values and tastes. Websites and discussion groups were creative and participatory, but were also carefully policed and relatively inaccessible, again acting 'to reinforce the boundaries of the grouping' (ibid.: 176) rather than to open things up in some sort of 'postmodern' way. Rather than replacing them, online resources and interaction also enhanced and facilitated 'real-life' activities and events and most participants 'focused their internet use on the British goth scene', gathering information about 'events they were able to attend', and interacting with 'individuals with whom face-to-face contact was a realistic possibility' (ibid.: 186–8). Their use of the internet illustrated that, 'rather than spelling the end of face-to-face interaction and community, on-line technologies can [instead] function to enhance off-line social activities and affiliation' (ibid.: 186).

Taken as a whole Hodkinson's research is interesting and important, in part because of the way it offers a detailed account of how the subculture actually works. Far from a CCCS-style reading of the subculture in terms solely or predominantly of the semiotics of subcultural style, it instead demonstrates in some detail how the subculture actually operates, what holds it together and how a series of different aspects of subcultural practice together cohere into a meaningful whole. In addition to providing a careful account of the workings of a particular subculture, Hodkinson's research also contributes to a number of wider themes. First, in demonstrating that goth possesses a considerable degree of 'cultural substance', Hodkinson attempts to illustrate both the continuing relevance of the concept of 'subculture', when reformulated in these terms and the concomitant difficulties with alternative concepts such as 'neo-tribe'. Describing the four key indicators of cultural substance in a related article as 'a *consistent distinctiveness* in group values and tastes, a strong sense of *shared identity*, practical *commitment* among participants, and a significant degree of *autonomy* in the facilitation and operation of the group' (Hodkinson 2004b: 141–2), Hodkinson's research indicates that goth fulfils each of these criteria and can thus be conceived of in 'subcultural' rather than 'tribal' terms. Suggesting that the latter concept be confined to 'contemporary lifestyles and affiliations which, in contrast to subcultures, are fundamentally ephemeral and partial' (Hodkinson 2002: 196), he also points out that, without implying they are wholly inaccurate, 'the case of the goth scene certainly raises questions about attempts to apply such models across the board' (ibid.: 73).

Similarly, the 'translocal' nature of the subculture also indicates difficulties with a separate tendency to focus recent youth or subcultural research on specific, locally based scenes. Facilitated by specialist retailers, traditional and online media, and travel to events throughout the UK, the 'translocal consistency' of the goth scene meant that participants tended to feel 'that they had more in common with ... goths hundreds of ... miles away than they did with most nonaffiliated members of their immediate locality' (Hodkinson 2004a: 134). Traditional and online media helped to facilitate local connections and participation, but were arguably more significant in terms of the provision of translocal connections, and 'rather than consisting of a series of highly separate, distinctive and clearly bounded local scenes, [goth] comes across more as a singular, relatively coherent movement, whose translocal connections were of greater significance than its local differences' (ibid.: 141–4).

While illustrating the continued relevance of the concept of subculture when reformulated in relation to indicators of subcultural substance, as well as the apparent inappropriateness of concepts such as 'tribe' or 'scene', Hodkinson's work also indicates difficulties with earlier understandings of the term. These difficulties include what he regards as the CCCS tendency to conceptualize subculture as prior to or apart from media and commerce. As has already been indicated, Hodkinson notes the importance of 'external' media and commercial interests in the initial 'facilitation and construction of the subculture' (Hodkinson 2002: 119, 155) and the subsequent growth in importance of subcultural media and entrepreneurs. Noting, too, the importance of consumption to 'participants' experience of the goth scene' (ibid.: 131), Hodkinson points out that goth cannot be considered 'as occupying an authentic position outside or in opposition to consumerism', and that rather than being seen as antithetical, media, commerce and subculture must instead 'be regarded as highly compatible' (ibid.: 121–2).

Finally, Hodkinson's research also contributes to debates over the internet, contradicting some of the claims that have been made about its potential effects. Addressing the idea that easy access to the variety of information available on the Web may encourage fluidity, playfulness and the breaking-down of cultural boundaries, as well as 'the trying on and casting off of multiple styles and selves' (Hodkinson 2003: 287), Hodkinson points out that amongst his participants internet use was actually highly selective and 'usually functioned, in the same way as goth events, to concentrate their involvement in the goth scene and to reinforce the boundaries of the group' (Hodkinson 2002: 176). Mailing lists and discussion groups were carefully policed and inaccessible to outsiders, and the internet also tended to enhance rather than reduce offline involvement, encouraging and facilitating face-to-face interaction at local and translocal events. The 'desire to utilize virtual connections to facilitate "real life" activities rather than as an end in themselves' also limited goths' 'interest in non-British internet content' (Hodkinson 2004a: 143), and Hodkinson argues that, overall, goths' use of the internet helps to illustrate the point that, rather than being necessarily transformative, such technologies may instead serve to reinforce 'life as it is' (Castells, quoted in Hodkinson 2003: 296).

In acknowledging the part played by media and commercial interests in the construction and facilitation of the subculture Hodkinson's research provides a helpful corrective to the overly romanticized version of 'subculture' – as authentic, pre-commodified and necessarily resistant or subversive – found in CCCS and related accounts. Hodkinson also made considerable use of the internet as a research tool and in so doing was able to contribute to a series of wider debates about online technologies. Issues of interpretation and conceptualization will be addressed in the sections that follow. First, though, consideration is given to an aspect of his research that Hodkinson himself devotes considerable attention to: his status as a member of the subculture he was investigating.

On Being (or Not Being) a Goth

As is indicated by the photograph on the back cover of his book, and as he also discusses in the book and elsewhere, Hodkinson was directly involved as a participant in the goth subculture, both before and during his research (and indeed continues to be involved in it). Along with other researchers who have recently conducted 'insider' research of this sort, he also suggests that this was a significant advantage, although he does not go as far as Roseneil (1993) – who conducted research on the Greenham Common women's peace camp of the early 1980s on the basis of her own direct involvement – in suggesting that his research might not have been possible had he not been so directly involved (see also Hodkinson 2005: 137).

Hodkinson acknowledges in a recent paper that the notion of 'insiderness' has been problematized by accounts of identity and subjectivity as fluid, multiple and unstable (2005: 133). He notes further that, in the context of research into youth or subculture, this position is further complicated by an emphasis in post-subcultural accounts of the open, superficial and ephemeral nature of contemporary tribes. At the same time, however, he also maintains that 'committed and bounded' youth cultural groupings may 'remain more prevalent' (ibid.: 135) than such work suggests, and that in this context the insider or outsider status of the researcher remains significant. He also argues for a pragmatic interpretation of 'insider research as a non-absolute concept intended to designate ... situations characterized by a significant degree of *initial* proximity between the sociocultural locations of researcher and researched' (ibid.: 134).

Whilst rejecting the idea that insider researchers 'have privileged access to a single insider truth', and that only insiders can access 'the worldview of those they study' , Hodkinson nonetheless maintains that avoidance of essentialist positions of this sort does not mean that we should not consider the implications of researcher proximity for the 'types of understanding produced' (ibid.: 141–2). He also argues that 'we can accept the absence of absolute certainties and of exclusively correct "ways of seeing" without abandoning the notion that ... some forms of ethnographic interpretation should be regarded as more plausible ... than others' (ibid.: 142). On the basis of his own experience Hodkinson suggests that insider status can confer advantages – in terms of issues such as access, trust and rapport – which are not simply practical but also affect the sorts of data one is able to produce and that whilst 'competent non-insiders' are still likely to 'generate persuasive and valuable interpretations', 'social distance can create obstacles, uncertainties and hazards that may [otherwise] be bypassed' (ibid.: 142–3). These include being fed exaggerated, inaccurate or distorted accounts, which an insider would not only be more likely to spot but would also be less likely to be provided with in the first place (ibid.: 140). That is not to say that Hodkinson's insider status was always immediately apparent: one of the points he makes about his internet-based research is that it was initially more difficult to communicate his insider status online, although the careful use of particular conversational strategies, 'website photographs and eventual face-to-face acquaintance with some subscribers' (ibid.: 138; see also 2002: 5) also meant that he was also able to overcome such difficulties with time. Hodkinson's position in relation to insider research is actually quite close to Roseneil's arguments in relation to her own research on women peace campaigners at Greenham Common. Roseneil has argued that 'it was strongly advantageous ... to have been involved in Greenham' herself, that 'being an insider "acts as a built-in truth check"' or as a 'form of triangulation', and that, whilst she would not want to claim that her account is necessarily definitive, it is certainly 'better than' [anything] produced by an outsider could have been' (Roseneil 1993: 189, 192).

Despite emphasizing the benefits of insider research, however, Hodkinson also acknowledges some of its potential difficulties. These include complacency and the taking of issues for granted, as well as a failure to acknowledge how one's degree of proximity is likely to vary from one respondent to the next (Hodkinson 2005: 139). Although it may help to prevent exaggerated or distorted accounts, the presence of an insider interviewer may also place pressure on participants to provide answers that are subculturally 'correct' (ibid.: 140). Just as in relation to its potential advantages, then, insider status does not simply have practical implications or effects, but also raises questions surrounding 'the kinds of ... knowledge ... produced' (ibid.).

It is important therefore to exercise 'caution, awareness and ongoing reflexivity' (ibid.: 132) with regard to one's status and, as an insider *researcher*, to appreciate that both aspects of one's position are of equal significance. Being an insider researcher allows for an empathetic yet critical perspective in relation to one's research, and in the transition from insider to insider *researcher* it is important that sufficient critical distance is achieved. The 'position of insider researcher may offer significant ... benefits in terms of ... issues such as access and rapport', whilst enhancing 'the quality of the eventual understandings produced', but Hodkinson argues that it is also important to ensure that one avoids the position of 'subcultural spokesperson' and to employ a 'careful, reflexive ... approach to ensure that' the benefits of one's 'initial proximity are realized without the emergence of significant difficulties' (ibid.: 146).

Whilst acknowledging the need to achieve critical distance, there is arguably something of a tension in Hodkinson's work between accepting his participants' accounts and adopting a more critical and/or theoretical perspective, and this will be returned to in relation to issues of interpretation in the section that follows. Despite his acknowledgement of some of the difficulties associated with insider research, and his arguments in favour of a reflexive approach, certain other issues also remain unacknowledged or underexplored – including the potential impact of his subcultural status on the sorts of academic work Hodkinson felt able to produce (again, these are returned to below). As already indicated, Hodkinson's work helps to redress some of the difficulties with earlier work on subcultures by avoiding CCCS-style overtheorizing and focusing instead on what it is that subculturalists actually *do*. At the same time, however, it can also be argued that his work goes too far in the former direction and not far enough in the latter. These and related difficulties will now be addressed.

Interpretation and Critical Distance

In the first place, it can be argued that for all of its detail – and its important contribution to our understanding of how the subculture actually works – Hodkinson's work contains certain significant omissions, not least a full sense of what his participants actually get out of being a goth and why they take part. It was noted above that some of the work arguing for a greater focus on subcultural practice has also argued for more attention to be paid to issues around experience, embodiment and affect (Macdonald 2001; Sweetman 2001), linked to more general work within cultural studies which has argued that we need to pay greater attention to the pleasures of consumption rather than simply the meanings of texts. Whilst providing a great deal of information about the mechanics of the subculture, Hodkinson does not provide us with much of a sense of the motivations or experiences of his participants, what they get out of it and the *pleasures* of being involved. He does note the importance of things such as shopping and 'hanging around' (Hodkinson 2002: 149), as well as of attending events such as the Whitby Gothic Weekend; but exactly what his participants got out of such practices and activities remains unclear, and we do not learn much, if anything, about the *particular* pleasures involved.

Some of these pleasures may plausibly be centred around transgressive performances of gender and sexuality, yet, while Hodkinson notes that he was impressed by this aspect of the subculture (ibid.: 197) and draws our attention to 'femininity and ambiguity' as a key aspect of goth style (Figure 6.1), this issue is underexplored. Paradoxically, perhaps, this may also reflect the second difficulty indicated above, which relates to Hodkinson's wish to avoid CCCS-style overtheorizing in favour of an account his participants would recognize and endorse. It is unclear how much data Hodkinson collected on these sorts of issues – and this would, of course, have reflected both the methods he employed and the sorts of questions that he asked – but, assuming it was limited in scope, this may also have limited his willingness to move beyond his participants' accounts. This also arguably affects his treatment of a second aspect of goth style, the appropriation of 'fragments of related styles'. There is a clear issue of interpretation here, as this might, alternatively, be taken to indicate the porousness of subcultural boundaries or be regarded as a form of 'bricolage'. From the CCCS perspective, when punks wore Teddy boy style drape-coats or brothel-creepers they were not so much borrowing 'fragments of related styles' as engaging in a form of bricolage through which, in a process of recontextualization, new meanings were assigned (Hebdige 1979).

Hodkinson also rejects the idea of a homological relationship between different aspects of subcultural style, or a semiotic approach as a whole, noting his participants' own reluctance to read anything beyond straightforward

Figure 6.1   Femininity and ambiguity
Source: Hodkinson (2002: 49).

aesthetic preferences from particular aspects of goth style (Hodkinson 2002: 62).
Whilst there is some strength to this argument, however – and to Hodkinson's
point that 'without wanting to endorse an uncritical reliance upon the accounts
of insiders, we should surely be wary of interpretations which … take little
account of them at all' (ibid.: 61) – there may be times when insiders' comments are not entirely forthcoming and when it is legitimate to read more into
things than is actually acknowledged in one's participants' accounts. Just because
participants do not regard their actions as overtly political or transgressive, for
example, does not mean they should not be interpreted as such. Further, while

there are very real dangers in privileging theory over one's participants' own understandings and accounts, there are also very real dangers in privileging experience over interpretation (Frith and Savage 1997: 13) and assuming that a particular theoretical perspective cannot be employed simply because it does not tally with lay understandings of the phenomena under investigation. This would, of course, be particularly problematic from the sort of perspective that explicitly suggests that lay participants are likely to *misunderstand* the nature of their own position, and would automatically rule out whole swathes of Marxist theory in this regard. As Dick Hobbs points out in relation to his own insider research in London's East End, an acknowledgement that academic work is produced in a particular context and for particular sorts of audiences also problematizes what Hobbs would regard as somewhat naïve attempts to present an 'authentic' account that would necessarily be recognized and/or endorsed by one's fieldwork participants (Hobbs 1993).

There is a definite tension here because Hodkinson (i) notes that one needs to be careful to avoid accepting participants' statements at face value; (ii) criticizes others for adopting an 'uncritical approach' in this regard; and (iii) suggests that being an insider can help in weeding out exaggerated or distorted accounts. In relation to his participants' comments about their appearance, he points out, for example, that 'many interviewees exaggerated the extent of their stylistic differences from other goths', and notes that 'an over-reliance upon the ways in which ... participants choose to respond to ... questioning can sometimes result in debatable conclusions' (Hodkinson 2002: 39). He also notes the importance of his sociological background to his interpretation of his data – pointing out that through his 'academic reading' he began to question whether his participants' 'emphasis on individualism might [instead] be interpreted as a form of subcultural ideology or rhetoric' – and makes the point that critical distance is required in order to ensure that one avoids taking on the role of '"subcultural spokesperson", rather than that of critical analyst' (Hodkinson 2005: 144–5). Hodkinson's *overall* position is clearly weighted towards an emphasis on his participants' own interpretations and accounts, however, and there are times when he does appear to take their statements somewhat at face value, such as when he suggests that aspects of their identities such as class and ethnicity took a back seat to subcultural identification. However, he fails to interrogate sufficiently this finding in relation to the largely white, middle-class nature of the subculture as a whole (Hodkinson 2002: 70–1).

To return to the issue discussed in the previous section, it may be that each of these difficulties reflects not simply Hodkinson's overall approach but also his position as an insider researcher. It is certainly plausible, for example, that as a conspicuous member of a subculture, Hodkinson felt under some pressure to prove his seriousness as an academic researcher and as a result deliberately or otherwise toned down his account in certain respects (for example, downplaying issues around transgression, embodiment and affect). Whilst stressing the need for a 'careful, reflexive ... approach' (Hodkinson 2005: 146), he focuses his discussion of being an insider researcher on his position within the field, not on the potential implications of his subcultural affiliation to his status as an academic and on the sorts of work he felt able to produce. He also overlooks the way in which his own investment in the subculture may have influenced him to produce a largely positive portrait, in the same sort of way that Hobbs's 'personal closeness' to his own East End informants may have led him 'to paint a relatively benign view of their activities' (Devine and Heath 1999: 8), and that Roseneil may have toned down her critical findings about Greenham Common out of a 'sense of personal loyalty' (Devine and Heath 1999: 193). Although it constitutes a strength insofar as he reflects critically on his insider status vis-à-vis his research participants, it might also be argued that in these respects Hodkinson is not reflexive enough. It is also the case that although he addresses some of the potential disadvantages of insider research, he does not directly address the advantages of being an *outsider*, not least being able to approach things as a stranger in an anthropological sense.

(Re)conceptualizing 'Subculture' and Questions of Purpose or Significance

Hodkinson's wish to avoid CCCS-style overtheorizing in favour of an account that lends greater weight to the experiences of subculturalists themselves also affects a further set of issues surrounding his reconceptualization of 'subculture' itself, and there is arguably something rather circular about his retention of the term, albeit in a modified form. This is because, on the one hand, the concept is reformulated around a set of criteria – identity, commitment, autonomy and consistent distinctiveness (Hodkinson 2002: 29) – and, on the other hand, the fulfilment of these criteria is then taken as indicative of the continuing relevance of the term. He also, and more importantly, sidesteps the issue as to whether it is actually appropriate to retain the term whilst denuding it of most of its previous connotations. In the first place, the full implications of and background to the CCCS understanding of the term are not properly set out; so what the concept is being stripped of is not clear, and the legitimacy of doing so is not adequately addressed. *Is* it appropriate to retain the term when so much of what it formerly represented has been lost? Second, what is one actually left with? What does the concept actually mean if all that it implies is the fulfilment of a set of relative criteria indicative of '(sub)cultural substance'? How, in this respect, does goth differ from a suburban golf club or the Young Conservatives? And, if the latter two groups fulfil all of Hodkinson's criteria, does that mean that they too should be regarded as subcultures?

From the CCCS perspective, of course, they should not – the concept itself having been formulated in relation to an overall theoretical framework which regarded subcultures as subversive, resistant, and so on. Hodkinson's wish to avoid CCCS-style overtheorizing whilst retaining their central concept – in part to distinguish groups such as goths from other contemporary formulations such as scenes and tribes – invites such questions, however. These in turn raise further questions about the overall purpose of subcultural studies (as considered below). It should be noted, though, that one can distinguish between more and less committed 'subcultural' groups, and in so doing indicate difficulties with attempts to apply a neo-tribal framework across the board, without necessarily retaining the term 'subculture' in an overly denuded form. In a recent paper, for example, I proposed a distinction between 'travellers' and 'tourists' – as more or less committed 'subcultural' types – whilst noting that, however the travellers may view themselves, both represent elective responses to contemporary cultural conditions and that neither should therefore be regarded as true 'subculturalists' in the CCCS sense of the term (Sweetman 2004). This framework would accommodate groups such as goths and allow them to be distinguished from more superficial 'tourists', whilst clearly demarcating both groups from CCCS-style subcultures and also allowing for the clear links between travellers and tourists to be adequately acknowledged and explored (Sweetman 2004).

Hodkinson notes the strong sense of collective identity and group distinction of goths and the importance to this of their stylistic distinctiveness (Hodkinson 2002: 65), but if one refuses to regard subcultural style as resistant or subversive how does it actually differ from any other marker of group affiliation such as a golf-club sweater or tie? He also refers to fanzines, for example, as a 'form of subcultural media as defined in this book – that is – written by, about and for enthusiasts of the same substantive lifestyle grouping' (ibid.: 161). Again, though, one might ask how this differs from a pamphlet written by steam-railway enthusiasts or fans of fly-fishing; and if the answer is that it doesn't, then additional reasons for singling out groups such as goths as deserving of particular sociological attention presumably have to be found. According to Hodkinson, his reworking of the concept 'avoids key problems with traditional subcultural theory, particularly its Birmingham School incarnations' (ibid.: 196), but what are we left with that is significant? And what is the point of looking at subcultural groups if almost any reasonably clearly demarcated lifestyle grouping can be so defined? One answer might be to do with issues around gender, sexuality and transgression, but, as has already been indicated, this is not an issue that Hodkinson really explores, and, in any case, such a rationale would need to be clearly spelled out.

All of this also means that Hodkinson's reworking of the concept is – in terms of superficiality if not in terms of commitment – considerably closer to

Maffesoli's understanding of neo-tribes than Hodkinson acknowledges. Indeed, one could argue that rather than unequivocally supporting the retention of the term 'subculture', Hodkinson's research is equally supportive of the neo-tribal framework he claims partially to refute, albeit with the latter concept partially reworked to allow for the greater commitment and durability that he identifies (see Bauman 1992; Sweetman 2004). As Hodkinson himself points out, in a manner largely consistent with Maffesoli's understanding of neo-tribal sociality, 'essentially, the goth scene ... functioned as a highly specialist consumer grouping' (Hodkinson 2004a: 139), amongst whom 'external political goals or effects were less important ... than the desire to feel distinctive and to belong to a community' (Hodkinson 2002: 196).

According to Hodkinson his research contributes significantly to our overall understanding of contemporary society: 'the detailed account of the process through which, in a society characterized by instability, most goths came to reject multitudes of fleeting affiliations in favour of a single intensive subcultural lifestyle, provides an important contribution to ... understanding, regardless of whether such a lifestyle is deemed virtuous' (ibid.: 197). And the 'considerable control exercised by goths over the facilitation and construction of their subculture' means that his work also makes 'an important contribution to ... debates over the general potential for grass-roots agency and active participation in contemporary society' (ibid.). In each case, however, such claims could also be made for a host of other groups, such as extreme right-wingers and fundamentalist religious groups in the former case, and environmental campaigners in the latter, and presumably an environmental campaign group would provide a better example of the 'potential for grass-roots agency' (ibid.) given goths' relative autonomy and apparent lack of political engagement?

From the CCCS perspective, subcultures were interesting not so much in their own right, but because of their assumed cultural significance and effects; yet underlying Hodkinson's work appears to be an implicit assumption that subcultures such as goth are necessarily interesting in and of themselves. This may well be the case: the point, however, is that they would no longer assume the same sort of political or cultural significance (thereby raising questions about retaining core conceptual terms), and if they are assumed to be interesting simply in and of themselves this assumption ought probably to be both acknowledged and interrogated. None of this is to suggest that Hodkinson's work is unimportant – it is not. However, having stripped the central concept of its wider connotations and implications, and failing to recontextualize his work in relation to an alternative set of wider debates – such as those surrounding consumption and globalization, or the politics of pleasure – the overall rationale for focusing his attention on this particular group remains unclear. In this sense it arguably replicates a problem within literary and cultural studies, where texts of different sorts are frequently explored in the absence of any explicit rationale or clear sense of why that particular text is significant. Is the rationale simply that the text is interesting in itself? That it is illustrative of a particular sort of cultural phenomenon? That it is indicative of wider developments or emergent trends? Or because of its presumed influence or effect? Hodkinson's research does, of course, contribute to debates about contemporary subcultures and to the other areas identified above, but why we should be concerned about 'spectacular subcultures' *at all* if they are not regarded as politically significant remains open to question.

Conclusion

As has already been noted, Hodkinson's research is interesting and important, in part because of the way it offers a detailed account of how the goth subculture actually works. Like other recent work in this area it moves away from a CCCS-style reading of the subculture in predominantly textual or semiotic terms, instead focusing on subcultural practice, or what it is that 'subcultures actually *do*' (Clarke 1990: 90). Moving away from a CCCS-type reading of the subculture in terms solely or predominantly of the semiotics of subcultural style, it instead explores how the subculture actually operates, and how different aspects of subcultural practice together cohere into a meaningful whole. In acknowledging the part played by the media and commerce in the construction and facilitation of the subculture it also provides a necessary corrective to the overly romanticized version of subculture found in CCCS and related accounts.

Whilst itself making an important contribution to the 'new subcultural studies', Hodkinson's work also indicates difficulties with other recent work in this area, including attempts to recast 'subculture' in tribal or other terms. Although goth may actually be somewhat closer to Maffesoli's neo-tribes than Hodkinson acknowledges, the degree of substance displayed does indicate difficulties with claims surrounding the superficiality of contemporary youth culture, and the translocal aspects of the subculture also indicate difficulties with alternative concepts such as 'scene'. As has been indicated, Hodkinson's work also contributes to a series of additional debates such as those surrounding the internet, which he suggests may not be as transformative as certain commentators have claimed, but may instead serve to reinforce 'life as it is' (Castells, quoted in Hodkinson 2003: 296).

That is not to say that Hodkinson's work is without difficulties. Not only do we not learn much about what goths actually get out of being goths or *why* they take part, but in abandoning the theoretical framework associated with CCCS understandings of the term and reframing the central concept solely in terms of (sub)cultural substance, it becomes quite difficult to see how 'spectacular subcultures' differ significantly from any other sort of relatively committed lifestyle grouping, and in this respect why we should be *particularly* interested in them at all. Such questions of overall purpose – important though they are – should not detract, however, from an acknowledgement of Hodkinson's significant contribution to the new subcultural studies and its increased attention to Phil Cohen's third level of subcultural analysis – what it is that subcultures actually *do*.

Additional Reading

Hall and Jefferson's edited collection *Resistance through Rituals* (1976) is *the* classic collection on post-war British subcultures. The book sets out the theoretical framework associated with the CCCS and includes both theoretical and more substantive contributions by key figures such as Dick Hebdige, Angela McRobbie and Paul Willis. Bennett and Kahn-Harris's *After Subculture* (2004) is a key collection of new work on youth and subculture – including chapters by both Hodkinson and Sweetman – which has gone a long way towards remapping the field. See also Muggleton and Weinzierl's edited collection *The Post-Subcultures Reader* (2003). Hobbs's 'Peers, Careers, and Academic Fears: Writing as Field-Work', in his edited collection with T. May, *Interpreting the Field* (1993), is an interesting, entertaining and informative account of research as an insider of sorts, focusing on criminals and coppers in London's East End. In the same collection, see also Roseneil's 'Greenham Revisited: Researching Myself and My Sisters', which is another helpful account of insider research although, in this case, of a retrospective sort. These examples are both discussed in detail in Devine and Heath's *Sociological Research Methods in Context* (1999).

Acknowledgements

I am grateful to Sue Heath and Fiona Devine, and also to Paul Hodkinson, for sharing with me their thoughts and comments on an earlier version of this chapter, many of which are incorporated here. I am also grateful to Paul for providing me with copies of one or two of his more recent articles.

References

Bauman, Z. (1992) 'Survival as a social construct', *Theory, Culture & Society*, 9: 1–36.
Bennett, A. (1999) 'Subcultures or neo-tribes? Rethinking the relationship between youth, style and musical taste', *Sociology*, 33 (3): 599–617.

Bennett, A. and K. Kahn-Harris (eds) (2004) *After Subculture: Critical Studies in Contemporary Youth Culture*, Basingstoke: Palgrave Macmillan.

Clarke, G. (1990) 'Defending ski-jumpers: a critique of theories of youth subcultures', in S. Frith and A. Goodwin (eds) *On Record: Rock, Pop, and the Written Word*, London: Routledge.

Clarke, J. (1976) 'The skinheads and the magical recovery of community', in S. Hall and T. Jefferson (eds) *Resistance through Rituals: Youth Subcultures in Post-war Britain*, London: HarperCollins.

Clarke, J., S. Hall, T. Jefferson and B. Roberts et al. (1976) 'Subcultures, cultures and class: a theoretical overview', in S. Hall and T. Jefferson (eds) *Resistance through Rituals: Youth Subcultures in Post-war Britain*, London: HarperCollins.

Cohen, P. (1997) 'Subcultural conflict and working-class community', in K. Gelder and S. Thornton (eds) *The Subcultures Reader*, London: Routledge.

Cohen, S. (1997) 'Symbols of trouble', in K. Gelder and S. Thornton (eds) *The Subcultures Reader*, London: Routledge.

Devine, F. and Heath, S. (1999) *Sociological Research Methods in Context*, Basingstoke: Palgrave Macmillan.

Frith, S. and J. Savage (1997) 'Pearls and swine: intellectuals and the mass media', in S. Redhead, D.Wynne and J.O'Connor (eds) *The Clubcultures Reader: Readings in Popular Cultural Studies*, Oxford: Blackwell.

Hall, S. and T. Jefferson (eds) (1976) *Resistance through Rituals: Youth Subcultures in Post-war Britain*, London: HarperCollins.

Hebdige, D. (1976) 'The meaning of mod', in S. Hall and T. Jefferson (eds) *Resistance through Rituals: Youth Subcultures in Post-war Britain*, London: HarperCollins.

Hebdige, D. (1979) *Subculture: The Meaning of Style*, London: Routledge.

Hobbs, D. (1993) 'Peers, careers, and academic fears: writing as field-work', in D. Hobbs and T. May (eds) *Interpreting the Field: Accounts of Ethnography*, Oxford: Clarendon Press.

Hodkinson, P. (2002) *Goth: Identity, Style and Subculture*, Oxford: Berg.

Hodkinson, P. (2003) ' "Net.Goth": internet communication and (sub)cultural boundaries', in D. Muggleton and R. Weinzierl (eds) *The Post-Subcultures Reader*, Oxford: Berg.

Hodkinson, P. (2004a) 'Translocal connections in the goth scene', in A. Bennett and R. Peterson (eds) *Music Scenes: Local, Translocal and Virtual*, Nashville, TN: Vanderbilt University Press.

Hodkinson, P. (2004b) 'The goth scene and (sub)cultural substance', in A. Bennett and K. Kahn-Harris (eds) *After Subculture: Critical Studies in Contemporary Youth Culture*, Basingstoke: Palgrave Macmillan.

Hodkinson, P. (2005) ' "Insider research" in the study of youth cultures', *Journal of Youth Studies*, 8(2): 131–49.

Macdonald, N. (2001) *The Graffiti Subculture: Youth, Masculinity and Identity in London and New York*, Basingstoke: Palgrave Macmillan.

Maffesoli, M. (1996) *The Time of the Tribes: The Decline of Individualism in Mass Society*, London: Sage.

Malbon, B. (1999) *Clubbing: Dancing, Ecstasy and Vitality*, London: Routledge.

McRobbie, A. (1990) 'Settling accounts with subcultures: a feminist critique', in S. Frith and A. Goodwin (eds) *On Record: Rock, Pop, and the Written Word*, London: Routledge.

McRobbie, A. and J. Garber (1976) 'Girls and subcultures: an exploration', in S. Hall and T. Jefferson (eds) *Resistance through Rituals: Youth Subcultures in Post-war Britain*, London: HarperCollins.

Muggleton, D. (2000) *Inside Subculture: The Postmodern Meaning of Style*, Oxford: Berg.

Muggleton, D. and R. Weinzierl (eds) (2003) *The Post-Subcultures Reader*, Oxford: Berg.

Pearson, G. (1993) 'Foreword: talking a good fight: authenticity and distance in the ethnographer's craft', in D. Hobbs and T. May (eds) *Interpreting the Field: Accounts of Ethnography*, Oxford: Clarendon Press.

Roseneil, S. (1993) 'Greenham revisited: researching myself and my sisters', in D. Hobbs and T. May (eds) *Interpreting the Field: Accounts of Ethnography*, Oxford: Clarendon Press.

St John, G. (2003) 'Post-rave technotribalism and the carnival of protest', in D. Muggleton and R. Weinzierl (eds) *The Post-Subcultures Reader*, Oxford: Berg.

Storey, J. (1993) *An Introductory Guide to Cultural Theory and Popular Culture*, Hemel Hempstead: Harvester Wheatsheaf.

Sweetman, P. (2001) 'Stop making sense? The problem of the body in youth/sub/counter-culture', in S. Cunningham-Burley and K. Backett-Milburn (eds) *Exploring the Body*, Basingstoke: Palgrave Macmillan.

Sweetman, P. (2004) 'Tourists and travellers? "Subcultures", reflexive identities and neo-tribal sociality', in A. Bennett and K. Kahn-Harris (eds) *After Subculture: Critical Studies in Contemporary Youth Culture*, Basingstoke: Palgrave Macmillan.

Thornton, S. (1995) *Club Cultures: Music, Media and Subcultural Capital*, Cambridge: Polity Press.

Turner, G. (1990) *British Cultural Studies: An Introduction*, London: Routledge.

CHAPTER 7

TV Soaps: Tufte's *Living with the Rubbish Queen*

HELEN WOOD

This chapter looks at issues of method in media studies. Research on the media is very interesting because it crosses disciplinary borders that demarcate the social sciences and the humanities. Helen Wood considers Thomas Tufte's Living with the Rubbish Queen (2000) which is an ethnographic study of a telenovela – a national form of soap opera – in Brazil. Methodological challenges of two kinds are considered in detail. First, Wood explores how Tufte combines different types of data and then arrives at a particular interpretation of a cultural process. Second, Wood reflects on issues of interpretation, validity and reflexivity in qualitative cultural research. Wood is impressed by Tufte's wide range of research material and the way in which it taps into different dimensions of media, ranging from production to consumption. She also applauds Tufte's reflections on being a European man studying Brazilian women. That said, she calls for a greater acknowledgement of the power relations at play to ensure reflexivity in practice.

Introduction

Television is considered so familiar and banal that its study has sometimes not been taken seriously. Yet even academic lives could not be experienced without it. If scholars were to exclude TVs from their homes, they would not be able to evade screens in waiting rooms, bars and even in our city squares. In an episode of the hit US sitcom *Friends*, Joey Tribbiani, whilst talking to a 'geeky' academic who proudly proclaimed not to have a television, asks the troubled question: 'but what does all your furniture point at?'. Joey is no philosopher, but his query gets to the heart of television's sociological enigma.

It lies at the centre of our household dynamics helping to order, as well as disrupt, daily ritual. It is still the most dominant medium for receiving news, offering an albeit distorted 'window on the world' at the very cusp of the private/public interface. The scene from *Friends* also alerts us to the politics surrounding television as cultural consumption. Choosing not to watch can be seen as a marker of higher cultural standards and a refusal of tabloid culture. Television is thus usually located at the bottom of systems of cultural value, providing a foil for distinctions of class and taste.

It would be wrong to assume, though, that TV research is uniform. The mass communications research tradition has been concerned with the messages of television and their potential impact upon belief systems; those more closely associated with television as an art form have concentrated on televisual aesthetics and usually the production of drama; sociological approaches have been concerned with the embedding of the technological object within the framework of modern living. But *all* of these aspects are germane to the way in which television has intimately located itself within the daily fabric of our existence, imbricating the macrostaging of world politics with the microeating of toast with breakfast-time news.

There are, therefore, numerous ways in which the technology impacts upon our experience, thereby providing us with a methodological challenge. Researching media often begins with a particular 'object', which might either be a medium (television) or a form (soap opera), requiring us to research 'around' them as particular empirical entities. This is a media-centric approach to media research that has largely dominated the field, but, of course, the media figure in social research when they crop up as an inevitable part of social life, which leads David Morley to argue for a 'non media-centric media studies' (Morley 2007). Television is more than a domestic appliance, although it has suited certain political ends in favour of deregulation to describe it as a 'toaster with pictures'. It is also a dominant storyteller, generating tales via the political and economic conditions of media organizations, networks and nation-state regulations.

Taking all of this into account means that the choice of research method or methods is not necessarily obvious because researchers are required to traverse disciplinary borders. We have to apply a humanities' eye to the interpretation of narratives and stories (texts) whilst deploying the 'sociological imagination' to evaluate their significance to everyday life (contexts). How these approaches can work together to illuminate social processes *around* television, and the responsibility this imparts upon the researcher, are the main foci of this chapter. I concentrate on the ethnographic study of television: the familiarity of television obscures its sociological significance, but taking up the challenge of ethnography to 'make the familiar strange' can serve to bring it back into view.

   This chapter will focus upon Thomas Tufte's *Living with the Rubbish Queen* as one of relatively few extensive ethnographic studies of television. The work brings a wealth of contextual information on the socio-political context of Brazil to bear on the institutional frameworks of television production, the narrative drives of the 'telenovela' (a national form of soap opera), and the role that television and the telenovela play in the lives of Brazilian women. The chapter will first offer a brief overview of developments in media reception research before outlining the details of Tufte's ethnography. I will consider the issues at stake in undertaking interdisciplinary research that involves combining different types of data and examine how Tufte uses his collection of research material to illuminate a 'cultural process'. Such an interpretive approach demands that researchers be reflexive about how they have arrived at their particular interpretation of lived culture; thus the final section of the chapter will interrogate the politics of reflexivity and its role in asking questions of validity in qualitative cultural research.

Researching Media Reception

There is not space here to offer a summary of all the varieties of media research since it has grown out of a number of disciplines with different emphases, but it has largely shown an interest in texts, institutions and audiences (see Branston and Stafford 2006). Instead it is useful to offer an overview of the research on media reception where the television audience has traditionally been subject to more scrutiny than the audience for any other medium.

   The early introduction of the television set into homes spawned concern for the maintenance of family values as it became part and parcel of suburban living. Women and children were seen to be at risk of television's perceived ability to engender both passivity and delinquency (see Spigel 1992). Early research on television was, therefore, mostly conducted as psychological experiments into television's negative effects. For example, a classic study by Belson (1978) found that high exposure to television violence increases the degree to which adolescent boys engage in serious violence. But results from this kind of approach, which seeks a direct correlation between behaviour and media exposure, have produced varying responses: some suggesting that viewing violence increases actual violence, others suggesting that it operates as a cathartic release-valve (Aronson 2003). This effect-led approach is still undertaken, but sociologists have argued that these experiments tend to remove television viewing from its broader social contexts, serving to locate blame with the media rather than tackling broader social trends. (For a wider discussion of the problems associated with this tradition of 'effects' research, see Boyle 2005.)

The overdeterministic 'media effects' model was countered by the functionalist 'uses and gratifications' research model which suggested that media use depends on the perceived satisfactions, needs, wishes or motives of the prospective audience (Katz et al. 1974). This type of research ignores both the significance of particular genre distinctions and broader social shifts that might account for the implications of social or cultural influences by focusing upon a universalized sense of human 'need'. The most significant criticism of 'uses and gratifications' research is that it fails to engage with questions of power (Moores 1993).

Studies of audience reception from sociology and cultural studies have been concerned to grasp the role of television in the circulation of cultural meanings and belief systems. They have therefore considered television in terms of its location within socio-cultural contexts, rather than in terms of establishing cognitive or behavioural models of reception. Breakthroughs made at the Birmingham Centre for Contemporary Cultural Studies (CCCS) – as discussed in the previous chapter – in the 1980s took into account the relative power of both text and reader in cultural struggles over 'meaning'. This development was initiated by Hall's (1980) influential 'encoding and decoding' model which acknowledged the interplay between the encoding of messages in production and the decoding of those messages in reception. This shifted the emphasis away from the older communication models of 'sender-message-receiver' into a situation whereby 'we must recognize that the discursive form of the message has a privileged position in the communicative exchange ... and that the moments of "encoding" and "decoding" though only "relatively autonomous" in relation to the communicative process on the whole are *determinate* moments' (ibid.: 129). Meaning therefore does not only reside in the message, but also in its reception. This indicates that the text might be open to alternative readings, but not in some relative way according to the needs of the individual. Hall's theoretical account suggests that the social make-up of the decoder is central, and he lays the groundwork for subsequent sociological audience research.

The social subjects implied in Hall's work make use of the symbolic resources around them to decode messages. Morley (1980) in *The Nationwide Audience* famously tested Hall's hypotheses through empirical audience research. He assessed the ways in which audience members incorporated, negotiated or resisted the preferred reading of the text according to their socio-economic position. His use of focus groups drawn from different socio-demographic backgrounds to generate responses to *Nationwide* (an early evening magazine news programme) supported Hall's thesis. This study is heralded as a landmark in media research because it proved relationships between ideological readings and social positions as part of a broader project to interrogate the media's hegemonic role in the maintenance of the status quo. Other studies have followed this tradition, utilizing the encoding-decoding paradigm and the focus group method, such as Corner et al's (1990) *Nuclear Reactions* on audience reception of television programmes on nuclear power; Jhally and Lewis's (1992) *Enlightened Racism* on the reception of *The Cosby Show*; and Schlesinger et al.'s (1992) *Women Viewing Violence*. All of these studies reveal group readings of material shown in an institutional context – usually the university department.

Morley's early work is acknowledged as leading the way for reception research that takes into account the social position of the viewer, but he does make clear some limitations inherent in his early method. Conducting focus group research in the university setting extracts research subjects from their usual viewing environments. The domesticity of television is central to its interpretation as a cultural form. This led to a change in direction, and audience studies began to focus upon the domestic conditions of media consumption and as a result began to draw methodological inspiration from 'ethnographic' approaches in anthropology. This involved spending time with informants in their local environments and homes, carrying out participant observation and usually semi- or unstructured interviews.

Key examples of early ethnographic media research include Hobson's (1980, 1982) study into young mothers' use of the media in the home and her research with soap opera viewers; Lull's (1980, 1990) extensive study involving the observation of over 200 family households; and also Morley's (1986) follow-up study *Family Television*. Research on media in the home has been considerably influenced by a feminist agenda framed around the politics of the domestic sphere and patriarchal power dynamics (e.g. Gray 1992). The 'ethnographic turn' in audience studies has led to research on the *technological* appropriation of media in the domestic environment (e.g. Silverstone et al. 1992), where the media texts have sometimes fallen from view. However, there are a few ethnographic studies of television that flesh out accounts of texts and their role in everyday life, of which *Living with the Rubbish Queen* is one. It is to this approach that we now turn.

Television Ethnography: *Living with the Rubbish Queen*

Ethnographies of television have attempted to capture a broad field of understanding media in social settings by bringing component elements together: an understanding of television's texts and products within national and institutional contexts, an exploration of how these texts get interpreted by viewers, and a consideration of how cultural meanings circulate around the television set within household dynamics. Studies of this kind include Gillespie's *Television, Ethnicity and Cultural Change* (1995), Mankekar's *Screening Culture*

(1999) and Abu-Lughod's *Dramas of Nationhood* (2005). These provide a more holistic picture of processes 'around' television by adopting a framework which recognizes a 'circuit of culture' where meaning is shaped around national contexts and media products, circulating through audiences and social contexts (see Johnson 1986).

Thomas Tufte's research concentrates on the role of telenovelas in the popular consciousness of Brazil. Telenovelas are Latin American melodrama serials that are screened six days per week and run for six or seven consecutive months with peak audiences of more than 50 million viewers. (In the UK, *Coronation Street*'s viewing figures peak at 27 million.) They are an everyday part of the cultural life of Brazil, and are very popular amongst women in a similar way that soap operas are in the UK. The entire telenovela is not filmed in advance as a complete text but it is developed through interaction with its audiences, through an understanding of the most popular characters, and sometimes by incorporating current news items into the narrative framework. To gather a rounded picture of this phenomenon, Tufte is keen to get beyond an analysis of telenovelas as only 'texts' because this literary reference tends to suggest bounded and unified works of art where meaning is located with the author's intention. Instead, he suggests:

> I am interested in them as cultural expressions which have an active part in the everyday lives of their viewers. Understanding telenovelas as cultural expressions requires an analysis of the socio-cultural and political-economic context from which they spring.
>
> (Tufte 2000: 2)

The book therefore outlines the way telenovelas have been important mediators in Brazil's process of urban development and capitalist modernization. Brazil has a population of more that 186 million and is one of the most densely populated countries in the world. It is made up of many racial groups because it has encouraged immigration since the late nineteenth century: mostly Europeans, Africans and Amerindians (the indigenous people of the Americas, sometimes referred to as Native Americans). As a former colony of Portugal, Portuguese is its main language. It has previously been governed by military rule, but is now one of the world's leading democracies and has undergone a period of rapid economic growth. Now one of the tenth largest economies in the world, Brazil has recently been grouped together with Russia, India and China (the so-called BRIC countries) as one of four economies set to become a world power.

One of the effects of Brazil's fast-growing economy has been extreme social inequality. The sites of Tufte's ethnography are large 'unofficial' dwelling sites – *favelas* – for the new urban poor. These are hillside shanty towns occupied by the vast number of rural migrants moving to the cities for work, but for whom there is a shortage of housing. Large numbers of residents live at the edges of the wealthiest cities for low-income employment, but their presence has largely gone unacknowledged by the state. These areas are characterized by the material problems of poor housing conditions, overcrowding, social deprivation and crime.

Telenovelas have therefore provided a backdrop to this picture of Brazil's uneven pattern of social change. They offer emotional narratives, typically stories of love, class struggle and overcoming difference, which highlight the rural to urban contours of population migration and the industrialization of the region. Narrative tension and often humour is derived from the distinctions between traditions of the agrarian countryside and the more high-tech city, or between the relative wealth of city dwellers as compared to those living at the margins.

Television itself has played a key role in negotiating such social change, in part giving coherence to Brazil's complex and mixed *mestizaje* culture. *Mestizaje* refers to the particular cultural and racial mixing that has historically produced Latino culture through the uneven processes of migration and modernization. Perez-Torres (2006) describes the way in which this form of racial hybridity has played a significant role in the development of expressive Latino culture more generally. Television in particular was seen to link Brazil to global economic markets, whilst the large-scale adoption of television in homes in the 1960s was seen as a symbol of the nation's progress. By 1980 more Brazilians had a television set than a fridge.

To consider within this wider portrait of Brazil the formation of *Rubbish Queen*, the telenovela at the centre of Tufte's study, Tufte employed a number of methods to capture the dynamic interplay between text and social context. Tufte's final work, therefore, offers an extremely rare insight into the social process around television. The main data for this project were collected during two months of fieldwork in 1991, followed by another month of fieldwork in 1993. The portrait of the place of television within the socioeconomic context of the nation is accompanied by a 'genre analysis' of the phenomenon of the telenovela. His discussion of the genre's trajectories and strategies is supported through interviews with seven writers and producers of telenovelas. He made two visits to the studios of the largest Brazilian TV network, Rede Globo, where he conducted interviews with representatives from different stages of the production process (editing, direction and production). He collected a series of secondary media texts in which the telenovela appears: magazines, newspapers and records, and he obtained 12 recorded chapters of the telenovela *Rubbish Queen*.

In humanities research the analysis of genre and their emergence sheds light on the shared set of agreements about cultural products as they are negotiated between producers and audiences at particular historical conjunctures (Neale 1980). Tufte charts the way in which the genre has evolved alongside the social contexts of the political and the urban and rural traditions, and the class distinctions between the new monied elite and the traditional aristocracy. This is carried out via the aesthetics of emotional drama and the classic romance narrative. He discusses how the genre has evolved and changed to incorporate the mood of the nation and different moments of political unrest, giving us insights into key popular telenovelas from the 1960s onwards, concluding that 'by drawing on well-known cultural matrixes of storytelling, and by exploring the needs and aspirations of the public, telenovelas serve as mediators of and socializers into the society of which they are at the same time a product' (Tufte 2000: 88).

To consider everyday life and media use, 13 women from different *favelas* were selected as key informants for the research. Tufte spent time and conducted participant observations in three low-income urban areas in Brazil: Santa Operaria in southern Brazil, Vila Nitro Operaria in São Paulo and Calabar in Salvador in north-eastern Brazil. This was followed by 13 qualitative interviews with women between the ages of 13 and 63. His qualitative research was supported by a quantitative data survey with 105 participants from the case study areas to establish the socio-economic conditions of the household, television viewing habits and other media use.

Such a complete approach to the context of a media form is hard to find in the field. Tufte's work into the institutions, texts and contexts allows him to build bridges between these aspects of media which are often researched as separate entities. His findings show how telenovelas have sometimes blurred the lines between fact and fiction and encouraged political action, suggesting that television fiction can become more politically influential than the news broadcast. Therefore, he concludes that telenovelas operate as sites for 'cultural citizenship'. This means that they give access to, and generate debates about, public life for those usually positioned outside of traditional modes of civic engagement, leading Tufte to argue for 'cultural citizenship' as a political project.

Multi-Method Interdisciplinary Research

As the description of Tufte's research demonstrates, media ethnographies tend to become interdisciplinary, relying on the analysis of different orders of data. A genre analysis belonging to a tradition more usually located in the arts and humanities is combined with empirical methods derived from the social sciences. Tufte describes his range as offering seven different groups of data through which the book plots a complex narrative of the telenovela as a 'cultural expression'.

Gray (2003) raises the question of whether we want to refer to such a spread of information as 'data' at all. In what sense texts constitute 'data' is a thorny issue depending upon your approach to analysis. For example, some researchers use content analysis to codify elements of texts in order to quantify certain recurrences when they are looking to measure bias. Gray, however, stakes a preference for the phrase 'research material' which encompasses all the 'stuff' of research that we might collect in ethnographic fieldwork: diaries, magazines, videos, notes, biographies, interview accounts and, importantly for media research, the products of our literary and visual textual analysis. Her point also relates to the claims to 'objectivity' that are conjured by the word 'data' – an issue to which we will return. First, let us concentrate on the purchase that all these methods, or aggregate of methods, might have upon finding out about the role of the telenovela in Brazilian culture.

It is common in social science research to use a number of methods in order to compare different data on the same phenomena. For example, quantitative surveys are often compared with qualitative interview data for methodological triangulation. This approach can throw light upon inconsistencies, allowing the researcher points of comparison in order to enhance validity. Triangulation can also combat any accusation of bias, of which researchers using only one method might be accused (Cohen and Manion 1985). There is an epistemological issue here since this position suggests that there *is* an observable and 'correct' reality that the researcher can access. However, researchers influenced by the theoretical thrust of post-structuralism and postmodernism think that research methods construct a 'version' of the reality that they seek to document. As Devine and Heath (1999: 49) suggest, for some the strength of triangulation 'lies in its capacity to reveal different, but equally valid, facets of a social phenomenon'.

In the case of the type of media research under discussion, usually influenced by the postmodern turn in the social sciences, different methods are deployed to give alternative vantage points around the 'cultural circuit', taking in production, text and audience. As discussed earlier this evolves from a mediacentric concern with a particular 'object', the telenovela, which provides the focal point for the particular socio-cultural conjuncture. The research, therefore, offers a dissection through the available materials. If this *is* a method of triangulation then the point of collecting comparative data is not to compare them *against* each other as oppositional sources, but it is rather to compare how they are *aligned with* each other so as to stitch together the relationships *between* the various points of contact.

To explain how this works let us take some examples of material from Tufte's research that demonstrate the benefit of this methodological approach extremely well. Telenovelas have offered an emotive melodramatic soundtrack to some of the social shifts occurring throughout Brazil's troubled process of modernity, where the twin developments of capitalism and democracy have not ushered in greater economic wealth for most of the population. Instead, capitalist accumulation has worked against a process of redistributing wealth, and urbanization has created a huge population living outside legitimate sites of recognition for citizenship.

Tufte's research on writers and producers of telenovelas revealed that, notwithstanding the pressures of the commercial generic formula, they felt the value of their writing was in the ability to contribute to public debate on political issues related to social inequality:

> Recognising that I had a powerful instrument in my hands penetrating into every home, and that the audience was a very important factor for the enterprise ... I wanted to build that in order to be valued as an author. But at the same time I did not forget with such a large audience I had a good opportunity to discuss certain matters which needed to be discussed, e.g. education. As I did in *Pe de Vento* criticising the Brazilian education system.
>
> (Ruy Barbaros, quoted in Tufte 2000: 133)

Tufte's subsequent genre analysis of the rise of the telenovela and his particular textual analysis of *Rubbish Queen* interprets their relationship to the class themes of social inequality that characterize Brazil at the time. The main character, Maria do Carmo, has made her fortune through reselling rubbish whilst in reality a growing number of people were surviving through working in the informal economy. The story was even rewritten to include events unfolding at the time. The newly elected right-wing president had frozen all savings accounts and in the telenovela Maria's love rival, Laurinha, married to an aristocrat, declares her despair at losing her money. The story reflects the conditions of social stratification of São Paulo – between traditional elites who were associated with aristocracy and the coffee trade, and the nouveau riche associated with lower cultural values and taste. Much of the humour in *Rubbish Queen* is made through these distinctions.

Tufte then wants to assess how these production strategies and textual features mobilize discourses of class and inequality in audiences. This becomes clear as he describes how the class consciousness of the women is central to their enjoyment of the programme. Here is one example from one of his informants:

> The poor are very humiliated, very stepped upon. We are not considered anything, we are considered animals. Society does not accept us, that is why we suffer as much as we do, you see. Her story was like ours. She rose thanks to a lot of suffering, renunciation and everything. But before, when she was bullied in school, like my children.
>
> (Eva, age 32, resident of Santa Operaria, quoted in Tufte 2000: 215)

Extracting snippets of his material does not really do justice to Tufte's level of analysis, but the point is to demonstrate how different types of data might be aligned with one another – here we are taking an even smaller slice through Tufte's larger picture. This helps us to see this particular process of mediation, allowing insight into how class discourses operate through the telenovela and the consciousness of the women of the study. To mobilize an analysis of production, text and context together allows us some purchase on the particular conjuncture. It leads Tufte to this more complete analysis:

> Two elements thus characterise the class discourse in the telenovela's texts and readings: on the one hand the women have been born into one of the socially most polarised societies of the world, on the lowest step of the social pyramid; on the other, every day they watch telenovelas showing a standard of living that is at the very least rather better than theirs, with a narrative that ends happily, every time. It is in this dichotomy between a harsh class polarization experienced in everyday life and their personal dreams of social mobility and change that we find a significant part of the explanation as to why so many low-income women watch three to four telenovelas every day.
>
> (Tufte 2000: 222)

Tracing and then aligning comparative elements around a circuit of culture allows us a cross-section of the process of mediation at work. But these findings rely on the 'thick description' of the researcher offering a narrow but deep portrait of a small group of people (Geertz 1973). This kind of data is therefore not meant to be representative in the scientific sense: there is no attempt to claim that the experiences of the 13 women of the study can stand in for the entire population of Brazil.

The figure of the 'population' has largely dominated the social sciences, and its methods have sought to quantify, interrogate or explore the attitudes of individuals. In media research like this, which takes its starting point as the object, the figure of the population is not the first point of contact in relation to questions of 'generalizability'. This is a product of breaching the distinction between the textual and the social and looking for the processes through which the two become entwined. Johnson, in his discussion of 'working the text/social split', argues that such studies

> can also prove to have a wider scope of reference than the 'size of sample' might suggest. This is because the object here is not really individual attitudes at all. Rather, the researcher, through a particular instance or case study, is attempting to tap into cultural structures or formations, which are precisely social or shared. They are likely to have a larger range of occurrence than the single example suggests.
>
> (Johnson 1997: 468)

The point, therefore, of comparing textual readings with empirical data is not as in the more scientific sense to use multimethod research to explore why different data about the same object throw up different things – and then using that information to get a better purchase on an observable reality. Researching the text and researching the consumption of the text here are separate projects. We would not necessarily expect a researcher's reading of a text to map onto an audience reading in order for us to understand what it *really* means: the differences in interpretation would not make us question their validity as interpretations. To understand that is to grasp the complexity of media products as complex cultural expressions, rather than as 'messages' that can be 'implanted' into audiences with ease. This involves working with the concept of 'process', which is not the same as saying that all inconsistencies can be explained away. In the next section I will consider how we can apply a notion of 'validity' to the analysis of cultural processes.

Interpretation, Validity and Reflexivity

The kind of ethnographic and 'interpretive' approach to research discussed here identifies 'processes' which may offer us some insights into media formations in different contexts. In audience studies, Morley (1992: 37) has suggested that we create a map of 'interpretive communities' whereby the workings of any particular texts might be tested across other sites. When Johnson (1997) described the text/social distinction as inherently 'phoney', this is partly because both are brought into view through a process of 'interpretation'. In his useful textbook for students starting out on textual analysis, Alan McKee states that

> textual analysis is a methodology for gathering information about sense-making practices, that is, how members of various cultures interpret the world around them. We analyse texts using a form of 'forensic analysis' – treating them like clues (or 'traces') of how people have made sense of the world.
>
> (McKee 2003: 63)

Ethnography has similarly been described as a type of interpretative textual analysis. Clifford Geertz (1973: 9) comments that 'what we call our data are really our own constructions of other people's constructions of what they and their compatriots are up to'.

Methodologically, textual analyses and ethnography have come to share similar epistemological principles, making it easier for us to incorporate them into media research. However, an interpretative map should not imply that 'anything goes' and that any interpretation is reliable. Morley uses E. H. Carr's argument about the nature of history:

> It does not follow that, because a mountain appears to take on different shapes from different angles of vision, it has objectively either no shape at all or an infinity of shapes. It does not follow that because interpretation plays a necessary part in establishing the facts of history, and because no existing interpretation is wholly objective, that one interpretation is as good as another.
>
> (Carr, quoted in Morley 1992: 179)

How can we assess the quality of the interpretation at hand? This is a difficult question that has vexed social researchers since the postmodern turn made us query how all methods, including quantitative ones, produce knowledge through their own particular set of discursive frameworks. The response has been to operate a greater degree of reflexivity over our methods. This means revealing all the variables at play in the research process so as to make it as transparent as possible. This is to acknowledge that the *way* knowledge has been produced should be meaningfully brought to bear upon any assessment of the quality of the findings.

In ethnography, this requires employing what Hammersley and Atkinson (1995: 21) call 'the reconstructed logic of enquiry' which importantly includes taking into account the role of the researcher in the research field. This also stems from a long tradition in the critique of anthropology where the studies of the white male 'going native' were found to instate powerful hierarchies which ideologically 'othered' the cultures that they sought to describe (see Said 1978).

More recently Marcus and Fischer (1986), in their discussion of interpretative anthropology, have emphasized that ethnography undoubtedly involves some type of 'vantage point' and that this must be made explicit in order to explain the research findings. For similar reasons, Gray (2003) calls for the use of the word 'material' to replace 'data', as it more adequately acknowledges the researcher's presence within the frame of the findings. The word 'data' tends to suggest sets of disembodied pieces of information 'extracted' from their contexts for analysis in keeping with the traditions of science. Gray argues that the word 'material' is

> also suggestive of substance and 'worldliness', if something is material then it is grounded and embodied. This neatly encompasses both the kind of research material we produce, and also the way in which we do it ... Thus neither the stuff of research, nor the researchers [sic] themselves, are free-floating or disembodied. Rather, both must be located and locatable.
>
> (Gray 2003: 79–80)

If one measure of the validity of any interpretation of culture is an awareness of how the presence of the researcher impacts upon the data then let us look closely at how Tufte frames his own participation in the study. His acknowledgement of the reflexive imperative is to provide an account of the 'project trajectory' which he suggests might help answer the question as to how 'a middle-class Danish man can conduct ethnographic studies among low-income Brazilian women' (Tufte 2000: 34). He charts a 17-year interest in Brazil and logs the various periods of time spent in the country. He talks about learning the language, living in *favelas* and experiencing the impact of various social movements. We get a picture of him working for Dutch NGOs, working in a seminary and conducting research in *favelas* even before the period of this particular study, which he suggests brought him in to 'all the classic and often difficult fieldwork situations that require flexibility, careful conduct and reflexivity regarding the role of the researcher in the field' (ibid.: 36).

For the most part this personal account is used as evidence of his having undertaken the necessary groundwork for the research:

> On the one hand this trajectory has provided me with knowledge and insight regarding Brazilian society, popular culture and everyday life. The fieldwork experiences in Brazil have given me the important methodological experiences regarding the practical use of ethnography, whether in interviews among low-income urban citizens, surveys in the field, or participant observation. Having spent more than two years in Brazil and more than four years in the region as a whole, living and working in a variety of contexts and with people of many distinct origins and natures, has given me a feeling for and insight into the characteristics and complexities of Latin American people, their cultural identity, their tastes and beliefs, their recent national history, and their dreams for the future.
>
> (ibid.)

Whilst Tufte is not naïve enough to suggest that he has the ability to 'go native', this reflexive account operates to convince us that he has done his homework, that he is qualified to undertake the empirical research and that his interpretation can be trusted. It works to position him as an authority which is a common way of using reflexivity but which does not entirely account for the 'presence' of the researcher in the field.

There is a growing debate about the use of the researcher's own reflexivity in qualitative research. Whilst there has been a general acceptance of the reflexive turn in social science, it has been accompanied by a discussion about the politics of its use. Adkins (2002) argues that in some studies reflexivity in the form of self-narration can operate to grant the author greater authority, thereby actually reinforcing the hierarchy between the researcher and the researched at the expense of any transparency in relation to the power involved in the research process. Similarly, Skeggs argues that 'there is a significant difference between being reflexive and accruing reflexivity to oneself through a process of attachment … and doing reflexivity: building sensitivity into the research design and paying attention to practice, power and process' (Skeggs 2002: 368).

From the extract above Tufte is certainly generating an account of himself from which he is able to claim the authority from which to write, but it is not the case that his book is littered with a confessional self-awareness. The problem is that there is relatively little reflection on his own presence in the description of his findings outside of the explanation of the 'project trajectory'. Whilst he cannot be accused of navel-gazing there is at least one point in the research where his lack of reflection on his own research practice might serve to obscure the clarity of his findings.

For example, one of Tufte's key interpretative findings is that of 'the hybrid sphere of signification'. He describes how the television set is located in the women's homes in rooms that occupy a space 'in-between' the public neighbourhood and the more private parts of the home. People come and go here as windows and doors are wide open to the street and the screening of telenovelas become social events. The spatio-temporal organization of the everyday around the television is a significant issue in media ethnography. This hybrid sphere comes to operate as an overarching metaphor for the whole of the study to describe the way in which the telenovela occupies a particular bridging of public and private spheres to those located outside of civic culture: offering a type of 'cultural citizenship'. The 'hybrid sphere of signification' is the key to unlocking the particular social grammar of the television set within Latin American modernity:

> The hybrid sphere of everyday life is a social, cultural and economic construct, an autonomous sphere of signification, defined by the specificity of the organisation of time–space relations. As I interpret the everyday life of the women in my survey areas, the hybrid sphere is a social and cultural field of everyday practices mediated by the contradictions between urban and rural life, between tradition and modernity, and finally between masculine and feminine norms and values. It thus becomes an important sphere in the development of hybrid cultures.
>
> (Tufte 2000: 192)

The 'in-between' room connects urban living with its television set to the more traditional and social aspects of the neighbourhood and combines the public and private space of gender relations (Figure 7.1). However, at least one

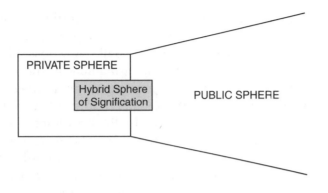

Figure 7.1   The hybrid sphere of signification
Source: Tufte (2000: 186).

description of the researcher's experience from the field alerts us to the potential impact of the researcher's presence:

> Eva always kept her front door open, except when not at home. Likewise with the window shutters (there is no glass). In the house next door her younger sister lived with her family. They often communicated across the wall. From the entrance one could look straight across at the television set. There was not much furniture in the living room; a sofa, a chair and the television set standing on a television table and a few pictures on the walls. Television viewing went on all day; in the daytime it was mainly the children watching, in the evenings the whole family. Sometimes the children sat on the staircase watching television a little and running around playing in between. It was only on the third visits to her house that Eva invited me further inside than the living room. I was a visitor and therefore kept in the living room, the 'visitors lounge'. Only by asking permission to follow Eva into the kitchen, did I get to move around the house. From the living room one entered a small hall, from where there were doors into two very small bedrooms and a small dining room which lead on to the kitchen and a very small toilet.
>
> The kitchen had a back door, leading out into the back yard. In the yard lived a dog and clothes were washed and dried. Eva's home had a clear frontier between the living room and the rest of the house, with the small hall constituting the invisible division.
>
> (Ibid.: 185)

Tufte's interpretative analysis is based on the organization of social space and the inhabitation of various social spheres. What difference does it make that at least one of the women does not really want him to enter into some parts of her home? He suggests that Eva does invite him further in, but this is not unsolicited because he asks and she agrees. He is mostly confined to what he (or she, we do not know) calls the 'visitors room'. How does this concur with the notion of the hybrid sphere? Were he a member of the neighbourhood and not a visitor would he be able to move around more freely?

The notion of the hybrid sphere is based upon the gendering of space, operating as the site where genders meet, whilst the bedrooms, the kitchen and the backyard are assigned as women-only social spheres. In terms of validity the same rules apply here that we might apply to quantitative research – is he interpreting what he thinks he is interpreting? Tufte is a male, European, university researcher: could it be that only he experienced these spheres in this way? We feel Eva's discomfort even in his description and get a sense of the gender, class and cultural distinctions that might lead her to want to control his access to her home. How do we know therefore whether this account supports his broader claim? Is the 'clear frontier between the living room and the rest of the house' one that she might have reasonably *created* in the situation of being the subject of ethnographic research? This one example does not necessarily deconstruct Tufte's broader reading of the social organization of household space, but it does highlight how the presence of the researcher and the power relations that entails might begin to have a determinate influence on findings.

Entering homes is often an awkward and uncomfortable process in ethnographic research. Taking that step over the doorstep imbues the researcher with a good deal of responsibility as he or she invades the private sphere and takes something away from it for his or her own analysis. Other studies discuss the politics of that process at some length, for example Skeggs (2002), but Tufte does not supply us with an account of how this process is negotiated – he simply frames himself as a 'visitor' who conjures up a certain level of polite civility. What is significant here though is that Tufte's overarching findings rely on an account of spatial organization of the home, but we need to know what impact his presence might have over that very space.

This is not to be understood as a plea for greater self-narration per se, but rather as a call for methodological transparency. To be able to judge the quality of any interpretation we need a full explanation of the practices of power in play when undertaking the research. In Skeggs's (2002) discussion, she draws upon Bourdieu's insistence that reflexivity should attend to the way in which authority becomes legitimized as he asks us to explore 'the relationship between the properties of discourses, the properties of the person who pronounces them and the properties of the institutions which authorises him to pronounce them' (Bourdieu 1992: 111, quoted in Skeggs 2002: 361). Tufte's account of himself in the methodology section of this book, whilst justifying his research on Brazilian women from his own social location, serves to legitimate his authority to describe them. He needed to acknowledge how that power relation operates in the field in order to account for it, and be truly reflexive, in *practice*.

Conclusion

In the conclusion to the first edition of this book Devine and Heath (1999) describe how they would have liked to have included an example of research more explicitly informed by postmodern influences but that their attempts were stymied by the fact that many of these studies lack methodological transparency. Media and cultural research studies derived from more textual/humanities traditions have often failed to consider that 'interpretation' could be framed in and by methodological protocols. This is still often the case, despite the urgency to describe how we go about doing textual analysis to our students.

In this chapter I have attempted to shed light upon how media research operates its particular mode of interpretation through looking for the points of contact between textual discourse, or object, and social practice. Thomas Tufte's ethnography of television in Brazil provides us with one of the richest examples of research that works in and through the triumvirate of production, text and context, mobilizing different sets of data to draw forth inferences from the conjunctures of these elements.

All too often, maintaining the focus on the media or cultural 'object' deflects concentration from social scientific questions of validity, reliability and generalizability. The focus of media and cultural research on a singular 'process' must involve a thoroughgoing and responsible reflexivity if we are to reach for rigour in this version of representativeness. We cannot stand outside of the groups that we observe and so cannot aspire to scientific objectivity; interpretation is part and parcel of the empirical description. Reflexivity, therefore, must be the regulator of interpretation, and its effective deployment must be achieved not through a greater concentration on the self of the researcher per se, but through a tighter focus on the politics of research *practice* in the pursuit of methodological transparency.

Arguments about the use of reflexivity and practice have moved on apace since Tufte conducted his ethnography in Brazil. None of these discussions here should detract from the considerable achievement of his work. There are a limited number of texts from which to choose when attempting to explain what is possible through an ethnographic approach to media research. Tufte offers us a rich bank of data, and his work moves intelligently through micro- and macrolevels of analysis, stitching in how broader socio-political contexts relate to the narrative developments of telenovelas as texts, the frameworks of their institutional production and their embedding within routines and practices of everyday life. Working the text/social split is not straightforward but *Living with the Rubbish Queen* gives us considerable insights into how it can be done.

Additional Reading

For other examples of ethnographies of television, see Gillespie's *Television, Ethnicity and Cultural Change* (1995) and Mankekar's *Screening Culture: Viewing Politics: An Ethnography of Television, Womanhood and the Nation in Postcolonial India* (1999). Gray's *Research Practice for Cultural Studies* (2003) explains the distinctiveness of a cultural studies approach to empirical research. Machin's *Ethnographic Research for Media Students* (2002) is a student text which explains ethnographic approaches to media through relevant case studies.

Acknowledgements

I would like to thank Thomas Tufte and the editors, Fiona Devine and Sue Heath, for very helpful suggestions for improvement on earlier drafts of this chapter.

References

Abu-Lughod, L. (2005) *Dramas of Nationhood: The Politics of Television in Egypt*, Chicago, IL: University of Chicago Press.
Adkins, L. (2002) 'Reflexivity and the politics of qualitative research', in T. May (ed.) *Qualitative Research in Action*, London: Sage.
Aronson, E. (2003) *The Social Animal*, 9th edn, New York: Worth Freeman.
Belson, W.A. (1978) *Television Violence and the Adolescent Boy*, Teakfield: Saxon House.
Bourdieu, P. (1992) *Language and Symbolic Power*, Cambridge, Polity.
Boyle, K. (2005) *Media and Violence*, London: Sage.
Branston, G. and R. Stafford (2006) *The Media Student's Book*, London and New York: Routledge.
Cohen, L. and L. Manion (1985) *Research Methods in Educational Research*, London: Routledge.
Corner, J., K. Richardson and N. Fenton (1990) *Nuclear Reactions: Form and Response in 'Public Issue' Television*, London: John Libbey.
Devine, F. and S. Heath (1999) *Sociological Research Methods in Context*, Basingstoke: Palgrave Macmillan.
Geertz, C. (1973) *The Interpretation of Cultures*, New York: Basic Books.
Gillespie, M. (1995) *Television, Ethnicity and Cultural Change*, London: Routledge.
Gray, A. (1992) *Video Playtime: The Gendering of a Leisure Technology*, London: Routledge.
Gray, A. (2003) *Research Practice for Cultural Studies*, London: Sage.

Hall, S. (1980) 'Encoding/decoding', in S. Hall, D.Hobson, A.Lowe and P.Willis (eds) *Culture, Media, Language: Working Papers in Cultural Studies*, London: Hutchinson.

Hammersley, M. and P. Atkinson (1995) *Ethnography: Principles in Practice*, London: Routledge.

Hobson, D. (1980) 'Housewives and the mass media', in S. Hall, D. Hobson, A. Lowe and P. Willis (eds) *Culture, Media, Language*, London: Hutchinson: 105–14.

Hobson, D. (1982) *Crossroads: The Drama of a Soap Opera*, London: Methuen.

Jhally, S. and J. Lewis (1992) *Enlightened Racism: 'The Cosby Show', Audiences and the Myth of the American Dream*, Boulder, CO: Westview Press.

Johnson, R. (1986) 'What is cultural studies anyway?', *Social Text*, 16: 38–60.

Johnson, R. (1997) 'Reinventing cultural studies: remembering for the best version', in E. Long (ed.) *From Sociology to Cultural Studies: New Perspectives*, Oxford: Blackwell.

Katz, E., J. Blumler and M. Gurevitch (1974) 'Utilisation of mass communications by the individual', in J. Blumler and E. Katz (eds) *The Uses of Mass Communication*, London: Sage.

Lull, J. (1980) 'The social uses of television', *Human Communication Research*, 6(3): 197–209.

Lull, J. (1990) *Inside Family Viewing*, London: Routledge.

Machin, D. (2002) *Ethnographic Research for Media Students*, London: Hodder Arnold.

Mankekar, P. (1999) *Screening Culture: Viewing Politics: An Ethnography of Television, Womanhood and the Nation in Postcolonial India*, Durham/London: Duke University Press.

Marcus, G. and M.M.J. Fisher (1986) *Anthropology as Cultural Critique: An Experimental Moment in the Human Sciences*, Chicago, IL: University of Chicago Press.

McKee, A. (2003) *Textual Analysis: A Beginner's Guide*, London: Sage.

Moores, S. (1993) *Interpreting Audiences: The Ethnography of Media Consumption*, London: Sage.

Morley, D. (1980) *The Nationwide Audience*, London: BFI.

Morley, D. (1986) *Family Television: Cultural Power and Domestic Consumption*, London: Comedia/Routledge.

Morley, D. (1992) *Television, Audiences and Cultural Studies*, London: Routledge.

Morley, D. (2007) *Media, Modernity and Technology: The Geography of the New*, London: Routledge.

Neale, S. (1980) *Genre*, London: BFI.

Perez-Torres, R. (2006) *Mestizaje: Critical Uses of Race in Chicano Culture*, Minneapolis, MN: University of Minnesota Press.

Said, E. (1978) *Orientalism*, London: Vintage Books.

Schlesinger, P., R.E. Dobash, R.P. Dobash and C. Kay (1992) *Women Viewing Violence*, London: BFI.

Silverstone, R., E. Hirsch and D. Morley (1992) 'Information and communication technologies and the moral economy of the household', in R. Silverstone and E. Hirsch (eds) *Consuming Technologies*, London: Routledge.

Skeggs, B. (2002) 'Techniques for telling the reflexive self', in T. May (ed.) *Qualitative Research in Action*, London: Sage.

Spigel, L. (1992) *Make Room For TV: Television and the Family Ideal in Post-War America*, Chicago: Chicago University Press.

Tufte, T. (2000) *Living With the Rubbish Queen: Telenovelas and Modernity in Brazil*, Luton: University of Luton Press.

CHAPTER 8

Post-Colonial History: Butalia's *The Other Side of Silence*

NAVTEJ PUREWAL

This chapter explores methodological issues thrown up in social history and, specifically, the post-colonial history of South Asia in the second half of the twentieth century. Navtej Purewal examines Urvashi Butalia's book, The Other Side of Silence (2000). The book draws on interviews with first-hand survivors – notably, women and children – of the partition of India and Pakistan in 1947. Two methodological issues are reflected upon. First, the presentation of the interview material, alongside other sources, and how a narrative is constructed from this material, is considered in depth. Second, the way in which Butalia includes her own personal experiences among the voices of the overlooked survivors is addressed. Purewal highlights the ways in which a story, even one with hard facts, is constructed and why students should look closely at the way in which narratives are created. She demonstrates how Butalia's personal interest in the story of partition enriched the analysis and insights. Subjectivity has vices and virtues. The challenges of researching memories and emotions in social history are revealed.

Introduction

Urvashi Butalia's book *The Other Side of Silence: Voices from the Partition of India* was published in 2000 during a period of immense recollection and reflection on the partition of India which had taken place nearly 60 years before the book's publication. The geographical, political and demographic division of the region of South Asia that had taken place in 1947 became a focus of much media, government and academic attention in an unprecedented way. Towards the end of the twentieth century, the partition came to signify much more than merely a historical period or event. It had become a focal point of critical reflection of both the past and present. The publication of *The Other Side of Silence* and the impact it subsequently had upon wider studies of contemporary South Asian societies represents this shift. It might be said that the book spoke to the popular sentiments of the time that sought to listen to the experiences of first-hand survivors of the partition as an attempt to recover a history largely lost to official narrations more concerned with containing rather than exploring ideas, responses and emotions about the partition.

What was so significant about the reflections of this time compared to the types of reflections that had been produced and published previously? One noticeable departure was that the commemoration of the fiftieth anniversary of India and Pakistan's independence from British colonial rule in 1997 had seen the themes of loss and recovery overtake previous celebrations of competing Indian and Pakistani nationalism. Personal and collective experiences and stories of pain, loss, regret and reconciliation around the events that surrounded the division of India into two countries, which had been previously ignored within academic and official discourse until that time, were utilized in order to draw attention to the human side of the events. This shift emerged out of a wider critique of the 'nation' as a constructed set of ideas around identity, nationalism and belonging. In line with this critical analysis of nationalism came a plethora of re-examinations of history which had been previously accepted as 'fact', raising questions as to whose perspective was being reflected and why 'official' accounts should be seen as more valid than 'unofficial' ones.

It is within the broader context of these questions as to how social history is produced and written that Butalia's book will be discussed in this chapter. I begin with a brief introduction to the partition of India by laying out the context and historical backdrop to the field that the book is engaging with, including the significance of the Subaltern Studies Group to the field of post-colonial history. The concerns shared by other areas of social history will also be reflected upon in terms of how previously ignored or overlooked groups have more recently been brought into or even rewritten into history as valid, if not pivotal, social actors. This is followed by a discussion of the book's approach to historical writing in its attempt to redress certain imbalances and omissions through the tools offered by contemporary social research.

In this respect, two specific methodological issues will be analysed in terms of how Butalia sets out the book at the onset and how she works through these in the research process. First, her presentation of the interview material alongside other sources will be analysed in terms of the format of presentation. The construction of a narrative from these various accounts presents a range of issues around how her own subjective position shapes the way in which the stories and 'facts' are told. Second, the chapter will look at the way in which she locates herself within the book, providing a view of how reflexivity can open the space between the researcher and the researched, both in the fieldwork and writing up stages. Her use of oral histories as her main methodological tool will be specifically discussed in terms of one of the book's central aims – to highlight voices previously and still often not considered worthy of being documented as 'fact'. Butalia's use of the notion of 'voice' throughout the book is particularly relevant to questions as to how a researcher committed to the subject area through connections of personal interest, academic enquiry, political perspective and family history can work through these in enriching the analysis and insights, rather than appearing defensive and wary of appearing subjective. The chapter ends with a discussion of the issues that emerge when writing and reflecting upon memory and oral histories, particularly addressing some of the challenges that this presents to contemporary social science research.

Rethinking the Partition of India

The political partition of India in 1947 resulted in the drawing of new national boundaries between India and Pakistan which caused an exodus, or 'transfer of populations' as government documentation of the time called it, which saw millions of Muslims leave their homes to go to newly formed Pakistan, and millions of Hindus and Sikhs relocating to newly demarcated India. The border area of Punjab in the north-west of South Asia, which is the focus of Butalia's book, holds a particular place in terms of the traumatic upheaval that the partition wreaked upon the region. It was divided across the new national boundaries of India and Pakistan, resulting in a Pakistani Punjab with a majority population of Muslims and an Indian Punjab with a majority of Hindus and Sikhs (Table 8.1).

Table 8.1   Punjab before and after the partition of 1947

	Area sq. km	Population (millions)	Muslim (%)	Hindu (%)	Sikh (%)	Other (%)
1941	256,600	28.4	53	31	15	1
1951*	122,500	16.1	2	62	35	1
1961	122,500	20.3	2	64	33	1
1966+	50,260	11.2	0	45	53	2
1971	50,260	13.5	0	38	60	2
1981	50,260	16.7	0	36	62	2

* After the creation of Pakistan.
+ After the separation of Haryana.
Source: Jeffrey (1994: 42).

Despite the evidence of such social and demographic change at local and regional levels, academic attention upon the events surrounding 1947 has been largely, up until the 1990s, dominated by a focus upon the high politics of the end of colonial rule and the birth of the new nations. The predominance of nationalist perspectives on this period was significant in that there was no central place for the personal experiences of the partition. Instead, the notion of India as Hindu majority and Pakistan as a safe haven for Muslims consistently appeared, relegating all personal stories as sacrifices for the nation. The defence of the sanctity of Pakistani and Indian national perspectives, as highlighted in the writings of Ahmed (1991) and Chandra (1979) respectively, offered little scope for voices and views which expressed disquiet with the formal outcomes of nationhood. Instead, they upheld the argument that, while colonialism had a degenerative impact, nationalism had a regenerative impact upon societies in South Asia. Thus, the righteousness of the nation-states that were created in 1947 produced a top-down view of the partition as a necessary, though negative, by-product of independence. Other conventional accounts, though less loyal to nationalism, still reaffirmed the colonial notion of primordial religious identities, such as Muslim, Hindu and Sikh, as the modes of identification that people hinged their lives and identities upon, before and during the partition (Singh 1991; Robinson 2000). This view of the partition continues to circulate in Pakistan and India in school textbooks, official government documentation and in wider official discourses on the partition which illustrates its pervasiveness even today.

The mounting critique of the dominance of overarching state perspectives on the partition culminated in the emergence of the field of partition studies which saw more critical analyses of the meanings and limits of religious categories as well as the 'nation' and which led towards a more penetrating view of the partition from a diversified range of perspectives and approaches. What has come to be known as 'partition studies' expanded the scope of enquiry towards other disciplinary interests, such as literature and poetry, cultural studies, film studies and regional studies, alongside the continuing social science and historical research. However, there are a few notable contributions to the field worth mentioning in charting this shift. The historian Gyanendra Pandey, in his book *Remembering Partition* (2001), argues that the violence that surrounded the partition, rather than being an anomaly within the nations of Pakistan and India, needs to be viewed as a founding narrative of the region. His analysis of news reporting and documentation of incidences of 'communal' violence across India, before and during the partition, uses discourse analysis to study different textual sources and their reporting on the same events. Menon and Bhasin (1998), and Butalia (1993), produced women-centred studies of the gendered nature of partition violence and abductions of women. Didur's *Unsettling Partition* (2006) uses the methods of literary criticism to analyse some of the literature that addresses the partition. However, well before the publication of this book, the base for expanding partition studies into the cultural and literary fields already existed. The richness of the fictional literature and poetry on partition which was being written even while the partition was taking place reflected a public sentiment that sought to express the emotions that accompanied the political division of India. Such examples as Manto's short story *Toba Tek Singh*, Singh's novel *Train to Pakistan* and Sidwa's novel *Cracking India* have come to be seen as central 'texts' on the subject, offering important slices of understanding of the partition from fictional and literary perspectives. The expansion into other disciplinary areas has had a tremendous impact upon the types of research as well as on public discourse by opening a space for memories, emotions and people's experiences to be included in the way that partition is spoken about and reflected upon. Even historians such as Ian Talbot (2000), who has been a significant contributor to the earlier wave of research focusing upon the official archives and high politics, began to engage in the new disciplinary openness of the changing field of partition studies.

The questioning of official, national accounts of the partition did not occur in isolation. Within the various disciplines of the social sciences and history, the impacts that the expansion of *historiography* (i.e. that every history is a contested, debatable field rather than a reflection of fact) has had introduced the notion that every rendition of history represents a particular story from a contextual perspective. Published histories which had once been accepted as 'fact' have now been reviewed as representations worthy of rigorous critique and qualification. In this respect, the search for a history of the 'masses' is one which has had a strong current within this shift in highlighting how previous published accounts have by and large reflected elite or institutional histories. Overarching concepts such as the 'nation' have been particularly problematized in how they conceal internal social divisions and hierarchies (Hobsbawm 1987). The perspectives of 'ordinary people' have increasingly been seen as significant in this critique of macrohistories. Such perspectives often reveal tensions, conflicts, alternative and multiple perceptions and experiences, exclusion and even violence – thus raising questions not only with regard to *whose* history has been written and documented to date but in terms of what types of knowledge these official histories have constructed and other ways of knowing they have hence concealed.

The end of formal empire in many parts of the world through the decolonization process offered an important dimension to discussions of historical writing which had been centred around a Eurocentric sense of history. Critical readings of this resulted in a post-colonial critique of history (Asad 1987; Ahmad 1994). The foregrounding of marginal perspectives in the telling of history has seen fundamental questions being raised around the scope of current research to engage with history as a contestable set of narratives. During the early post-colonial and post-war era, new questions were being raised within intellectual traditions in the West, around the bias within historical writing towards dominant or elite class perspectives, inspired largely by British Marxist writers. Several books, including Thompson's *The Making of the English Working Class* (1963), Williams's *Culture and Society* (1958) and Hobsbawm's *The Age of Empire* (1987), were important in how they questioned previously accepted representations of history. Thompson's work was important for how it posited class neither as a category nor an outcome of a superstructure, but as a social formation having ownership of its own history, thus offering an example of how history can be told from non-elite perspectives. Similarly, Williams contributed to certain shifts that were taking place in how society and history were being approached by academic disciplines. Often cited as the founder of cultural studies, Williams had a conception of cultural materialism which resisted the classical Marxist notion of culture as merely derivative of superstructure and an economic base. He conceptualized the notion of culture as being an important political expression of social processes and thus presented an argument for studying culture as an embedded form of social organization within economic and political structures. Both Thompson and Williams proposed that political and social change are not external forces beyond the reach of popular culture or of 'ordinary people' and that social class and culture should not be interpreted as only including 'high culture' or that belonging to the 'elite or capitalist classes'. Such studies broadened the lens of the focus of social history towards 'ordinary people' as active agents in their contributions to the making of history.

The deepening of the methodological concerns of social history through such questions resulted in the emergence of critical historiography which was able to revisit the analogues and archives of previously documented and undocumented histories. The surge in the rewriting of histories gave the historical tradition a new lease of life. Central to these developments within writing on South Asia has been the Subaltern Studies Group, whose contributions have influenced the writing of history, even beyond South Asia. Established in the 1980s, the Subaltern Studies Group began by attempting to develop a new narrative or narratives on the history of India and South Asia, largely building upon the works of Stokes (1980) and Gramsci (1971). This narrative approach consciously sidelined elite political consciousness by focusing on non-elites or 'subalterns' as agents of social and political change in their own right. The manifesto of the group, from the onset, was to highlight and critically reflect upon previously undocumented histories. This aim was made explicit by the collective, made up of scholars working on various aspects of South Asian history, based in India, Britain, Australia and the US (Chakrabarty 1992; Kaviraj 1992; Pandey 1994; Amin 1995). By seeking to challenge certain overarching 'truths' about the analysis of Indian society, which had been generated by various historical traditions, the founding editor Ranajit Guha highlights the contentious nature of the terrain into which the Subaltern Studies Group entered:

> serious scholars, who have lived too long with well-rehearsed ideas and methodologies, find it disturbing that so many new questions should be addressed to problems which were supposed to have been studied, solved and closed ... For we know that by defying the elitist paradigms of historiography and the social sciences we are bound to give offence to the custodians of official truth entrenched within their liberal and leftist stockades.
>
> (Guha 1985: viii)

The popular, grassroots level was given centre stage in the studies appearing in the published volumes where the locations, perspectives and contributions of peasants, marginal castes and tribal communities, for instance, were elevated to the role of protagonists within the histories being reflected. This is an objective which requires a conscious effort to scour the archives for missing voices and experiences. While having a left-wing intellectual perspective, the group are also critical of the classical Marxist narrative on Indian history which views the history of development in India as one in which the British colonizing force and the Indian elites command agency in the narration of history – whereby a feudal society was colonized by the British and, as a result, the elites gain the political consciousness for resisting and standing up against the British. The masses are merely viewed as recipients of the consciousness handed on to them from the elites. Subaltern Studies represented the possibility of alternative varieties of Marxism, which could be Marxist while also located in the history of the colonized. Despite being missing from official colonial and nationalist records, the range of Subaltern Studies writers have shown how the peasantry were in fact integral to colonial modernity in India. Guha (1983) postulates that this academic exercise of recovering the voice of peasant insurgency in fact unsettles the telling of history by posing the insurgency not as marginal or futile, but as pivotal social actions of rebellion to class, caste and colonial hierarchies of power – thus representing a highly developed sense of political consciousness.

The contribution of Subaltern Studies to academic disciplines beyond, for instance to political science, sociology, development economics, literature, cultural studies and anthropology, has been perhaps even more revealing of its intellectual reach. The expanse of its intervention into seemingly disparate debates highlights its role in (a) sustaining critiques of Eurocentrism and orientalism within the various disciplines; (b) engaging with debates within and among Marxist and other historiographies; and (c) contributing to the emergence of post-colonial studies. Critiques of the linkages of some of the foundations of social science with empire (Asad 1973; Ahmad 1994) saw Subaltern Studies move far beyond a historiographic approach, to one which represented non-Western, post-colonial perspectives on imperialism, the writing of culture and understandings of history. Thus, the tools of Marxist analysis of 'economic base' and 'superstructure', or of traditional British history which used tools of social actors and groups to depict Indian society as following the West under the patronizing guidance of colonialism, were challenged by the Subaltern Studies' tools of voice, consciousness, resistance and autonomy.

Through the interventions of Subaltern Studies, post-colonial history has generated methodological tools for writing history and social science, opening up possibilities for new versions of history. In the next section, Urvashi Butalia's book, while not published within the Subaltern Studies series, will be focused upon as an example of the relevance of post-colonial history to contemporary social science.

Rewriting Social History from the Margins

There has been a mass recollection exercise in attempting to recover histories that had previously neither been recorded nor taken into account in how official histories have been told. Previous literature on the 1947 partition had rather uncritically adopted the religious labels of Muslim, Hindu and Sikh affirmed by the colonial and post-independence nationalist documentation available in their analyses. In a concerted attempt to move away from producing yet another 'community versus community' or 'us versus them' account of the partition, Butalia's book opens up the analysis through her use of a range of primary sources upon which to base the telling of the history of the partition. How does one begin to write a history from below when unwritten, 'marginal' perspectives are simply absent from the archives? Butalia begins by arguing the case for qualitative methods in the endeavour of both finding new sources and rewriting social history. She explains how interviews and oral testimonies were most appropriate for her particular project of exploring alternative perspectives on the partition in how they gave legitimacy to the voices of ordinary people. Her book emerges out of a long-standing interest which spans years of inquiry into the subject area. While in total she conducted 70 interviews, not all of them appear in the book. Some of them are with relatives, others are with strangers. There was also no selected sample in terms of the social background of interviewees. Instead, Butalia conducted the interviews over a period of several years. It is here that the reader is left wondering as to how she was able to gain access to the partition survivors whose interviews appear in the book. Was it that so many people have stories that they want to tell that they simply offered their time willingly? How did she represent herself to potential interviewees as a means of gaining access to their stories? While the story which begins the book is a blood relation, subsequent interviews are with strangers and non-related people. The presence of the author in the interview is often not made explicit in terms of how, for instance, a Dalit (low-caste) woman reacted when she was approached to be interviewed by an educated, articulate woman, and how this played out in the interview. Despite the effort to be transparent, there are questions such as this which remain in the reader's mind.

Interviews are the central but not the only method she uses. Her primary sources include interviews, oral histories, memoirs, diaries, autobiographies, newspapers and letters, which she utilizes as a means to access not only the reflections of people whose experiences generally do not feature within official histories but also the dominant narratives of the time. The value of using a mixed-method approach to highlight the significance of a people's history of the partition is made clearly in the book from the onset. Butalia begins by pointing out that despite the documentation of the estimated 'human costs' of the partition by Indian, Pakistani and British sources in terms of quantitative figures – 12 million displaced, between 200,000 and 2 million deaths, 75,000 abductions of women, and countless rapes – this *generality* has circulated publicly through history books. Yet the *particular*, which exists privately within households, families and communities in India and Pakistan through stories and reflections of what happened before, during and after 1947, is what had been missing from the large political facts and narrations:

> the 'history' of Partition seemed to lie only in the political developments that had led up to it. These other aspects – what had happened to the millions of people who had to live through this time, what we might call the 'human dimensions' of this history – somehow seemed to have a 'lesser' status in it ... Yet could it really be that they had no place in the history of Partition?
>
> (Butalia 2000: 5–6)

It is within this wider context of arguments in favour of including voices often previously not included within formal, official histories which Butalia's work can be situated. *The Other Side of Silence* utilizes oral histories to privilege the experiences of women, children and what she calls 'the margins' – Dalits or scheduled castes – to retell their experiences from a centre-stage position, as opposed to one relegated to the peripheries. Thus, Butalia's work does not merely view the perspectives of women, children and the margins as add-ons to official perspectives, but, rather, she achieves a Subaltern approach to the partition through the use of memory and oral histories as her primary tools.

The Other Side of Silence represents a restoration exercise of people's experiences of the partition of India to the dominant macrohistory told of the creation of the nation-states of India and Pakistan in August 1947. Butalia uses a number of different types of sources in her endeavour to redress the official–informal binary relationship within historical accounts and narratives on the partition. The book charts out a methodological approach to representing the oral histories alongside other sources in the rewriting exercise of the partition. In addition to interviews, the range of sources that Butalia draws from – diaries, memoirs, newspaper reports, letters, enquiry commissions, pamphlets and other documents – provide the foundations of her methodological approach which weaves together spoken stories through interviews, published and unpublished memoirs, as well as a range of other types of sources which bridge the informal–formal divide. *The Other Side of Silence* attempts to challenge the upheld distinction between official historical renditions and informal, personal recollections of the partition. Her attempt to challenge the notion of formal history as sacrosanct on the one hand and personal stories or oral histories as less worthy of formal documentation on the other is a thread which runs throughout the book. Central to the insertion of oral histories into the recollection exercise is the emphasis placed upon highlighting the previously ignored significance of 'ordinary' people's experiences and perspectives on the partition. Up until the publication of *The Other Side of Silence*, writings on the partition had focused primarily upon historical and official government documents which de facto adopted understandings of the partition firmly entrenched within the national frames of India or Pakistan. Such understandings were unable to acknowledge adequately the significance of voices of ordinary people which potentially could challenge the sanctity of the nation by emphasizing the loss and violence which marked the formative period of nation-building for the two countries. For Butalia, the 'margins' become essential dimensions of this previously undocumented history:

> Despite the recent opening up of Partition histories there are many aspects that remain invisible in official, historical accounts of the event. ... Among these are stories of very many people who inhabit a world that is somehow – falsely – seen as peripheral. These histories have remained hidden, to my mind because so much writing on Partition has focused on Hindus and Sikhs and Muslims – or more correctly on Hindu and Sikh and Muslim men – that it is as if no other identity existed ... Partition history has worked to render many others invisible.
> (Butalia 2000: 6–7)

Throughout the book, Butalia highlights a discrepancy between many ordinary people's own perceptions of their significance to the partition and how they elevate the importance of official discourses of the history which they see as carrying more weight and substance. This is poignantly highlighted when Butalia reflects upon meeting Damyanti, an 80-year-old woman, whom she asked if she could interview:

'Why do you want to talk to me?' she said, 'I have nothing to say. Just a few foolish stories here and there.' I persisted, saying I'd be happy to listen to her stories, foolish or otherwise, and eventually, reluctantly, she relented.

(Ibid.: 87)

As the interviews with Damyanti, which spanned several months, unfold, we come to learn about a 'hidden history' of the recovery efforts to locate abducted women during that time of inter-religious, communal turbulence and retribution. Under the Inter-Dominion Treaty of December 1947, the Central Recovery Operation was undertaken through an agreement between the newly formed Indian and Pakistan governments to mount a mass recovery of women who had been abducted and/or raped during the turmoil of the partition. The official history of how the two governments entered into this sensitive area has been largely told through the documentation of the state recovery operations which shows teams of social workers, army and police officials executing an operation to 'take back' women from the other side. Such accounts fail to give a sense of *women's* experiences and the multitude of survival strategies which saw many so-called abducted women interpreting their own circumstances as 'refuge' from a communally charged period of civil strife where women's bodies became territorialized between communities of men.

While official reports provide approximate figures and a matter-of-fact summation of the relief efforts which the Central Recovery Operation embarked on, the operation has been criticized for defending a masculinist notion of community and nation (Das 1995). The heightened nature of sexualized violence during this time saw women's bodies become territorialized by communities, with individuals and officials responding in their own capacities as to how the operation should treat women's positionality, both as victims and agents. Conflicts of gender interests from within the recovery operations are highlighted in Butalia's history on this time, which shows how the execution of 'recovery' was often less concerned with women's well-being as it was with defending community possession or ownership of women. Butalia unpicks the official history of recovery and exposes it for the complicity of many men within the gendered violence, both as perpetrators in the acts of abduction as well as in the sabotage of rescue missions. Butalia's narrative casts a critical eye on the official history of relief and recovery, and the state's efforts in addressing the issue of abducted women, as one of women's interests and concerns. On the surface, the Indian and Pakistan state efforts showed concern for the recovery of the women. However, the execution of these operations saw how this actually unfolded in practice, with men and women acting as agents of the state in the recovery operation. Damyanti's own accounts as a social worker involved in these recovery teams, alongside male army and police counterparts, provides insights into how women working in professional capacities engaged and negotiated with the awkward and problematic task of locating abducted women:

> We'd go selling eggs. We'd go into the villages, and we'd ask people for *lassi* (yoghurt drink), saying *amma* (mother), *amma*, we have come from very far, please give us some *lassi* ... Then, we'd tell stories, we'd say we have come from Hindustan and you know, my younger brother, these bastard Sikhs have taken his young wife away, they've abducted her. He is bereft, and lonely. Do you know of any daughter of kaffirs in this area – if there is any such girl do tell us, maybe we can buy her and the poor man, at least he can set up home again. And the old women would know and they would often tell us there's a girl in such and such place ... So there was all this about selling eggs and asking, *amma*, give us some *lassi*.
>
> (Butalia 2000: 115)

Thus, Butalia writes the history of the recovery operation of abducted women with the insertion of a perspective including the fraught experiences of women, not merely as victims of the time but also as agents. Her insertion of a women-centred focus is one which the oral history, produced out of Damyanti's interviews, enables. Thus, such oral histories can provide an empirical source for the grounding of that history in 'fact', while also locating the microlevel of an individual experience within the wider contexts of the regional and national frames. Butalia's rewriting of history not only centres the voice of Damyanti's account, but is also able to highlight and foreground the complexities illustrated by her story. Yet, as Damyanti's life history reveals, not least in her role as a social worker, her subsequent life course was dramatically affected by the partition, which in itself has something very significant to contribute to the historical record. Butalia not only centres Damyanti's interview in her retelling of the history of the partition, but she also uses the interview to shed light on the gendered nature of the violence surrounding the time of the partition, and the subsequent recovery operations, in a manner which counters the objectifying, essentializing documentation of the government records available from that time.

Constructing a Narrative

One of the methodological issues which *The Other Side of Silence* raises is the format in which the various sources and interview material are represented.

In more practical terms, how does one write a social history when utilizing a mixed range of sources and methods? What form should it take? While Butalia draws upon a range of different types of sources, she is also conscious to avoid labelling any source as official, factual, historical or fictional; as she states: 'how do we know this event except through the ways in which it has been handed down to us' (ibid.: 8). Thus, for Butalia, every social history is a narrative, or a story, with a subjective position told from a particular perspective. She acknowledges that her social history of the partition is no exception and is laden with her own views and perceptions:

> In the beginning, I thought it better to simply put together a book of oral accounts, without any explanation or commentary. Gradually, I came to believe otherwise: as a reader and a publisher ... As I got more involved in the work, I found there was a great deal I wanted to say ... There were their stories, as they told them, and there was what I learnt and understood from those stories. I then began to think of a way of meshing the two together.
>
> (Ibid.: 14)

Butalia inserts herself as the narrator, who has licence to select what is reflected and whose standpoint and ideological position becomes the frame of the story. From the beginning of the book, she works through her embracement of the narrative method as a means for her to organize the data she had collected in a way that reflected her own understandings of how the various strands of data fit together. Having done the interviews and collected the source material for a number of years out of personal interest, she had access to a vast amount of material and 'data' – yet this also created a challenge to the writing-up process in terms of structuring the book, considering what to include or exclude and whether to present interviews as separate stories or to present them in other ways. Her headings of 'Blood', 'Facts', 'Women', 'Honour', 'Children', 'Margins' and 'Memory' are themes which she uses to organize the interviews and secondary data, and it is across these different themes that the interviews transcend. Thus, no single story is told in one account, but rather appears across a number of different themes over the book's course. It could be argued that the limit of this strategy is that, by the end of the book, the rich specificities of each particular story can begin to merge with one another to the reader. This effect of the narrative approach also reinforces the underlying voice of the narrator, who holds the agency of voice in the telling of the stories. However, it could also be argued that unlike other depictions of history, the narrative approach is more upfront about its subjective nature and thus only claims to present a history from the eyes of the author/narrator.

Perhaps, most significantly, the narrative approach offers a method for presenting alternative narratives on history. As discussed earlier, the Subaltern Studies School created a space for critiques of nationalist, overarching and other historical approaches previously not concerned with the representation of marginal groups. The narrative approach, by viewing every story or rendition of history as valid, allows for the status of even marginal voices to be elevated to that of history maker. A critical point of thought, however, is that even in the narrative approach the author is not exempt from being blamed for occupying central stage in a narration of history. In this instance, Butalia highlights this in acknowledging that her voice is present throughout the book, but that its perspective needs to be understood from her position not only for its insights but also for its limitations.

This question around the narrator's own subjectivity also presents questions as to what extent this is concealed or made explicit. In presenting the interviews in the book, there is an absence of the interview questions and even of the interviewer, which leads one to wonder about the dynamics of the interview from the perspective of the interviewed and to what extent the interviewer guided the conversations and shaped the interview material. None of the interviews in the book stand on their own, but instead are woven into the historical backdrop that Butalia draws from the secondary material and from her own narrations and analyses. The overall format of the book emerges as a series or web of stories with overlapping themes in which the interviewer/narrator is omnipresent and where the licence to represent the stories is held solely with the author herself. However, Butalia's positioning of herself in the book in other ways, as will be discussed in the following section, strengthens the use of the narrative form.

Writing Reflexively: Oral Accounts and Historical Writing

The subjectivity of the narrative approach draws attention to how Butalia locates herself within the book. 'Reflexivity' is the circular and cause–effect relationship that researchers have with their fields in not only observing them, but also in shaping them, in affecting change and, in turn, in the research being shaped and changed by the field itself. Foucault (1970), one of the most well known theorists of reflexivity, highlights in his critique of the pursuit of knowledge in the social sciences that one can be both a knowing subject but at the same time an object of one's own study. Butalia takes the reflexive position in the book by continually highlighting issues and problems of power and asymmetry within the research process. She uses this as her rationale for adopting the tools of feminist historiography in this project:

> Oral history is a methodological tool that many feminist historians have found enormously empowering ... But while oral history has been empowering, it has also brought its own problems ... After all, the telling is always only one-sided. How, further, can such historians ensure that the subjects of their interviews are not simply the 'raw material' on whose experiences they will build their theories?
>
> (Butalia 2000: 16)

The politics of power in the research process emerge as one explores the tools of memory and oral history where the interviewer/author/researcher is clearly a part of the story being told in one sense or another, whether in terms of how the interview is directed, conducted, analysed or presented. However, what feminist approaches to methodology offer, which is where Butalia clearly locates herself, is in the possibilities for the researcher to locate consciously her- or himself in the research process, with a subject position which can be worked through in the manner in which the history is told and documented.

The reflexivity which Butalia employs from the onset of the book supports this approach by immediately directing the reader to her intellectual, political and personal interest in the subject matter of the partition:

> I can only say that I have always had a deep suspicion of histories that are written as if the author were but a mere vehicle, histories that, to use Roland Barthes' phrase, 'seem to write themselves'. The absence of the 'I' in such histories helps perhaps to establish distance, even to create the illusion of objectivity, perhaps to establish factuality. I have no wish to pretend that these histories, these stories, are in any way an 'objective' rendering of Partition. I do not believe such a thing is possible.
>
> (Ibid.: 15–16)

Her methodological approach goes beyond a justification for how her 'voice moves in and out of these stories' (ibid.: 16) in the analysis and presentation of the histories. Quite significantly, the first of the oral accounts is that of Butalia's visit to her long-lost maternal uncle who she meets and interviews in Pakistan. This is the first oral history to be told in the book and comes under the thematic heading of 'Blood'. The interview is with 'Ranamama', her mother's brother who had stayed behind in Pakistan – keeping his mother (Butalia's maternal grandmother) with him – as the rest of his siblings migrated to India at the time of the partition. The personal family story which is told is tied with issues around property, separation, estrangement and perceived betrayal, which open up questions which Butalia explores throughout the presentation of the story. The story takes us on a journey that Butalia makes across the border to Pakistan from India for a first-time meeting with her uncle, who none of her relatives has seen since the partition. As the interview unfolds, Butalia reflects on a family history of pain, loss and dislocation which, by the end of the story, leaves more unresolved questions than when it had begun. Thus, the story is told as a means of exploration, rather than one of arriving at answers, and is done within a reflexive oration of a story close to the author. Through Butalia's explicit location of herself within the story, both in her relationship to the interviewee and in how she analyses and presents the story, this private, personal story of partition becomes one which is shared and collectively owned in its written, published form.

As a narrative on partition, Ranamama's story simply does not fit within national discourses of belonging or identity. His conscious decision to stay behind, rather than migrate to India along with the wave of Hindus and Sikhs, as official accounts would tell us, reflects a dimension of the partition which would only circulate within private reflections. That Ranamama chose to remain in Pakistan to maintain the ancestral property in itself symbolizes the contributions that subaltern, marginal histories provide to our understandings of the social world, offering glances of social experience often not visible within dominant perspectives. Butalia's reflexive narration allows readers to be privy to her exploration of a story not accessible or present in official accounts yet which is close to her own personal, political and intellectual interests. Thus, Butalia's reflexivity not only opens up the terrain for her own access into the field but also guides the reader to new avenues of questioning and exploration, making the possibilities for future social research on a period of history long past seem infinite.

Conclusion

The Other Side of Silence has been influential in expanding the lens and scope of research and writing in the field of partition studies. What is perhaps most exemplary of *The Other Side of Silence* as a piece of social research is its manner of addressing the issues of voice, silences, omissions and marginality while not being patronizing to the interview subjects or material. One of the most significant contributions of the book is the manner in which social history is presented as a dynamic field of inquiry for addressing contemporary social questions. Her approach to post-colonial history in this book is not one of recovering a 'lost' or 'missing' history, but rather is one which shows how understandings of contemporary social worlds cannot be removed from the historical backdrop out of which they are borne. Hence, broader understandings of the present can only be conceptualized through a broadened view of how history can be written and told. On another level, *The Other Side of Silence* also fills an empirical gap by documenting experiences, tales, narratives and reflections which show how a critical view of the historical record can, with the help of the tools of oral history and memory, build an alternative databank of knowledge.

There are two issues of method concerning the book which this chapter has raised. The first is the narrative approach which presents questions as to how one writes up the interview material and the form it should take. Butalia had to make a conscious decision as she began to write the book, as she explains, not to relegate the interviews to an appendix in the back of the book, which she felt would not give them the status in the book that they deserved. However, in the form that the book takes, Butalia's voice overarches the many stories that are told, as well as the secondary material, which she integrates into the narrative that emerges. The second issue discussed is reflexivity. Butalia's approach to this does not appear in a mere discussion about method, but instead is part and parcel of how she is present in the narrative throughout the book, making *The Other Side of Silence* as much of a personal journey as a serious piece of social research. She utilizes her position as interviewer and the method of the interview as an entry point into a sensitive and often uncomfortable or painful subject matter.

The book presents a social history of the partition which, by using a narrative approach, engages with discourses of location and belonging of the past, while also highlighting how legacies of exclusion continue in the present. The book tells us Butalia's 'story' of partition through multiple stories that come out of her interviews. Without making claims to expose or discover an authentic or hidden history of the partition, the book alerts us to the imperatives of social research that we should look beyond the written, official and documented word towards other rich sources of social life.

Additional Reading

Didur's *Unsettling Partition: Literature, Gender, Memory* (2006) offers an insightful analysis of literary texts, novels, short stories and testimonies which address the theme of partition. Menon and Bhasin's *Borders and Boundaries: Women in India's Partition* (1998) filled a void at the time it was published by highlighting the locations of women during the partition around violence and territoriality over women's bodies. Pandey's *Remembering Partition* (2001) is one of the most seminal works produced on the partition to date. Pandey illustrates the ways in which critical historiography attempts to 'read between the lines' when utilizing material drawn from archives and documented collections.

Acknowledgements

I would like to thank Urvashi Butalia for graciously reading and commenting on an earlier version of this chapter and to the editors for their suggestions.

References

Ahmad, A. (1994) *In Theory: Class, Nations, Cultures*, London: Verso.

Ahmed, A. (1991) *Resistance and Control in Pakistan*, London: Routledge.

Amin, S. (1995) *Event, Metaphor, Memory. Chauri Chaura 1922–1992*, Berkeley, CA: University of California Press.

Asad, T. (1987) 'Are there histories of peoples without Europe? A review article', *Comparative Studies in Society and History*, 29(3): 594–607.

Asad, T. (ed.) (1973) *Anthropology and the Colonial Encounter*, New York: Ithaca Press.

Butalia, U. (1993) 'Community, state and gender: on women's agency during partition', *Economic and Political Weekly*, 24 April.

Butalia, U. (2000) *The Other Side of Silence: Voices from the Partition of India*, Durham, NC: Duke University Press.

Chakrabarty, D. (1992) 'Postcoloniality and the artifice of history: who speaks for "Indian" pasts?', *Representations*, 37, Special Edition: Imperial Fantsaies and Postcolonial Histories (Winter): 1–26.

Chandra, B. (1979) *Nationalism and Colonialism in Modern India*, Delhi: Orient Longman.

Das, V. (1995) 'National honour and practical kinship: of unwanted women and children', in V. Das (ed.) *Critical Events: An Anthropological Perspective on Contemporary India*, Oxford: Oxford University Press.

Didur, J. (2006) *Unsettling Partition: Literature, Gender, Memory*, Toronto: University of Toronto Press.

Foucault, M. (1970) *The Order of Things: An Archaeology of the Human Sciences*, New York: Pantheon Books.

Gramsci, A. (1971) *Selections from the Prison Notebooks*, New York: International Publishers.

Guha, R. (1983) *Elementary Aspects of Peasant Insurgency in Colonial India*, Delhi: Oxford University Press.

Guha, R. (1985) *Subaltern Studies*, vol. IV, New Delhi: Oxford University Press India.

Hobsbawm, E. (1987) *The Age of Empire: 1875–1914*, New York: Vintage.

Jeffrey, R. (1994) *What's Happening to India? Punjab, Ethnic Conflict and the Test for Federalism*, 2nd edn, Basingstoke: Macmillan.

Kaviraj, S. (1992) 'The imaginary institution of India', in P. Chatterjee and G. Pandey (eds) *Subaltern Studies*, vol. VII, Oxford and Delhi: Oxford University Press,.

Manto, S.H. (2005) *Toba Tek Singh and Other Stories*, Singapore: Educational Publishing House.

Menon, R. and K. Bhasin (1998) *Borders and Boundaries: Women in India's Partition*, Chapel Hill, NC: Rutgers University Press.

Pandey, G. (1991) 'In defence of the fragment: writing about Hindu.– *Subaltern, 26 (11–12):559–73*.

Pandey, G. (1994) 'The prose of otherness', in D. Arnold and D. Hardiman (eds) *The Aftermath of Partition in South Asia*, London and New York: Routledge.

Pandey, G. (2001) *Remembering Partition*, Cambridge: Cambridge University Press.

Robinson, F. (2000) *Islam and Muslim History in South Asia*, Delhi: Oxford University Press.

Sidwa, B. (1991) *Cracking India*, Minneapolis, MI: Milkweed Editions.

Singh, K. (1994) *Train to Pakistan*, New York: Grove Press.

Singh, K. (ed.) (1991) *Select Documents on Partition of Punjab: 1947, India and Pakistan*, Delhi: National Bookshop.

Stokes, E. (1980) *The Peasant and the Raj: Studies in Agrarian Society and Peasant Rebellion in Colonial India*, Cambridge: Cambridge University Press.

Talbot, I. (2000) 'Literature and the human drama of the 1947 partition', in I. Talbot and G. Singh (eds) *Region and Partition: Bengal, Punjab and the Partition of the Subcontinent*, Delhi: Oxford University Press.

Thompson, E.P. (1963) *The Making of the English Working Class*, London: Vintage.

Williams, R. (1958) *Culture and Society, 1780–1950*, New York: Columbia University Press.

CHAPTER 9

News Interviews: Clayman and Heritage's *The News Interview*

CHRISTIAN GREIFFENHAGEN

This chapter considers issues of method with reference to research on the news. Christian Greiffenhagen presents a review of Clayman and Heritage's The News Interview (2002). The book is based on a detailed investigation of talk between interviewers and interviewees and draws on conversation analysis (CA) which sees discourse as a form of interaction. Three topics are considered. First, there is a discussion of the relationship between the perspective of the participant and the researcher. Second, the ways in which the practices that make the talk produced by an inter-viewer and interviewee recognizable as news interview talk is explored. Third, the similarities and differences between television and radio inter-views, one of which is visual and the other which is not, is considered. Greiffenhagen looks at how Clayman and Heritage understand the inter-view from the participants' perspectives, especially when they are evasive. He applauds the way in which the authors contrast interview talk with ordinary conversation to show the distinctiveness of news inter-view discourse. Finally, he considers the way in which the visual dimen-sions of television news interviews could be extended within CA.

Introduction

The news interview is a phenomenon familiar to all of us, not only as a tool through which journalists gather information, but also as a media product in its own right. Many broadcast programmes do not just include reports that summarize what journalists have learned through interviews, but consist of interviews with public figures themselves. This novel use of news interviews has led to changes for both journalists and public figures. While journalists previously gained face and status through their investigative skills (e.g. the *Washington Post* reporters Bob Woodward and Carl Bernstein during the Watergate scandal in the 1970s), today journalists are often known for their skills of questioning. For example, Jeremy Paxman is known for his aggressive style of questioning on BBC's *Newsnight*, famously asking in a 1997 interview with former Home Secretary Michael Howard the same question 12 times. Conversely, public figures do not only have to know how to deliver speeches in an engaging manner, but also how to perform well in interviews.

Clayman and Heritage's *The News Interview: Journalists and Public Figures on the Air* (2002) aims to study the methodic practices that are at play in the modern broadcast news interview. Since interviews are predominantly enacted through talk, they do so from the perspective of conversation analysis (CA), a sociological approach to studying discourse as a form of interaction. The aim of CA is to uncover the procedural properties of 'talk-in-interaction', where this is understood as the ways in which participants organize their talk so that they can be understood and in turn display this understanding to each other. Consequently, Clayman and Heritage study the news interview as a methodically produced course of interaction, emphasizing that the content of the interview (*what* is being talked about) is achieved through the interaction between interviewer and interviewee (*how* it gets talked about).

This chapter begins by placing the book in the context of studies of discourse and media, before summarizing some of its main findings. The methodological assessment will focus on (1) the relationship between the perspective of the participant and the researcher and the ways in which Clayman and Heritage ground their analysis in the *endogenous analysis of participants*; (2) the ways in which the *institutional specificity* of the news interview can be established; (3) the similarities and differences between radio and television interviews, in particular, the question of how television interviews can be studied as a *visual phenomenon*.

Studies of Discourse and Media

Clayman and Heritage's book contributes to a number of fields, including sociology, linguistics and mass communication. However, the book is most usefully seen in the context of two fields.

Discourse

Firstly, the book is a contribution to socio-linguistic studies of discourse (often simply referred to as 'discourse analysis'), an interdisciplinary field originating in a variety of disciplines, including linguistics, anthropology, sociology, psychology and philosophy. The emergence of these studies is often seen as a result of the 'linguistic turn', which in Britain is associated with philosophers such as Wittgenstein (1953), Austin (1962) and Winch (1958) and on the continent predominantly with French structuralism (e.g. Saussure 1959 [1916]; Barthes 1967 [1964]). While philosophers had previously seen language as simply a reflection of reality (prompting questions as to whether language is a true reflection of reality), it was now seen as, in an important sense, defining reality, since our ways of enquiring and approaching reality are conducted in and through language.

Within the human and social sciences the linguistic turn led to a view that saw sociological topics (such as work, gender or race) as investigable as 'worded entities' (Sharrock and Watson 1989: 431), that is as sustained and reproduced through the linguistic practices of members of society. The focus in studies of discourse is thus not so much on the language itself, but upon how language is used, that is what is accomplished in and through talking and writing (hence the term 'discourse' rather than 'language').

There are a large variety of approaches to studying discourse (for overviews, see Schiffrin 1994; Cameron 2001; Wetherell 2001), working with a diverse range of materials and using a number of different methods. To mention just a few: originating in linguistics and using predominantly quantitative methods, the *variationist approach* (Labov 1966) tried to connect the study of linguistic variables (e.g. pronunciation) with the study of social variables (e.g. class). In contrast, the *ethnography of speaking* (e.g. Hymes 1971) originated in anthropology and consequently used the method of participant observation to detail how people's way of speaking relates to the kind of situations they are in. In recent years, Foucault's notion of discourse has led to an increasing number of studies, which predominantly work on written (often historical) materials (e.g. Macdonald 2003). Also influential have been 'critical' approaches such as *critical linguistics* (Fowler et al. 1979) and *critical discourse analysis* (Fairclough 1989), which have aimed at exhibiting how linguistic features are shaped by ideological frameworks.

The CA approach adopted by Clayman and Heritage is perhaps distinctive since it did not originate as a result of a specific interest in language, but rather as an attempt to develop a thoroughly systematic and empirical approach to studying social action (for introductions to CA, see West and Zimmerman 1982; Lee 1987; Heritage 1995; Drew 2005; ten Have 2007). The originator of CA, Harvey Sacks (1984, 1992), focused on talk simply as a result of the fact that in the 1960s tape recorders had become both affordable and portable, which allowed the recording of naturally occurring conversations. Early studies analysed aspects of the most 'ordinary' kinds of conversation, for example the way speakers organize and coordinate taking turns at talking (Sacks et al. 1974) or correct their own or others' mistakes (Schegloff et al. 1977). Subsequently, CA researchers extended this approach to the study of institutional discourse (Heritage 2005; Arminen 2005), for example courtrooms (Atkinson and Drew 1979), political speeches (Atkinson 1984) and medical encounters (Heritage and Maynard 2006). Clayman and Heritage's book thus adopts a particular approach to studying discourse (CA) to a particular social institution (the news interview).

Media

The book is, secondly, a contribution to media studies – the academic study of mass communication. Most media studies have been preoccupied with the concept of 'ideology' (cf. Masterman 1985: 187), trying to exhibit how ideologies are transmitted and reproduced through the media.

A huge influence has been the critical theory of the Frankfurt School (see e.g., Horkheimer and Adorno 2002 [1947]; Marcuse 1964). Critical theory was a development of Marxism, arguing that capitalist modes of production had penetrated into the sphere of culture, which had led to the liquidation of differences and individuality. People in modern societies were seen as not only economically, but also culturally, alienated. Furthermore, while the culture industry promotes a view according to which individuals are free to do what they want (e.g. Nike's slogan 'Just do it!'), this freedom is largely illusory, since most 'choices' are limited to a very few (and only marginally different) mass-produced items. According to critical theory, the mass media thus promote a view of liberty and freedom, but in fact contribute to their demise by persuading people to be happy with these very limiting conditions.

In Britain these ideas were revitalized in the 1970s, in particular through an analysis of the news. The Glasgow University Media Group (1976, 1980) challenged the view that news representations of what is happening in the world are impartial and neutral. By exhibiting discrepancies between the coverage of industrial disputes and official statistics of them, these studies tried to demonstrate that television reports are not a straightforward representation of reality, but rather a distorted representation of it. The argument was not that journalists are deliberately biased, but rather that despite their best efforts journalists cannot help but reproduce the dominant assumptions of our society. The problem with the news was not so much that they produced partial accounts, but that they presented these partial accounts *as if* they were 'neutral' and 'objective' (Glasgow University Media Group 1976: 267–8).

The Centre for Contemporary Cultural Studies in Birmingham, led by Stuart Hall (1980, 1982), as discussed in previous chapters, also challenged the notion of a neutral or objective media. Drawing on critical theory as well as semiology, Hall showed that the relationship between 'represented' and 'representation' (between what happened and how we talk about what happened) is not straightforward or automatic, but rather influenced by social and cultural norms. There are always different ways of representing the 'same' object and the choice of representation was seen as a result of power. The media, by choosing a particular representation of reality, thus helps to reproduce the current dominant ideology, which becomes accepted as 'natural' or 'obvious'. Again, the argument was not that the media were biased in any straightforward sense (e.g. by favouring the Conservative Party over the Labour Party), but rather that it was, unwittingly, helping to reproduce and stabilize the currently dominant political system (Hall 1982: 87).

In these early studies of the social construction of the news, linguistic factors got 'relatively meagre treatment' (Fowler 1991: 8). Subsequent studies thus tried to focus explicitly on the linguistic aspects of media products, predominantly in the tradition of critical linguistics (e.g. Fowler 1991) and critical discourse analysis (van Dijk 1988a, 1988b; Fairclough 1995). The focus of these critical studies was to show how the media has the power to 'influence knowledge, beliefs, values, social relations, social identities' (Fairclough 1995: 2) and how this is accomplished through linguistic representations, for example through the ways that people are categorized as 'poor' or 'oppressed', or by portraying processes as having an agent or not (e.g. 'life gets harder' versus 'the profiteers are making life harder'; ibid.: 104). These studies are 'critical' in the sense that their explicit aim is to demonstrate that what is supposedly accepted by many people as 'natural' or 'obvious' is, in fact, only one way of portraying reality and most commonly a way that favours those currently in power (Fairclough and Wodak 1997: 258).

Apart from such 'critical' approaches to media discourse, there has also been a variety of what is often referred to as 'descriptive', but which perhaps should better be called 'explicative', studies of media discourse. Put very simply, while critical approaches aim to exhibit what people are *not* aware of, explicative approaches study what people *are* aware of (Hutchby 2006: 33). Examples of such studies include a participant observation study of the journalists working on newspaper reports (Bell 1991), a CA study of radio talk shows (Hutchby 1996), a phenomenological study of both radio and television output (Scannell 1996) and a variety of studies of the interaction on television talk shows (Tolson 2001). Clayman and Heritage's book is in the tradition of these latter, 'explicative', studies.

The News Interview

Clayman and Heritage's book is based on recordings of approximately 250 American and British news interviews broadcasted on radio and television over the past 20 years. British data were drawn, for example, from *Newsnight* (BBC2) and *Today* (BBC Radio 4). Clayman and Heritage analyse these data from the perspective of CA with the aim of uncovering the cultural practices that interviewer (IR) and interviewee (IE) draw upon to understand each other and to coordinate their talk. It is these practices that allow us (as listeners and viewers) to identify the talk that we see or hear, often within seconds, *as* someone interviewing someone else.

News Interview Turn-taking

Because the central framework of CA analyses talk in terms of turn-taking arrangements, Clayman and Heritage pay central attention to the turn-taking structure of news interviews. Many activities that we engage in can be considered as involving a 'turn-taking system', for example, playing games, standing in a queue or talking to each other. In the paper which defines the nature of CA, Sacks et al. (1974) describe in detail how in ordinary conversation there is no specification as to who initiates a new topic, who will talk about that topic and for how long they will talk about it. In contrast, in other ('institutional') activities turns may be preallocated and specifically constrained.

Clayman and Heritage demonstrate that turn-taking in news interviews consists largely in the IR asking questions and the IE producing answers. That is to say, although IRs' turns may include several statements, the great majority of turns will end in a question of some kind. Furthermore, IEs are sensitive to this, that is they wait until the IR has completed a question before beginning their own turn. This can be illustrated by looking at Excerpt A, taken from an interview with a left-wing trade union leader, in which the IR is trying to get the IE to admit that he is a Communist. What is happening in this example is readily recognizable, in the sense that the IR saying that the IE is a Marxist can be heard as an accusation, while the IE's response is a denial. However, the interest lies in the ways in which the two parties organize their talk so that one is asking questions and the other is answering them.

Excerpt A UK BBC Radio *World at One*: 13 March 1979: Election

IR: Robin Day, IE: Arthur Scargill National Union of Mineworkers

1	IR:	.hhh er <u>W</u>hat's the difference between <u>y</u>our
2		Marxism and Mister McGahey's communism.
3	IE:	er The difference is that it's the <u>press</u> that
4		constantly call me a <u>M</u>arxist when I do <u>not</u>, (.)

5		and never <u>have</u> (.) er er given that description
6		of myself .[.hh I-
7 IR:	1→	[But I've <u>heard</u> you-
8	1→	I've heard you'd be very <u>happy</u> to: to: er .hhhh
9	1→	er de<u>scribe</u> yourself as a Marxist.
10	2→	<u>C</u>ould it be that with an election in the <u>o</u>ffing
11	2→	you're anxious to play down that you're a
12	2→	Marx[ist.]
13 IE:	3→	[er] Not at all Mister Da:y.=And I:'m (.)
14		<u>so</u>rry to say I must disagree with you,=you have
15		<u>ne</u>ver <u>heard</u> me describe my<u>self</u> .hhh er as a
16		Ma:rxist.=I have o:nly ((continues))

*CA has devised a number of transcription conventions to indicate the sequential structure of utterances (they can be found in Clayman and Heritage 2002: 347–53). The most important are the following: underlined items (e.g. 'not' in line 4) are audibly stressed; numbers in parentheses denote a silence in tenths of seconds, while '(.)' denotes a micropause of less than 0.2 seconds (see line 5); square brackets mark the onset and termination of simultaneous speech (lines 6 and 7, 12 and 13).

Source: Clayman and Heritage (2002: 106).

The IR in Excerpt A starts with a question about the IE's political position (lines 1–2). The IE responds by denying that he is a Marxist (3–6), which prompts the IR to ask the question again in a different way (7–12), starting with a statement that counters the IE's denial that he is a Marxist (7–9). In ordinary conversation the IE would be likely to initiate a disagreement directly after the completion of the first statement (i.e. the exchange would 'jump' from 9 directly to 13). However, in the news interview context, the IE *waits* until the IR has produced a question (arrow 2), before starting to answer (arrow 3). The IE thus orientates himself to the fact that the IR's first utterance (arrow 1), while constituting a complete 'ordinary' turn, does not constitute a complete 'interview' turn (since it does not include a question).

While the way it is relatively easy for IEs to recognize the end of IRs' turns (since questions are marked in various ways, e.g. their grammatical form or rising intonation), it is more difficult for IRs to recognize the end of IEs' answers. IEs thus attempt to make it apparent that they have finished their answer, for example, by repeating words from the original question at the end of their answer. However, this does not always work. In Excerpt B, an interview with a US presidential candidate, the IE answers the IR's question in such a concise manner that the IR does not immediately treat the answer as completed.

Excerpt B US PBS *Newshour*: 18 September 1992: Candidacy

IR: Judy Woodruff, IE: Ross Perot

```
1    IR:    So why don't you go ahead and (.) say: I'm (.) a
2           candidate for pr[esident?
3    IE:                    [Because that's not (.) where
4           the organization is now. Our organization (.)
5           is to:tally focused on try:ing to get both
6           parties to do the job.
7           (0.7)
8  →  That's why.
```

Source: Clayman and Heritage (2002: 116).

The IE produces a very succinct answer to the IR's question (lines 3–6), beginning the answer with 'because' which is the responsive term to 'why'. The pause (7) indicates that the IR does not treat the answer as complete, but seems to expect more talk from the IE. The IE orientates himself to this lack of response by the IR and recompletes his answer through the formulation 'That's why' (8).

Clayman and Heritage's achievement is not the 'discovery' that news interviews follow a question–answer format, but that they show how *participants* organize their talk so that it fits this pattern. Thus in Excerpt A the IE is demonstrably waiting for the IR to produce a question before starting to answer, while in Excerpt B the IE is showing that he treats the pause as a noticeable absence of the IR's next question.

Producing Talk for an Overhearing Audience

A lot of activities have pre-allocated turn-taking systems. In fact, even extended question–answer exchanges are not distinctive to news interviews, since they are also constitutive of other forms of interviews, for example courtroom interrogations (Atkinson and Drew 1979) and medical consultations (Frankel 1990). In order to detail what is institutionally distinctive about news interview talk, Clayman and Heritage argue that it is characterized by a special 'footing' (Goffman 1973; Levinson 1988) in which participants do not just talk to each other, but do so for an *overhearing audience*.

They demonstrate this by noting a number of differences to ordinary conservation. Firstly, while in ordinary conversations listeners typically produce a variety of 'acknowledgement tokens' (such as 'mm hm', 'uh huh', 'yes' or 'really') to indicate that the speaker may go on talking, these are largely absent in news interview talk. Clayman and Heritage argue that this absence demonstrates that the IR is not the primary recipient of the IE's response. Although the IR is the addressee of the IE's talk, it is the overhearing audience who is the intended recipient, which is why it would inappropriate for the IR to produce acknowledgement tokens.

The special footing of interviews is, secondly, marked by the fact that speakers often refer to each other in the third person. For example, in situations with more than one IE, IEs will refer to other IEs in the third person (e.g. 'I disagree with Sam Brittan in a most fundamental way about this' (Clayman and Heritage 2002: 122)). Again, this is a marked departure for how we talk to copresent others in ordinary conversation and points to the fact that speakers are talking for the benefit of an audience.

Maintaining Neutralism

Clayman and Heritage also address a central topic of media studies: the supposed neutrality of the media, which is shown to be of central concern to journalists themselves. In other words, IRs work at maintaining an impartial or 'neutralistic' stance during interviews. One common practice is to express views not as personal ones, but as those of other people, either of specific individuals (e.g. another public figure) or someone quite unspecific. Thus in the following interview with the South African Ambassador (which was still under apartheid rule and had just declared a state of emergency as a result of increasing civil unrest), the IR expresses a particular view (that the purpose of the state of emergency is to suppress political dissent) not as his own but as that of 'critics'.

Excerpt C US PBS *Newshour*: 22 July 1985: South Africa

IR: Jim Lehrer, IE: Herbert Beukes

1 IR: Finally Mister Ambassador as you know the

2   →   critics say that the p<u>u</u>rpose <u>o</u>f the state of

3		emergency the <u>re</u>al purpose of the state of
4		'mergeh- uh state of emergency is to sup<u>press</u>
5		political diss<u>ent</u>. th<u>o</u>se who are opp<u>o</u>sed to the
6		apartheid government of South Africa. Is th<u>a</u>t so,
7		(.)
8	IE:	I would <u>have</u> to: uh- take <u>i</u>ssue with
9	→	that pr<u>e</u>mise. because…

Source: Clayman and Heritage (2002: 164).

The IR is here expressing a strong opinion, which could bring his neutralistic stance in to jeopardy. By expressing the opinion as one of 'critics' (line 2), the IR can be seen as merely reporting that opinion. The IR is thus able to express a view directly in opposition to that of the IE without positioning *himself* as opposing the IE. This stance is furthermore accepted by the IE, who only challenges the premise of the question (8–9), but not the IR himself (i.e. he speaks of 'that premise' rather than 'your premise').

A particularly aggressive line of questioning may on occasion be treated by IEs as the IR expressing her or his personal opinion. However, in such cases the IR will work to reassert a neutralistic stance. Thus in the following interview with the Director of the Office of Management and Budget, the IR is asking about the way that the Office has handled the saving of US Savings & Loan. The IR is pursuing a relatively aggressive line of questioning, but when the IE accuses the IR of expressing a personal opinion, the IR quickly reasserts his neutralistic stance:

Excerpt D US ABC *This Week*: October 1989: Savings & Loan Rescue

IR: San Donaldson, IE: Richard Darman

1	IR:	Isn't it a fact, Mister Darman, that the taxpayers
2		will pay more in interest than if they just paid
3		it out of general revenues?
4	IE:	No, not necessarily. That's a technical
5		argument –
6	IR:	It's not a – may I, sir? It's not a technical
7		argument. Isn't it a fact?
8	IE:	No, it's definitely not a fact. Because first
9		of all, twenty billion of the fifty billion is

10	→	being handled in just the way you want –
11		through treasury financing. The remaining –
12 IR:	→	I'm just asking you a question. I'm not
13	→	expressing my personal views.
14 IE:		I understand.

Source: Clayman and Heritage (2002: 129–30).

The IR is pressing the IE on whether a decision by the IE's Office will cost taxpayers (lines 1–3) to which the IE responds by arguing that answering this question is not straightforward and based on 'technicalities' (4–5). The IR directly challenges this assertion and states that it is a fact (6–7). In response, the IE reaffirms his position (8–11) and insinuates that the IR is expressing a *personal* opinion (10). This prompts the IR to interrupt the IE's turn in order to state that he is only asking questions and not expressing his personal views (12–13).

None of this is to say that IRs may not have very strong personal views on a particular topic – or that IEs may not feel that the IR is in fact pursuing a rather one-sided line of questioning. What Clayman and Heritage are arguing is that *both* sides commonly maintain a stance in which the IR is understood not to be asking the questions because he or she is personally interested, but is doing so as a way of soliciting the interview*ee's views*.

Evasive Answers

Clayman and Heritage also discuss the widespread perception that public figures often try to avoid giving a direct answer to questions (which, of course, is partly a result of the fact that journalists spend a lot of time figuring out questions that IEs cannot easily answer). Again, this is dealt with in terms of the practices that IEs have developed in order to deal with questions that they do not want to answer directly.

One frequent practice is to repeat some words from the question in the answer in order to appear to give a straightforward answer to the question – while actually reinterpreting the question. One example of this is Excerpt A above, where the IR asks about 'the difference between your Marxism and Mister McGahey's communism' (lines 1–2). The IE starts his answer with a repeat of some of the words of the IR's question: 'The difference is that ...' (3). The repeat of the words 'the difference' allows the IE to tie his answer to the IR's question. However, the IE is in fact trying to undercut the question: the IR was asking about the difference between two political positions (trying to force the IE to admit that he is on the radical left), while the IE's response is about the difference in interpretation of what he has said in the past (the press describing the IE as a Marxist, the IE insisting that he has never described himself in that way). Of course, this is only a mild readjustment of the question's agenda, but it nevertheless allows the IE not to answer the question in the way it was framed.

Some IEs operate on the IR's question in even more subtle ways. A famous example occurred in an interview with then US President Bill Clinton about the suggestion that he had an affair with Monica Lewinsky, an intern at the White House:

Excerpt E UK PBS *Newshour*: 21 January 1998: Monica Lewinsky

IR: Jim Lehrer, IE: Bill Clinton

1 IR: You had <u>no</u> sexual relationship with this

2   [young wo[man.]

3 IE: [ml [Th-]

4 IE: There is not a sexual relationship. That

5   is <u>a</u>ccurate.

Source: Clayman and Heritage (2002: 295).

Here Clinton seems to answer the IR's question. However, note that Clinton actually shifts the time frame of the action, from something that has happened in the past to something that is still happening. Clinton only denies that there is *currently* a sexual relationship – which leaves open the possibility that there was one in the past (which has now been terminated).

Alternatively, an IE may try to shift the particular action that the IR is inquiring about. Thus in the famous Paxman–Howard interview the following exchange occurred:

Excerpt F UK BBC *Newsnight*: 13 May 1993: Michael Howard

IR: Jeremy Paxman, IE: Michael Howard

10 IR: Did you threaten to overrule him.

11 IE: I did <u>not</u> overrule Der[ek (Lewis).

12 IR: [Did you <u>thr</u>eaten to overrule him.

Source: Clayman and Heritage (2002: 256; abridged by the author).

Paxman questions whether Howard had threatened to overrule the prison director (line 10) to which Howard responds that he did not overrule him

(11). This seems to be an answer to Paxman's question. However, as in the previous case, a shift has taken place: Howard is acknowledging that he did not overrule the prison director – but does not specifically deny that he had *threatened* to do so. On this occasion, this is picked up by the IR who repeats his question, emphasizing the word 'threaten' (12).

The overview so far has focused on some topics of Clayman and Heritage's book that will allow us to discuss their methodology in more detail. In their book, they also investigate the historical development of news interviews (Chapter 2), how news interviews are opened and closed (Chapter 3), IRs' ways of producing adversarial questions (Chapter 6) and how these practices change in the case of panel interviews (Chapter 8).

Endogenous Analysis

There are many advantages of studying media discourse: materials are easily accessible, they are available in good quality and they are not distorted by an observer effect, since being recorded is a natural and essential feature of this activity (and not an external 'research' constraint on it). Rather than spending time collecting data, researchers can therefore focus on analysing their materials. However, since materials are not produced for research purposes, they do not speak for themselves and the challenge is to find ways of analysing them. Given a piece of data (for example, from a news interview), how can a researcher decide between the different possible interpretations of it?

In an important exchange on different ways of approaching discourse materials (Schegloff 1997, 1999a, 1999b; Billig 1999a, 1999b), Schegloff argues that there are two possible sets of standards which can be employed to analyse materials, either those of the researcher or those of the participants. According to Schegloff, most researchers investigate data according to their own (the researcher's) academic, political or aesthetic interests, whereas CA aims to uncover the relevances that *participants themselves* orientate towards.

CA tries to do this by taking advantage of the fact that its materials are 'interactive', in the sense that what the participants do next implements and displays their understanding of the previous action. What participants say or do next depends crucially on their understanding of what another participant has said previously – and furthermore displays how those prior utterances have been taken (i.e. understood). In that sense, 'conversation analysis' is not just a name for something done by researchers, but also for the analysis produced by participants: we are all 'conversation analysts' in the lay sense.

The fact that participants themselves display their understanding to each other can be used by researchers as a 'proof procedure' (Sacks et al. 1974: 729; Schegloff 2005: 476) for their professional analysis. Thus in the interview context, Clayman and Heritage ground their analysis in the fact that both IR and IE display in each subsequent turn an understanding of the other's prior turn. Their claim that the turn-taking structure of interviews follows a question–answer format is demonstrated by showing that participants *orientate* themselves towards this: in Excerpt A it can be shown that the IE is waiting to begin his turn until the IR has produced a question; and Excerpt B exhibits that the IE is analysing the IR's silence as an indication that the IR has not picked up on the fact the IR has completed his answer.

Clayman and Heritage's emphasis on the endogenous analysis produced by participants allows them to treat the central topic of media studies, the neutrality of the media, in a new light. Within critical approaches, it is typically the researcher who evaluates what is to be treated as 'not neutral' and that the ideology or bias of news reports may be 'hidden' or 'invisible' for the participants themselves (see Fairclough 1995: 54; Wodak 2001: 10). In contrast, Clayman and Heritage treat the issue of neutrality as one of central importance to participants themselves: IRs work at demonstrating their neutralism and IEs may, on occasion, challenge this. Thus Excerpt C shows that when IRs wish to oppose an IE's statement, they do so by speaking on behalf of others (e.g., 'critics'), so that they are not seen as expressing their own opinion. Furthermore, Excerpt D demonstrates that when an IE challenges the IR's neutralism, the IR quickly reasserts her or his independence.

The requirement to demonstrate that the feature that the researcher is talking about is orientated to by participants is not always easily to fulfil (cf. Schegloff 1991 on 'procedural consequentiality'). Clayman and Heritage face this as a problem in their efforts to deal with evasive answers. They note that although both IR and IE might agree that an IE is evading a particular question, they might both decide to let it pass (i.e. the IR may not address this through a follow-up question). Consequently, Clayman and Heritage 'reserve the term "evade/evasive" for actions that are treated as inadequately responsive by at least one of the participants' (2002: 242). Thus in Excerpt E, although Clayman and Heritage argue that the IE accomplishes a shift in the time frame that the question is enquiring about, they do not say that he is trying to 'evade' the question (since this would require either IR or IE to address this manoeuvre). In contrast, in Excerpt F, Clayman and Heritage claim that the IR is interpreting the IE's response as an evasive one, since it prompts the IR to repeat the question.

The issue of evasiveness points to a possible limit of Clayman and Heritage's way of approaching news interviews. However, it is perhaps more a 'limitation' of their data than their analytic approach, because the study could be easily extended by considering additional materials to the broadcast itself. It could be argued that the question of whether an IE is being evasive is not just decided by the IR and IE *in* the interview, but also by how audiences evaluate the interview and how other types of media subsequently report it. One could envisage studies that investigate how other media products report on the performance of the IE. For example, how were (in Excerpt F) Howard's reactions to Paxman's repeated questions assessed in the media? Was Clinton's manoeuvre (in Excerpt E) picked up and reported on directly after the interview – or only at a later stage? By investigating how the 'evasiveness' of IEs gets treated in subsequent media reports one could extend Clayman and Heritage's study – without relinquishing their aim to ground such analysis in the endogenous analysis of participants.

Clayman and Heritage (2000: 345) are also explicit that with their data it is impossible to investigate how *audiences* analyse the news interview: 'the impact that all of this may or may not have on audiences and on the course of public opinion also remains to be explored'. How could this be done? The classical way of investigating the reception of media products is through quantitative surveys, telephone interviews, focus groups or experimental studies of recall and comprehension (e.g. Morley 1980; Robinson and Levy 1986; Gunter 1987, 2000; Bertrand and Hughes 2005). Keeping in line with Clayman and Heritage's methodology, what would be more 'naturalistic' ways to study how audiences analyse the media?

In the case of a co-present audience, researchers have used the behaviour of the audience (e.g. clapping or booing) to see how the audience is analysing the action in front of them. This has been exploited by CA researchers in analysing political speeches (e.g. Atkinson 1984; Heritage and Greatbatch 1986). However, during most interviews there is no audience that claps or boos in specific response to what IRs or IEs are saying. One possibility would be to study people watching the news (perhaps with others) and record their reactions. For example, Wood (2006) recorded the comments made by women during daytime television. Another possibility would be to try to find situations in which people *talk* about what they have seen or heard on the news, for example at workplaces, pubs or cafes. This, however, would not be easy: there is, firstly, the problem of access to such settings, and, secondly, the need to collect a lot of materials, since people talk about the news relatively infrequently.

Although there are some limitations to Clayman and Heritage's study of news interviews, these are acknowledged and are predominantly a result of the data they have been working with. However, critics of CA (e.g. Fairclough 1995; Billig 1999a, 1999b; Wetherell 1998) argue that CA's methodological approach is unduly restrictive and uncritical, since it seems simply to reproduce what people do or say and thereby, at least implicitly, accept the status quo and convey 'an essentially non-critical view of the social world' (Billig 1999a: 552). In other words, how can we square the emphasis on endogenous analysis with the existence of social inequality in the world (Billig 1999b: 576)?

For example, Clayman and Heritage are relatively silent on the question as to *who* gets to talk in news interviews, that is whether the choice of IEs is in any sense representative. In their study of the guests on ABC's *Nightline* and PBS's *NewsHour*, Croteau and Hoynes (1994) showed that these were predominantly government officials and other established elites, while leaders of labour and racial/ethnic groups appeared only infrequently. This is clearly not an issue that Clayman and Heritage explicitly address. However, neither is it absent from their analysis. For example, the IR's practice of speaking on behalf of others, as in Excerpt C, can be seen to invoke non-present parties. Furthermore, the question of 'representativeness' is one that is not only addressed by researchers, but also by participants themselves; not necessarily in the interview, but in other settings, for example in editorial conferences where editors discuss what topic to address and whom to invite. Clayman himself conducted a study, based on audio recordings of newspaper editorial conferences that analysed how editors decide which story will make it to the front page (Clayman and Reisner 1998). A similar study could be conducted for news interviews.

Thus although Clayman and Heritage do not explicitly address questions of 'representativeness' or 'inequality', it would be possible to extend their study to address these issues, while holding on to their main methodological principle of grounding the professional analysis in the endogenous analysis of participants.

Institutional Analysis

The aim of Clayman and Heritage is to uncover the institutional specificity of news interviews, that is to determine the practices that make the talk produced by IR and IE recognizable *as* news interview talk. Doing so is by no means straightforward, since researchers face the problem that not everything that happens in a particular setting is related to the institutional character of that setting. Take a school building as an example. Although some of the interaction that will happen there will be related to institutional roles, there will also be conversations between teachers and pupils where they do not interact as teachers and pupils but as, for example, men and women, adults and children, British and Chinese, or teammates. The problem, as Schegloff (1991: 51) points out, is to demonstrate from the specifics of the talk that participants are speaking *on the basis* of their institutional identities.

Clayman and Heritage (2002: 20–1) address this problem by contrasting the characteristics of interview talk with those of ordinary conversation, that is they compare the ways in which IR and IE organize their turns at talk in the interview with how participants would do so in ordinary conversation. Firstly, they argue that, in contrast to ordinary conversation, the turns in news interviews are pre-allocated, that is IRs ask questions which IEs answer. If Excerpt A were taken from an ordinary conversation, a co-participant would initiate a disagreement directly at the point where it occurred and not wait until a question has been introduced as the IE does in the interview context. Secondly, Clayman and Heritage distinguish the news interview from other kinds of interviews, such as medical interviews (Frankel 1990) or research interviews (Button 1987), by highlighting the ways in which both IR and IE produce their talk for an overhearing audience. This is again demonstrated through a comparison with ordinary conversation, for example the absence of acknowledgement tokens in the interview context. The news interview departs from natural conversation in ways that differ from other types of interviews.

These two features certainly apply to the news interview. However, are they detailed enough to capture what is distinctive about it? It might be possible to go further in specifying what makes the talk interview talk, that is to make more 'of the fact that a news interview is not just *any* interview, but one specifically concerned with some topic or issue *defined as news*' (Hester and Francis 2001: 213; see also O'Connell and Kowal 2006).

It is not that the 'newsworthy' character of the news interview is entirely absent from Clayman and Heritage's study, but that their focus is on the forms in which turns at talk are organized in interviews and less so at what makes the identity of the IE or the subject matter of the interview 'news'. The *news* character of the talk configures many aspects of the news interview, in particular who is invited and what the participants will be talking about – as well as whether people will want to listen to what the IE has to say. They acknowledge this in the subtitle of their book when they characterize the IEs as 'public figures' and in their discussion of 'interview genres' (Clayman and Heritage 2002: 68–72), where they distinguish between 'newsmaker interview', 'background interview' and 'debate interview' and note the corresponding characterization of the IE as 'participant', 'expert' or 'advocate'. The 'newsworthiness' is also present in their analysis of the openings of interviews (Chapter 3), where they detail that these typically consist in headlines and background information, which are often 'selected so as to highlight the dramatic or newsworthy character of the subject matter' (ibid.: 61). Finally, that the interview is related to events in the news is of course visible in the interview itself. Thus in Excerpt C we can see from the IR's question that South Africa has just declared a state of emergency, which is the reason why the IR is talking to the South African ambassador.

There is therefore no need to reject Clayman and Heritage's mode of analysis and adopt another (such as critical discourse analysis) in order to answer questions about what makes things 'news'. One can easily extend Clayman and Heritage's analysis to cover the way in which interviews are set up in the context of how a news story is introduced, placed in a series of reporter statements, other interviews, and so on. One could also extend their study by considering other types of data, for example (as already suggested) to investigate how a particular interview is placed in a variety of media products. For example, Barthélémy (2003) investigates the temporal structure of media reports by showing how a particular newspaper story changes during the course of one year. Nekvapil and Leudar (2002, 2006) use the concept of 'dialogic network' to study the interplay of different kinds of media, for example newspaper articles, television debates and ordinary conversation about news events. Other studies have investigated the question of 'quotability' (Atkinson 1984; Clayman 1995), that is which bits of political speeches are 'picked up' in subsequent media reports.

In sum, Clayman and Heritage have made a start at getting to grips with the institutional specificity of news interviews. However, it would be possible to extend their study – possibly by considering other types of data.

Visual Analysis

CA was originally developed using audio-recorded conversations, often of telephone calls (e.g. Sacks 1967; Schegloff 1968). Especially in the case of the latter, participants and researchers can be said to have access to the same resources, since participants can only hear (not see or touch) each other. The CA approach is thus very appropriate for studying *radio* news interviews: the audience only has access to what participants say – and very often IR and IE may themselves be conducting the interview over the phone and can only hear each other.

However, in the case of *television* news interviews, the participants and audiences do not only pay attention to what participants say, but also to their bodily conduct (whether someone is smiling or frowning, looking confident or stressed – as well as the clothes they wear, their general appearance, etc.). These 'embodied' or 'non-verbal' aspects may, on occasion, have an impact on how participants react to each other or how they are perceived by the audience. A very dramatic example of this is reported by Atkinson (1984: 174) who remarks that after the 1960 Kennedy–Nixon presidential debate in the US, radio listeners thought that Nixon won the debate, while television viewers considered Kennedy the winner.

It is not that Clayman and Heritage do not make any reference to visual elements in their analysis of news interviews: they remark that IEs may on occasion respond through a nod rather than a verbal response or that an IR's frown may prompt an IE to reshape the answer in progress (2002: 291). They also mention the physical setting in which the interview is conducted (ibid.: 223). Finally, they refer to the work of the editor and cameramen who have to analyse the talk between IR and IE in order to anticipate whether they should change their 'shot' or not (ibid.: 76).

However, Clayman and Heritage's focus is clearly the talk, and visual features are considered more as an add-on to their analysis. In other words, the analysis of television interviews seems to follow the 'audio logic' of the analysis of radio interviews (cf. Ayass 2004; O'Connell and Kowal 2006). How could one extend Clayman and Heritage's analysis to take into account more explicitly the *visuality* of television interviews?

The first possibility would be to extend their focus on the ways that IR and IE analyse each other, but to pay more explicit attention to their visual behaviour. This line of research would follow other attempts that have extended CA from an analysis of spoken discourse to an embodied one (e.g. Goodwin 1981, 2001; Heath 1986, 1997), for example by investigating the role of gaze. One could imagine studies that focus on the bodily conduct of IR and IE (nodding, raising eyebrows, smiling, etc.). Results from such studies are unlikely to 'falsify' any of the findings of Clayman and Heritage, but would show how issues such as 'neutralism', 'evasiveness' or 'aggressiveness' are not just achieved through verbal, but also 'embodied', means. For example, in his study of public speaking Atkinson (1984: 69–72) shows that getting audiences to clap is not just achieved through verbal rhetorics but also through embodied conduct (e.g. hand movements or moving the head up or down).

A second possibility would be to investigate the role of editing and the *mise en scène* (the design aspects) of the television broadcast (cf. Ayass 2004). For example, during live broadcasts with several cameras available, production editors have to decide which shot to select during each moment of the broadcast. When interviews are recorded for later broadcast, they are often edited. A perspicuous feature of editing was discussed in the British press at the time of writing this chapter: it turned out that production staff regularly insert 'noddy shots' of IRs nodding during an IE's turn of talk to give the impression that the IR was reacting to the IE's immediate comment. However, these shots of the IR had been filmed *after* the interview had taken place (often only one camera is available for the interview) and were therefore seen as giving a false impression of what 'actually' happened.

One could investigate editing or the *mise en scène* using the same data as Clayman and Heritage, but investigating explicitly the ways in which the broadcast is edited. For example, during live broadcasts each switch from one shot to another tells us something about how production editors are analysing the unfolding interview. In his analysis of political speeches, Atkinson (1984: 50–2) remarked that not only does the audience listen for signals of the speaker to anticipate a completion, but so do the television producers in order to make a decision to switch from one camera to another. Two more recent studies of television panel debates and talk shows by Bovet (2007) and Mondada (2009) also investigate the moments at which particular shots are selected. Both studies show that production staff often switch from one participant to another at exactly the same moment that speaker change occurs, that is not only are the participants in front of the camera listening to each other in order to anticipate the end of a turn, but so do the people *behind* the camera in order to anticipate when they can – smoothly – change the shot. In an important sense, these studies extend Clayman and Heritage's attempt at uncovering the endogenous analysis of participants, but here not of IRs or IEs, but rather of editors in control of the broadcasted image.

By focusing upon the overall composition of the television image, one could also investigate how the visual presentation contributes to the production of the current 'footing' of the interaction, for example who is talking to whom. There have been no such studies of interviews, but in the context of talk shows Mondada shows that when all the participants may be sitting in a row next to each other, the editor may use a 'split screen' image to pick up two of the participants, which may be sitting at a distance but are now displayed side by side. A split-screen image is then not just a 'zoom' into the interaction, but an active reorganization of it.

An alternative to working with broadcast products would be to study the very process of *production*, that is to investigate the 'behind the scenes' of news interviews. The most common way of doing such studies would be through participant observation, and ethnographers have, for example, investigated the production of newspapers (Tuchman 1978), television programmes (Elliott 1972) and talk shows (Grindstaff 2002). However, one could also try to get audio or video recordings of the way that news interviews are edited. As already mentioned, Clayman and Reisner (1998) worked on audio recordings of newspaper editorial conferences. More recently, Broth (2004, 2008) gathered video recordings made of the work in the control room during a live broadcast panel interview. Broth shows that the very placement of the cameras (two at the front facing the guests, two at the back facing the journalists, one portable camera) anticipates the organization of the talk in terms of the categories 'interviewer' and 'interviewee'. He also shows how production staff avoid the danger of switching to a camera while it is moving or zooming: camera operators usually move their camera directly after a switch to another camera, while directors may talk to a camera operator to announce that a switch is forthcoming.

The attempt to develop methods for visual analysis has gained increasing importance in the last decade (see van Leeuwen and Jewitt 2001; Knoblauch et al. 2006; Rose 2007). There are several ways in which researchers can build on Clayman and Heritage's study to investigate the visual elements of broadcast interviews. However, it should be noted that although moving from audio to video allows new questions to be asked, such a move comes with a price.

One of the central innovations of CA was to produce transcripts of the materials that the researcher had been investigating. The inclusion of these transcripts in research articles means that CA works with 'openly available data' (Billig 1999a: 548), which allows readers to check whether the researcher's description of the materials is persuasive or not – and invites readers to launch and document their own alternative analysis (cf. Watson 1994: 178). Furthermore, the transcript system developed by Gail Jefferson was meant to capture not only features that are relevant for the current analysis, but also features that may only subsequently become relevant. In other words, CA transcripts are 'research generative' (Jefferson, quoted in West and Zimmerman 1982: 515) in the sense that a transcript produced to investigate question–answer sequences could also be used to study other phenomena, for example overlaps.

No such transcription system has emerged for analysing visual elements of interaction and it is unlikely that one will emerge, since embodied conduct is just too complex to capture all that might be relevant (there are too many details). As a result, researchers have developed transcription systems for *specific* aspects of embodied conduct, for example gaze direction (Goodwin 1981; Heath 1986) or typing at the keyboard (Luff and Heath 1993; Greiffenhagen and Watson 2009). As a result, transcripts are much more closely tied to the particular analysed 'non-verbal' features than in the case of purely verbal transcripts (cf. Mondada 2007). If one wants to reanalyse a particular fragment one therefore has to get back the original videotape, for the transcript alone is not rich enough. A focus on the visual aspects of the interaction therefore means that the data are no longer 'openly available'.

The great achievement of CA was its ability to describe and analyse certain aspects of talk-in-interaction in a *systematic* manner. Extending this approach to visual aspects has proven rather more difficult, because it is almost impossible to describe these in a similar systematic fashion (except by being very selective in one's analytic focus). Thus although visual studies remain to be done (to see how the basic turn-taking structure of news interview talk interacts with other features of the news interview), these are likely to be less systematic than the analysis provided by Clayman and Heritage.

Conclusion

Clayman and Heritage's book is the first systematic analysis of news interviews as a course of interaction: they demonstrate how interviews are opened and closed; how the turns of talk follow a pre-allocated format (according to which the IR asks questions and the IE answers them); how the IR aims to displays a 'neutralistic' stance, while nevertheless producing 'adversarial' questions; and how the IE may attempt to evade answering. Clayman and Heritage's greatest achievement is that they are able to demonstrate that these are not just features found by sociological analysis, but rather are ones that are used by *participants themselves*. As a consequence, the perennial topic of media studies, the questionable neutrality of the news, is given a new twist: it is not the researcher who is investigating whether or not a news report is neutral or not – but rather neutrality is shown as a concern for both IR and IE during the interview.

While Clayman and Heritage's data and way of analysing the data have produced some impressive findings, several ways in which their analysis could be extended have been mentioned. These include the possibility of seeing a particular interview in the context of other media products and of investigating how particular aspects of interviews get taken up in subsequent media reports – or are taken up by people listening or watching them. Another possible extension is to focus more explicitly on the differences between radio and television news interviews, that is to analyse the visual aspects of television broadcasts.

Additional Reading

Sacks's *Lectures on Conversation* (1992), transcripts of lectures held between 1964 and 1972, are still the most stimulating starting point for an introduction to CA. Ten Have's *Doing Conversation Analysis* (2007) provides a good practical introduction. For other case studies of the media, see Scannell's edited collection *Broadcast Talk* (1991), while Hutchby's *Media Talk: Conversation Analysis and the Study of Broadcasting* (2006) offers a good overview of methodological questions.

Acknowledgements

I would like to thank Rod Watson, Wes Sharrock, Lorenza Mondada, Alain Bovet and the editors, Fiona Devine and Sue Heath, for their helpful comments and suggestions during the preparation of this chapter. An earlier version was presented at a seminar at the Moscow School of Social and Economic Sciences (14 June 2007) and I would like to thank Dmitry Rogozin, Victor Vakhshtayn and the other participants for their comments and criticisms. I gratefully acknowledge the support of the British Academy through a Postdoctoral Fellowship and a Small Research Grant.

References

Arminen, I. (2005) *Institutional Interaction: Studies of Talk at Work*, Aldershot: Ashgate.
Atkinson, J.M. (1984) *Our Masters' Voices: The Language and Body Language of Politics*, London: Methuen.

Atkinson, J.M. and P. Drew (1979) *Order in Court: The Organization of Verbal Interaction in Judicial Settings*, London: Macmillan.

Austin, J.R. (1962) *How To Do Things With Words*, Oxford: Clarendon.

Ayass, R. (2004) 'Conversation analysis studies on mass media materials: what a consequential medialization of transcription can do for analysis', unpublished manuscript, Bielefeld: University of Bielefeld.

Barthes, R. (1967 [1964]) *Elements of Semiology*, tr. A. Lavers and C. Smith, London: Jonathan Cape.

Barthélémy, M. (2003) 'Temporal perspectives in the practical-textual handling of a European public problem', *Social Science Information* 42(3): 403–30.

Bell, A. (1991) *The Language of News Media*, Oxford: Blackwell.

Bertrand, I. and P. Hughes (2005) *Media Research Methods: Audiences, Institutions, Texts*, Basingstoke: Palgrave Macmillan.

Billig, M. (1999a) 'Whose terms? Whose ordinariness? Rhetoric and ideology in conversation analysis', *Discourse & Society* 10(4): 543–58.

Billig, M. (1999b) 'Conversation analysis and the claims of naivety', *Discourse & Society* 10(4): 572–6.

Bovet, A. (2007) 'Donner à voir le débat politique. La réalisation en direct d'un débat télévisé' ['Making political debate "watchable": the live production of a TV debate'], *Bulletin Suisse de Linguistique Appliquée* 85: 181–201.

Broth, M. (2004) 'The production of a live TV-interview through mediated Interaction' in C. van Dijkum, J. Blasius, H. Kleijer and B. van Hilten (eds), *Recent Developments and Applications in Social Research Methodology*, Proceedings of the Sixth International Conference on Logic and Methodology, 17–20 August 2004, Amsterdam. Amsterdam: SISWO.

Broth, M. (2008) 'The "listening shot" as a collaborative practice for categorizing studio participants in a live TV-production', *Ethnographic Studies* 10, 69–88.

Button, G. (1987) 'Answers as interactional products: two sequential practices used in Interviews', *Social Psychology Quarterly* 50(2), 160–71.

Cameron, D. (2001) *Working with Spoken Discourse*, London: Sage.

Clayman, S. E. (1995). 'Defining moments, presidential debates, and the dynamics of Quotability', *Journal of Communication* 45(3), 118–46.

Clayman, S. and J. Heritage (2002) *The News Interview: Journalists and Public Figures on the Air*, Cambridge: Cambridge University Press.

Clayman, S.E. and A. Reisner (1998) 'Gatekeeping in action: editorial conferences and assessments of newsworthiness', *American Sociological Review* 63(2): 178–99.

Croteau, D. and W. Hoynes (1994) *By Invitation Only: How the Media Limit Political Debate*, Monroe, ME: Common Courage.

Dijk, T.A. van (1988a) *News Analysis: Case Studies of International and National News in the Press*, Hillsdale, NJ: Lawrence Erlbaum.

Dijk, T.A. van (1988b) *News as Discourse*, Hillsdale, NJ: Lawrence Erlbaum.

Drew, P. (2005) 'Conversation analysis', in K.L. Fitch and R.E. Sanders (eds) *Handbook of Language and Social Interaction*, Mahwah, NJ: Lawrence Erlbaum.

Elliott, P. (1972) *The Making of a Television Series: A Case Study in the Sociology of Culture*, London: Constable.

Fairclough, N. (1989) *Language and Power*, Harlow: Longman.

Fairclough, N. (1995) *Media Discourse*, Arnold: London.

Fairclough, N. and R. Wodak (1997) 'Critical discourse analysis', in T.A. van Dijk (ed.) *Discourse as Social Interaction*, vol. 2, London: Sage.

Fowler, R. (1991) *Language in the News: Discourse and Ideology in the Press*, London: Routledge.

Fowler, R., B. Hodge, G. Kress and T. Trew (1979) *Language and Control*, London: Routledge.

Frankel, R. (1990) 'Talking in interviews: a dispreference for patient-initiated questions in physician-patient encounters', in G. Psathas (ed.), *Interaction Competence*, Washington, DC: University Press of America.

Glasgow University Media Group (1976) *Bad News*, London: Routledge & Kegan Paul.

Glasgow University Media Group (1980) *More Bad News*, London: Routledge & Kegan Paul.

Goffman, E. (1973) 'Footing', *Semiotica* 5(1/2): 1–29.

Goodwin, C. (1981) *Conversational Organization: Interaction between Speakers and Hearers*, New York: Academic Press.

Goodwin, C. (2001) 'Practices of seeing visual analysis: an ethnomethodological Approach', in T. van Leeuwen and C. Jewitt (eds) *Handbook of Visual Analysis*, London: Sage.

Greiffenhagen and R. Watson (2009) 'Visual repairables: analyzing the work of repair in human-computer interaction', *Visual Communication, 8(1): 65–90*.

Grindstaff, L. (2002) *The Money Shot: Trash, Class, and the Making of TV Talk Shows*, Chicago: University of Chicago Press.

Gunter, B. (1987) *Poor Reception: Misunderstanding and Forgetting Broadcast News*, Hillsdale, NJ: Erlbaum.

Gunter, B. (2000) *Media Research Methods: Measuring Audiences, Reactions and Impact*, London: Sage.

Hall, S. (1980) 'Encoding/decoding', in S. Hall, D. Hobson, A. Lowe and P. Lewis (eds) *Culture, Media Language: Working Papers in Cultural Studies, 1972–79*, London: Hutchinson.

Hall, S. (1982) 'The rediscovery of "ideology": return of the repressed in media studies', in M. Gurevitch, T. Bennett, J. Curran and J. Woollacott (eds), *Culture, Society, and the Media*, London: Routledge.

Have, P. ten (2007) *Doing Conversation Analysis*, 2nd edn, Los Angeles, CA: Sage.

Heath, C. (1986) *Body Movement and Speech in Medical Interaction*, Cambridge: Cambridge University Press.

Heath, C. (1997) 'The analysis of activities in face to face interaction using video', in D. Silverman (ed.) *Qualitative Research: Theory, Method and Practice*, London: Sage.

Heritage, J. (1995) 'Conversation analysis: methodological aspects', in U.M. Quasthoff (ed.) *Aspects of Oral Communication*, Berlin: De Gruyter.

Heritage, J. (2005) 'Conversation analysis and institutional talk', in K.L. Fitch and R.E. Sanders (eds) *Handbook of Language and Social Interaction*, Mahwah, NJ: Lawrence Erlbaum.

Heritage, J. and D. Greatbatch (1986) 'Generating applause: a study of rhetoric and response at party political conferences', *American Journal of Sociology* 92(1): 110–57.

Heritage, J. and D. Maynard (2006) *Communication in Medical Care: Interaction between Primary Care Physicians and Patients*, Cambridge: Cambridge University Press.

Hester, S. and D.W. Francis (2001) 'Is institutional talk a phenomenon? Reflections on ethnomethodology and applied conversation analysis', in A. McHoul and M. Rapley (eds) *How to Analyse Talk in Institutional Settings: A Casebook of Methods*, London: Continuum.

Horkheimer, M. and T.W. Adorno (2002 [1947]) *Dialectic of Enlightenment*, tr. by E. Jephcott, Stanford, CA: Stanford University Press.

Hutchby, I. (1996) *Confrontation Talk: Arguments, Asymmetries, and Power on Talk Radio*, Mahwah, NJ: Erlbaum.

Hutchby, I. (2006) *Media Talk: Conversation Analysis and the Study of Broadcasting*, Maidenhead: Open University Press.

Hymes, D. (1971) 'Sociolinguistics and the ethnography of speaking', in E. Ardener (ed.) *Social Anthropology and Language*, London: Tavistock.

Knoblauch, H., B. Schnettler, J. Raab and H.-G. Soeffner (eds) (2006) *Video Analysis: Methodology and Methods*, Frankfurt am Main: Peter Lang.

Labov, W. (1966) *The Social Stratification of English in New York City*, Washington, DC: Center for Applied Linguistics.

Lee, J.R.E. (1987) 'Prologue: talking organisation', in G. Button and J.R.E. Lee (eds) *Talk and Social Organisation*, Clevedon: Multilingual Matters.

van Leeuwen, T. and C. Jewitt (eds) (2001) *Handbook of Visual Analysis*, London: Sage.

Levinson, S.C. (1988) 'Putting linguistics on a proper footing: explorations in Goffman's concepts of participation', in P. Drew and A. Wootton (eds) *Erwing Goffman: Exploring the Interaction Order*, Cambridge: Polity Press.

Luff, P. and C. Heath (1993) 'The practicalities of menu use: improvisation in screen based activity', *Journal of Intelligent Systems* 3(2–4): 252–96.

Macdonald, M. (2003) *Exploring Media Discourse*, London: Arnold.

Marcuse, H. (1964) *One Dimensional Man: Studies in the Ideology of Advanced Industrial Society*, London: Routledge & Kegan Paul.

Masterman, L. (1985) *Teaching the Media*, London: Comedia.

Mondada, L. (2007) 'Commentary: transcript variations and the indexicality of transcribing practices', *Discourse Studies* 9(6): 809–21.

Mondada, L. (2009) 'Video recording practices and the reflexive constitution of the interactional order: some systematic uses of the split-screen technique', *Human Studies, 32(1): 67–99*.

Morley, D. (1980) *The Nationwide Audience: Structure and Decoding*, London: British Film Institute.

Nekvapil, J. and Leudar, I. (2002) 'On dialogical networks: arguments about the migration law in Czech mass media in 1993', in S. Hester and W. Housley (eds) *Language, Interaction and National Identity*, Aldershot: Ashgate.

Nekvapil, J. and I. Leudar (2006) 'Sequencing in dialogical networks', *Ethnographic Studies* 8: 30–43.

O'Connell, D.C. and S. Kowal (2006) 'The research status of Clayman and Heritage's (2002) *The News Interview*', *Journal of Psycholinguistic Research* 35(2): 147–65.

Robinson, J.P. and M.R. Levy (1986) *The Main Source: Learning from Television News*, Beverly Hills: Sage.

Rose, G. (2007) *Visual Methodologies: An Introduction to the Interpretation of Visual Materials*, 2nd edn, London: Sage.

Sacks, H. (1967) 'The search for help: no one to turn to', in E.S. Shneidman (ed.) *Essays in Self-Destruction*, New York: Science House.

Sacks, H. (1984) 'Notes on methodology', in J.M. Atkinson and J. Heritage (eds) *Structures of Social Action: Studies in Conversation Analysis*, Cambridge: Cambridge University Press.

Sacks, H. (1992) *Lectures on Conversation*, ed. G. Jefferson, Oxford: Blackwell.

Sacks, H., A. Schegloff and G. Jefferson (1974) 'A simplest systematics for the organization of turn-taking in conversation', *Language* 50(4): 696–735.

Saussure, Ferdinand de (1959 [1916]) *Course in General Linguistics*, ed. C. Bally and A. Sechehaye, tr. W. Baskin, New York: McGraw-Hill.

Scannell, P. (ed.) (1991) *Broadcast Talk*, London: Sage.

Scannell, P. (1996) *Radio, Television and Modern Life: A Phenomenological Approach*, Oxford: Blackwell.

Schegloff, E.A. (1968) 'Sequencing in conversational openings', *American Anthropologist* 70(6): 1075–95.

Schegloff, E.A. (1991) 'Reflections on talk and social structure', in D. Boden and D. H. Zimmerman (eds) *Talk and Social Structure: Studies in Ethnomethodology and Conversation Analysis*, Cambridge: Polity Press.

Schegloff, E.A. (1997) 'Whose text? Whose context?' *Discourse & Society* 8(2): 165–87.

Schegloff, E.A. (1999a) ' "Schegloff's texts" as "Billig's data": a critical reply', *Discourse & Society* 10(4): 558–72.

Schegloff, E.A. (1999b) 'Naivete vs sophistication or discipline vs self-indulgence: a rejoinder to Billig', *Discourse & Society* 10(4): 577–82.

Schegloff, E.A. (2005) 'On integrity in inquiry … of the investigated, not the investigator', *Discourse Studies* 7(4–5): 455–80.

Schegloff, E.A., G. Jefferson and H. Sacks (1977) 'The preference for self correction in the organization of repair in conversation', *Language* 53(2): 361–82.

Schiffrin, D. (1994) *Approaches to Discourse*, Oxford: Blackwell.

Sharrock, W.W. and D.R. Watson (1989) 'Talk and police work: notes on the traffic in information', in H. Coleman (ed.) *Working with Language: A Multidisciplinary Consideration of Language Use in Work Contexts*, Berlin: Mouton de Gruyter.

Tolson, A. (ed.) (2001) *Television Talk Shows: Discourse, Performance, Spectacle*, Mahwah, NJ: Erlbaum.

Tuchman, G. (1978) *Making News: A Study in the Construction of Reality*, New York: Free Press.

Watson, D.R. (1994) 'Harvey Sacks's sociology of mind in action', *Theory, Culture & Society* 11(4): 169–86.

West, C. and D.H. Zimmerman (1982) 'Conversation analysis', in K.R. Scherer and P. Ekman (eds) *Handbook of Methods in Nonverbal Behavior Research*, Cambridge: Cambridge University Press.

Wetherell, M. (1998) 'Positioning and interpretive repertoires: conversation analysis and post-structuralism in dialogue', *Discourse & Society* 9(3): 387–412.

Wetherell, M. (2001) 'Debates in discourse research', in M. Wetherell, S. Taylor and S.J. Yates (eds) *Discourse Theory and Practice: A Reader*, London: Sage.

Winch, P. (1958) *The Idea of a Social Science and its Relation to Philosophy*, London: Routledge.

Wittgenstein, L. (1953) *Philosophical Investigations*, tr. G.E.M. Anscombe, Oxford: Basil Blackwell.

Wodak, R. (2001) 'What CDA is about: a summary of its history, important concepts and its developments', in R. Wodak and M. Meyer (eds) *Methods of Critical Discourse Analysis*, London: Sage.

Wood, H. (2006) 'The mediated conversational floor: an interactive approach to audience reception analysis', *Media, Culture & Society* 29(1): 75–103.

CHAPTER 10

Family: Bengtson et al.'s *How Families Still Matter*

VANESSA MAY

Longitudinal studies provide an important window on the nature of social change over time – and sometimes, as is the case in the study under the spotlight in this chapter, across generations within the same family. In this chapter, Vanessa May considers some of the strengths and weaknesses of the Longitudinal Study of Generations (LSOG), a multigenerational study of American families, conducted by Vern L. Bengtson and colleagues, which began life in the 1970s. May highlights three important issues. First, she considers an important issue for survey-based research of any kind: the issue of sample representativeness. Second, May considers an issue which has particular relevance to longitudinal studies, namely the problem of sample attrition over time and how best to minimize this. Third, she tackles another issue which lies at the heart of the longitudinal approach: how to provide plausible accounts of social change when dealing with complex data. May concludes that Bengtson and his colleagues have done justice to the complexity both of their data and of the issues which they are examining, and have succeeded in making an important contribution to contemporary debates about family life

Introduction

How Families Still Matter: A Longitudinal Study of Youth in Two Generations by Vern L. Bengtson, Timothy J. Biblarz and Robert E. L. Roberts (2002) is based on the Longitudinal Study of Generations (LSOG) which began in California in 1970. The LSOG is unique because of its multicohort

193

longitudinal design which incorporates several generations of the same families. The book engages with the American debate over whether or not 'the family' is undergoing a 'decline' or 'breakdown' and what this might mean for future social development. Although the study and the specific debates it engages with are American, *How Families Still Matter* has relevance for the British context as well because of the similar concerns that have been expressed in the UK around 'family decline'. The study by Bengtson and colleagues is crucial in shedding empirical light on some of the claims that have been voiced in this debate. The particular focus of *How Families Still Matter* is on family influence and intergenerational transmission: that is, the extent to which families have been and are central in shaping individuals, their aspirations, attainments and values. Bengtson and colleagues compare two generations of late adolescents and young adults: 'Generation Xers' (as the authors refer to them) born between 1978 and 1985 and their parents, the 'Baby Boomers', born between 1945 and 1955.

In this chapter, I first provide a brief overview of the 'family decline' versus 'family solidarity' debate with which the authors engage and summarize the methodological traditions in this research field, before outlining the longitudinal study on which *How Families Still Matter* was based and the central findings presented in it. In the main body of this chapter, I discuss three methodological issues related to longitudinal studies – representativeness, attrition and the providing of plausible accounts of social change – and how these have affected the findings of *How Families Still Matter*.

Family Decline or Family Solidarity?

How Families Still Matter explicitly addresses the debate between those who argue that the most prevalent trend in recent decades in the US has been family decline and those who argue that American families continue to be typified by family solidarity. An early example of this debate is the dialogue held in the *Journal of Marriage and the Family* in 1993 (Cowan 1993; Glenn 1993; Popenoe 1993a, 1993b; Stacey 1993). On both sides of the Atlantic, the proponents of the family decline perspective interpret the demographic changes that have occurred in the last decades, such as decreasing marriage and birth rates, increasing rates of cohabitation, extra-marital births and divorce, and a rise in the proportion of single-person households, as signalling serious problems within the family. The family decline discourse declares that social changes have impeded the ability of families to socialize their children appropriately, contributing to a gradual breakdown of social order (e.g. Wallerstein et al. 2000; Popenoe 2006; for overviews of these debates in the US and the UK, see Furstenberg 1999b; Lewis 2001). These academic discourses are further reflected in public concerns over family change (Coltrane and Adams 2003).

In contrast, proponents of the family solidarity argument do not agree with such pessimistic visions of social deterioration. They point out that demographic shifts of the kind we are experiencing in Western societies are nothing new. 'The family' as understood by family decline theorists – that is, the two-parent nuclear family with clear gender roles – was a product of a particular age (post-World War II) and therefore signs of its diminished prevalence need not necessarily signal social doom (Furstenberg 1999a). Family solidarity theorists understand change as inevitable rather than problematic in and of itself, and tend to focus on how families adapt to changing circumstances. They do not necessarily deny that divorce has some negative impacts on family life, but at the same time they stress that other, positive, changes have also occurred in families (Houseknecht and Sastry 1996) and draw attention to how social change has also led to a shift in the criteria that are generally used to evaluate how well families are doing (e.g. Stacey 1996; Waite 2000). It has, however, also been emphasized – particularly by British researchers – that despite significant demographic shifts, families and family relationships continue to be central in individuals' lives (Finch and Mason 1993; Scott 1997; Smart and Neale 1999; Ribbens McCarthy et al. 2003; Smart 2007). In other words, according to this view, even under the pressure of demographic change, family solidarity prevails.

It is possible to detect a preference for different methodological approaches among family decline and family solidarity theorists. The family decline side tends to rely on hypothesis testing and the creation and analysis of large datasets with which to test their hypothesis, the hypothesis often being that parental divorce and maternal employment impact negatively on children's development and attainment. It is perhaps not surprising that such problem-oriented studies conclude that family change is harmful to children. The family solidarity corpus consists of a larger proportion of inductive and in-depth qualitative studies. The aim of qualitatively oriented researchers is to gain an understanding of the meanings that people give to their family relationships, to understand the complexity of how family life is experienced and to explore what demographic changes mean for the everyday lives of individuals. Studies using such an inductive approach often come to the conclusion that the doom-laden projections of family life that are part of the popular discourse do not necessarily represent how people are living their family lives.

This is of course an oversimplification and it is by no means the case that all quantitative studies adopt a problem-oriented approach, as demonstrated by Bengtson and colleagues' research, nor are all qualitative studies based on an agnostic outlook on social change. It is nevertheless refreshing to find a study such as *How Families Still Matter* that bucks the overall trend by being a large-scale quantitative study that does *not* set out to pronounce the imminent doom of 'family as we know it', despite the significant demographic shifts that have affected American families in the past decades.

How Families Still Matter

The 'decline' versus 'solidarity' debate hinges on the issue of change – whether families in the US have changed for the better or for the worse. The best way to address this question is of course to study developments over time, to which end longitudinal data are best suited. The findings presented in *How Families Still Matter* are derived from data from the LSOG based at the University of Southern California. The work began in 1970 as a cross-sectional study, and the longitudinal element was added in 1985 when the second wave of data gathering began. At the time of writing the book, the study comprised longitudinal data from four generations (G1–G4), with retrospective data from G0, that is, the parents of G1.

The LSOG is a unique dataset because it contains data from several generations *in the same families* spanning three decades, with each generation having been asked the same questions at the same stage in life. This has allowed the authors the rare opportunity to track what has changed and what has stayed the same across different generations and the extent to which families influence younger generations' values and aspirations. As the authors point out, the lack of such coherent data has been a weakness of much previous debate on how to interpret family change:

> Claims about family weakness or strength have been based on comparing what amounted to one-time snapshots of *different* families taken in *different* historical periods, by *different* researchers guided by *different research questions*. Faced with what amounts to comparing apples and oranges, family scientists have been unable to conclude whether differences in socialization outcomes from period to period were due to historical changes in family structure, differences in the research questions from study to study, or change in something the researchers failed to examine.
>
> (Bengtson et al. 2002: 9)

The data collection for the first LSOG survey was begun in 1971 as a one-off study of 561 members of a health maintenance organization for steel workers in Southern California. In other words, the sample is regional and not representative (I will return to the issue of sampling and representativeness below). This original sample comprised the grandparent generation or G1 of the study, born between 1896 and 1911 (see Table 10.1). The study

Table 10.1   The number of LSOG respondents by generation and wave

Generation	Wave 1 (1971)	Wave 2 (1985)	Wave 3 (1988)	Wave 4 (1991)	Wave 5 (1994)	Wave 6 (1997)
G1 b. 1896–1911	516	221	175	137	102	61
G2 b. 1916–1931	701	556	567	495	524	506
G3 b. 1945–1955	827	554	740	698	666	692
G4 b. 1978–1983	–	–	–	199	290	464

Source: Adapted from Bengtson et al. (2002: 170).

also surveyed 701 middle-aged children of the base sample (G2s born between 1916 and 1931) and 827 of their early adult or late adolescent grandchildren (G3s born between 1945 and 1955).

The original cross-sectional study became longitudinal in 1985 when the first survey (Wave 1) was repeated (Wave 2). The survey was then administered at three-year intervals – Wave 8 had been completed when *How Families Still Matter* was published, while the book is based on data from the first six waves. In 1991 LSOG began adding G4s at the age of 16 (born between 1978 and 1983), that is, the biological, adopted and stepchildren of G3s. As can be seen in Table 10.1, the number of respondents in all generations – except G4 – decline over time. This question of attrition is the second key methodological issue discussed in this chapter.

The LSOG data were gathered through self-administered questionnaires sent out by mail. At each wave, the respondents were asked identical questions relating to educational and occupational aspirations and attainment, value orientations, self-esteem and perceptions of the quality of their family relationships. This has allowed a comparison of, for example, social mobility, self-esteem, family solidarity, marital quality, attitudes and the quality of parent–child relationships across different generations in the same family (Glass et al. 1986; Biblarz et al. 1996; Roberts and Bengtson 1996; Mills 1999; Feng et al. 1999; Bengtson et al. 2002).

The LSOG also includes qualitative studies conducted with subsamples of the dataset, but, because these studies have not addressed any of the key questions that *How Families Still Matter* focuses on, the findings from them are not included in the book. These studies have, for example, focused on caregiving (Gatz et al. 1990; Mellins et al. 1993; Pyke and Bengtson 1996); how the death of a G1 family member affected the surviving members of that family (Troll 1996); single parenthood (Richards and Schmeige 1993); and stepfamilies (Schmeeckle 2001). This mismatch between the qualitative and quantitative foci is to some degree disappointing. Despite the richness and complexity of the data in *How Families Still Matter*, the findings would have gained more depth had there been qualitative data available to illustrate how the developments portrayed have been experienced and interpreted by individuals in their every-day lives. This is an issue I will return to in the conclusion.

Turning to the central findings of *How Families Still Matter*, the key focus is to examine the effects of family change on young adults' aspirations, self-esteem and values by comparing G4s in 1997 with their parents, G3s, at the same age in 1971. Bengtson and colleagues examine two aspects of family change in particular, parental divorce and maternal employment, both of which are presented by proponents of the family decline hypothesis as major causes behind the perceived deterioration in families. The authors address both aspects of this discourse: first, the claim that family transmissions have weakened over time; and second, that contemporary young people are faring worse than previous generations.

When measuring the effect that family change has had on educational and occupational aspirations, as well as on self-esteem, Bengtson and colleagues found that overall G4s had higher aspirations and expressed higher rates of self-esteem than G3s had at the same age. Despite this overall improvement, the authors found that when comparing G4s whose parents had divorced with those whose parents had stayed together, increases in aspirations and self-esteem have been 'suppressed' by rising parental divorce rates. In other words, parental divorce did have a negative effect on children's aspirations and self-esteem, and the G4s would have done even better had fewer of their G3 parents divorced. The authors also found that mothers' employment had a positive effect on the self-esteem of their sons. The authors conclude that there is thus some support for the family decline hypothesis (parental divorce does have negative effects), but that on the aggregate level this is largely offset by strong period effects, for example changes in opportunity structures and an increasing cultural emphasis on entrepreneurial success, the result of which is an 'unambiguous desire among G4s to excel' (Bengtson et al. 2002: 73).

The study further examined changes in the degree to which parents influ-ence their children's social priorities and to what extent these changes can be explained by increases in parental divorce and maternal employment. The authors compared the value orientations of G2–G3s in 1971 with those of G3s–G4s in 1997, focusing on two sets of value orientations – individualism/collectivism and materialism/humanism – and found that G4s expressed higher rates of individualism and materialism than G3s had at the same age. Divorce and maternal employment have contributed to the rise in individu-alism, but, with regards to the increasing levels of materialism, the picture is slightly more complicated. Divorce and maternal employment increased the scores for materialism for mothers, fathers and sons but increased daughters' scores for humanism. Interestingly, Bengtson and colleagues mention that G3s had become more collectivistic over time, but they do not speculate as to what this might mean in terms of possible future developments of the values of G4s. These results do, however, raise the question of whether G4s could become less individualistic in the future as they grow older (ibid.: 118).

Overall, Bengtson and colleagues found evidence of family solidarity in that G3s and G4s shared similar values which indicate that parents pass their values on to their children (cf. Bengtson and Roberts 1991). The authors are able to make this claim – that parents do pass on their values to their children – because the LSOG dataset contains information on successive generations in the same families. However, they could have perhaps done more with this unique aspect of their data by exploring more closely trajectories in individual families rather than merely presenting aggregates.

In sum, Bengtson and colleagues identify elements of family decline and family solidarity in their data, a good example of how change rarely if ever occurs only in one direction but rather in many and often contradictory ways. They emphasize that overall the importance of families has not significantly declined across generations and that family transmission processes continue to operate much as they did for previous generations, despite the many changes that families have undergone. In other words, families still matter.

There is, however, an apparent contradiction that runs through *How Families Still Matter*, or what could be interpreted as a contradiction by family decline theorists, that is never explicitly tackled by Bengtson and colleagues. It is nevertheless a key issue in the debate between family decline and family solidarity theorists and an issue that goes to the root of social science epistemology: that is, the role that theoretical frameworks play in the construction of knowledge. While Bengtson and colleagues maintain that increased rates of parental divorce and maternal employment have not led to family decline (in general), they do admit that their data indicate that parental divorce (and to a lesser degree maternal employment) has some negative effects on how well individual children do. Thus family decline theorists could argue that the LSOG data are proof of the deleterious effects that increasing divorce rates have on families.

Whereas family decline theorists would probably stop at the finding 'divorce has negative effects on children', Bengtson and colleagues argue that these negative effects have to be seen together with the many positive changes that have also had an impact on families in the US in the past decades (these are discussed below). In other words, despite the negative effects of divorce, increased rates of divorce have not led to an *overall* decline in how families are doing and therefore do not necessarily spell disaster for the family as a social institution. Thus the disagreement between family decline and family solidarity theorists does not seem to be so much about how particular data are to be interpreted (as both seem to agree that divorce does have negative effects on children) but rather whether these data are to be examined alone or as part of a more complex picture of families.

In the following three sections, I focus on the key methodological issues relevant to the LSOG study, and I discuss how these have been dealt with by the authors. These issues are: first, representativeness and the ability to make generalizations; second, attrition; and third, studying social change.

Representativeness and the Ability to Make Generalizations

A common problem with longitudinal data is lack of representativeness (e.g. Karney and Bradbury 1995). Only data that are random probability samples can call themselves representative and allow generalizations to populations (Dale 2006). There are some longitudinal studies, such as the National Child Development Study and the Millennium Cohort Study in the UK, and the National Longitudinal Study of Youth 1997 in the US, that are nationally representative. The costs of conducting such enormous surveys over time are however in many cases prohibitive and, consequently, many longitudinal datasets are *not* nationally representative (e.g. Karney et al. 2004). This has implications for the ability to make generalizations on the basis of the data, though, as I discuss below, this does not render such longitudinal research worthless, as even non-representative samples can generate significant findings.

The sample used for the LSOG was not nationally representative: it was collected from the records of a health maintenance organization representing steel workers in Southern California. Most of the G1s were white and from working-class backgrounds. Bengtson and colleagues nevertheless make a strong case for the robustness of their data and findings. To assess the representativeness of the LSOG sample, they compared their sample to other nationally representative samples and found them to be similar in terms of such characteristics as age, gender, occupational status and marital status. However, the LSOG sample had a smaller proportion of ethnic minorities, had better educated individuals and had a higher median household income than nationally representative samples (Bengtson et al. 2002: 172). The LSOG sample thus highlights a central problem that many surveys suffer from, that is, non-diversity, with survey samples generally skewed towards white middle-class individuals (Karney et al. 2004).

Bengtson and colleagues further compared their findings to those from other studies using nationally representative samples and found them to be similar (Bengtson et al. 2002: 176–7). Although they readily admit that their data are limited, they maintain that 'conclusions concerning family relations and processes based on LSOG data are robust across a variety of geographically and ethnically diverse samples', indicating that their findings have some validity beyond the LSOG sample (ibid.: 177). However, the under-representation of non-white populations in the LSOG sample presents a particular problem because qualitative studies have shown there to be substantial differences in family behaviour between different ethnic groups (Karney et al. 2004). Arguably, Bengtson and colleagues could have added the caveat that, although their findings seem to be robust, they can only make tentative generalizations about the *white* population but not ethnic minority families.

More recent longitudinal surveys in particular try to ensure that their samples are representative of non-white populations by collecting ethnic minority booster samples, in other words, by conducting extra interviews with members of a specific subgroup in order to ensure a larger and more representative sample size for minority groups. Such booster samples have been collected by, for example, the Health Survey for England, 2004, which focused on the health of ethnic minorities, and which will be used in the new UK Household Longitudinal Study, entitled Understanding Society (see Chapter 1). The LSOG team, however, did not boost their sample in such a way, partly because the survey was begun in 1971 before ethnicity became an issue automatically taken into consideration by mainstream sociologists. This in turn highlights another potentially problematic issue with longitudinal data, that is, that in order to conduct comparisons for measuring change over time one is limited by the questions upon which the original survey focused. Therefore, new issues that later emerge as salient in the social sciences cannot necessarily be studied retrospectively with the help of longitudinal data. Thus, the long-term value of longitudinal studies rests on the continued relevance of the questions addressed by the original survey.

This issue of ethnic diversity aside, Bengtson and colleagues manage to present a strong case as to why their findings have some claims to generalizability. However, generalizability is not the only measure of quality in social science research (Goodwin and Horowitz 2002). In other words, the use of non-representative samples and the resultant inability to generalize does not necessarily render these studies without value. The findings from some classic longitudinal studies are considered significant despite not being based on statistically representative data. For example, Elder's (1974) study provided meaningful insights into the effects that the Great Depression had on the lives of children whose families had suffered economic hardship as a result of it. Another key longitudinal study, the Baltimore Study of teenage mothers which originated in 1966, charted the outcomes for children born into disadvantaged circumstances over a 30-year period (Furstenberg et al. 1990; Furstenberg and Hughes 1995). These studies, based on non-representative samples, have nevertheless offered important theoretical insights into the effects of deprivation on child development within particular subgroups of the population.

Bengtson and colleagues mainly address the limitations of their dataset on their ability to generalize to a population, but they do not consider their ability to generalize to theory to the same extent (cf. Williams 2000; Mason 2002). Even without a statistically representative sample, they are able to make an important contribution to sociological theorizing about family change by conceptualizing divorce as *one* element of family change that cannot be viewed in isolation.

The authors attention is so focused on the issue of statistical representativeness that they do not explore the positive epistemological consequences of the unique characteristics of their data, or how these could be taken into consideration. The skewed nature of the LSOG sample raises some interesting questions about the extent to which the data can explain *the particular*, for example, what they say about white middle-class American families, or about the extent to which local context shapes family life. Such alternative questions would have, however, required disaggregating the data to a larger degree than the authors do. It is nevertheless important to keep in mind that the role of sociology is not merely to provide generalized statements but also to seek explanations as to the contextualized nature of social reality (Mason 2002).

Attrition

So far I have discussed the issue of representativeness in terms of how well a sample represents the population from which it is drawn. There is, however, a second aspect of representativeness that is relevant to longitudinal data: that is, the extent to which subsequent samples are representative of the original sample. Attrition, which means the loss of sample members over time, occurs either because the research team is unable to trace a particular person or because the person refuses to take part, has emigrated or died (Farrington et al. 1990: 123; Trivellato 1999: 342). Whereas in cross-sectional surveys it does not matter who takes part in the survey as long as the sample meets the standards of representativeness determined for that study, such unit non-response is a particularly difficult problem for longitudinal studies because they tend to be based on a design where the same persons are expected repeatedly to take part in the study (Farrington et al. 1990: 122). Any persons who fail to take part in subsequent waves cannot be replaced and, as a result, the sample size diminishes over time; indeed attrition rates are likely to increase as time goes on (ibid.: 123). The rate of attrition varies widely among longitudinal studies – in some panels as much as 60 per cent of the original sample has dropped out from further waves of the study (ibid.; Menard 2002: 39).

In light of this, the response rate for the LSOG data used in *How Families Still Matter* is high, especially considering that the surveys have been conducted through mail rather than face-to-face contact and that the data span

Table 10.2   The response rate of the LSOG over Waves 1–6

	Wave 1 *(1971)*	*Wave 2* *(1985)*	*Wave 3* *(1988)*	*Wave 4* *(1991)*	*Wave 5* *(1994)*	*Wave 6* *(1997)*
Response rate	65	65	73	74	74	73

Source: Bengtson et al. (2002).

three decades. Table 10.1 showed that the number of respondents had diminished in G1–G3 over time. Some of that was due to attrition, while some was the result of individuals no longer being eligible for participation because they had died, become mentally incapacitated or that the LSOG team had not been able to locate them at Wave 2 after a 14-year gap from the first wave. Furthermore, one cannot speak of a simple attrition rate for the LSOG because over time the survey has added new respondents (such as new partners and a new generation G4) to the study. The response rates for the LSOG are shown in Table 10.2, that is, the proportion of eligible respondents at each wave who took part in the study. The lowest response rate was experienced in Waves 1 and 2 when 65 per cent of those who were eligible for participation took part in the study – in other words, the highest rate of attrition ever experienced by the LSOG is 35 per cent. The lowest attrition rate of the LSOG was 26 per cent in Waves 4 and 5. A good indication of the LSOG's success in retaining its study participants is the fact that over 85 per cent of those G1s who were still eligible took part in Wave 6 of the study in 1997 (Bengtson et al. 2002: 170–1).

At the data gathering phase there are ways of trying to ensure that as many participants as possible take part in subsequent waves of the study, such as staying in touch with research participants between waves of data collection, for example by providing regular updates on the progress of the study (Farrington et al. 1990; Murphy 1990; Fox and Fogelman 1990: 236; Ruspini 1999; Hauser 2005). Bengtson and colleagues attribute their success in retaining respondents to two main factors: the nominal fee that all respondents received for participation and the efforts the study made to ensure that the respondents stay in contact with the study team and vice versa. The LSOG sent respondents newsletters twice a year and set up a free telephone 'hotline'. Respondents could also contact the research team via the project's website, which includes information about the study and its findings. The website (see Figure 10.1) also contains a 'Change Address' page which provides study participants an easy way to keep the research team up to date concerning their whereabouts.

Thus the LSOG has been relatively successful in retaining its research participants. However, it is not only the magnitude of attrition but also its pattern that is of importance. The main problem resulting from attrition is bias due

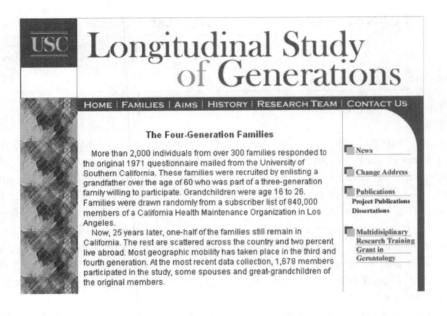

Figure 10.1   The website of the Longitudinal Study of Generations
Source: http://www.usc.edu/dept/gero/research/4gen/index.htm

to systematic non-participation of sample members, which leads to a situation where subsequent samples are not representative of the original sample (Miller and Wright 1995: 921; Menard 2002: 39). If attrition is random, then the analysis can proceed as normal and attrition does not need to be modelled for or taken into consideration in the interpretation of the results (Ahern and Le Brocque 2005). If attrition is systematic, the resulting bias has to be corrected if the results are to be appropriately interpreted (Miller and Wright 1995: 921; Trivellato 1999: 342). An advantage with longitudinal research as compared to cross-sectional research is that it is possible in further sweeps to determine *who* is missing from the survey and thus attempt to take any resulting bias into account (Farrington et al. 1990: 124). It is possible to determine whether attrition has occurred in a particular section of the original sample, for instance whether it is particularly men or women, or individuals from a specific class or ethnic background, who have been lost between waves of data collection (Duncan and Kalton 1987: 110; Menard 2002: 40). For example, studies on illegal behaviour, such as drug use, have found that it is usually the persons who take most drugs who fail to take part in subsequent interviews (Farrington et al. 1990: 124). Such systematic attrition means that researchers have to be careful when drawing conclusions from their data. It could also be argued that a sample may not necessarily be biased in terms of easily detectable socio-demographic variables but along other, but no less salient, qualities. For example, in family research, it might be that in all socio-demographic groups, those who are less family oriented are less likely to take part in a study, which would have important implications for the results. Such biases are of course difficult to detect but researchers should nonetheless consider them as a possibility.

Miller and Wright (1995) maintain that most longitudinal studies on families do little to detect and correct for attrition bias. This also seems to be the case for most of the studies published out of the LSOG data, with some exceptions (e.g. Roberts and Bengtson 1996; Silverstein et al. 1996; Parrott and Bengtson 1999). All of these, however, come to the same conclusion, namely that the sample selection bias that has occurred in the LSOG data does not significantly impact upon any results. This assertion is repeated by Bengtson and colleagues in the methodological appendix of *How Families Still Matter*. Although it is difficult to determine on what basis they make this claim – the authors do not detail which tests they have applied in order to determine that no significant attrition bias is at work – it is given extra weight by the more detailed examination of attrition bias in the LSOG conducted by Miller and Wright (1995). Miller and Wright (1995), at the University of Kansas (though Miller had previously been connected to the LSOG and published out of the data), examined the effects of attrition on a subsample of the LSOG dataset. Although they did discover attrition bias, they concluded that it had little effect on the validity of the final results.

Miller and Wright (1995) determined the external validity of a subsample of the LSOG by employing logit analysis to measure the probability of a Wave 1 respondent taking part in Wave 2 and to establish whether those G1s and G3s who took part in Wave 2 systematically differed from the original sample. For G1s, they found that Wave 1 and Wave 2 samples differed on gender, age, health, education, religiosity and the number of grandchildren, so that women, younger G1s and those with better health and education, lower religiosity and more grandchildren were more likely to participate in Wave 2. For G3s, they found only one variable on which the two samples differed, that is gender, with women more likely to take part in Wave 2. Furthermore, when they used chi-square tests and Fisher's *z* to determine the internal validity of the longitudinal sample, they also detected attrition bias. They then proceeded to correct this using Heckman's procedure which consists of calculating the probability that someone from the original sample will participate in subsequent waves, and then including the value of this probability in the dataset in order to correct for the attrition bias. Significantly, however, they found that correcting had little effect on the final results, thus corroborating Bengtson and colleagues' later assertions that, although there is some attrition bias in the data, the effects of this are minimal. Ahern and Le Brocque (2005: 58) cite Miller and Wright's (1995) article as an example of how

sample attrition should be controlled for, lending further support to the claim
that the LSOG findings are not significantly affected by attrition.

Providing Plausible Accounts of Change

One of the major benefits of working with longitudinal data is the ability not
only to study processes of social change and dynamic relationships (Ruspini
1999; Trivellato 1999; Frees 2004: 5), but also to determine the direction
and magnitude of change (Menard 2002: 3). Longitudinal research also offers
a way of capturing the complexity of change and continuity. For example, the
findings from the LSOG show that the same events, such as, for example,
parental divorce or maternal employment, can have different effects on sons
compared to daughters. Furthermore, change rarely if ever occurs in only one
direction. In the case of family change, there are different forces at work.
Some, such as parental divorce, have had a negative impact on the aspirations of youth, while others, such as parents' increased levels of education
and an increase in general prosperity, have helped raise aspirations
(Bengtson et al. 2002: 77–8).

Trends over time are best studied with the help of age-specific comparisons, that is, over time measuring different cohorts of the same age (Menard
2002: 9). *How Families Still Matter* has done this by examining, for example,
how the experiences of contemporary young adults differ from young adults
30 years ago. Multiple-cohort longitudinal studies such as the LSOG allow
an examination of period effects, that is, how sociohistorical context impacts
on individual lives (Mayer and Huinink 1990: 213; Ruspini 1999: 223;
Menard 2002: 4–5). Hallinan (1998: 23) argues that 'the ability to identify
and conceptualize the contextual determinants of social action' is one of the
main contributions of sociology, allowing it to specify 'how context interacts
with individual behavior within a system'. Each generation experiences particular social shifts and conditions which help shape that generation
(Mannheim 1952). For example, Elder's (1974) work showed that the psychological effects of experiencing the Great Depression varied according to
age. Similarly, the different historical circumstances under which the G3s and
G4s of the LSOG sample came of age will have affected their life chances,
values and aspirations. In other words, individual development and an individual's life course are partly shaped by the social and historical context.
Bengtson and colleagues (2002: 22) use the metaphor of biographical and
historical timelines to capture this complexity – an individual's life course is
shaped by both macro- and microhistorical events.

It nevertheless remains difficult to determine what exactly has caused any
particular change. Longitudinal data can chart change over time, but cannot

necessarily pinpoint why this particular change has taken place or what specifically in the social context has caused the change. The researcher's task is then to provide a plausible-sounding contextualized story for why change has occurred and what the possible contributing factors to change have been. Although Bengtson and colleagues stay mostly within the limits of their data, in most cases measuring the effects of particular microhistorical events such as divorce and maternal employment on children's aspirations, self-esteem and values, they also link their findings to the historical timeline, that is, to macrosocial changes that have occurred in American society, in order to account for some of the changes they identify in the LSOG data.

The four generations of the LSOG have lived in societies with differing opportunity structures. The G1s faced World War I and the 'Roaring Twenties', the G2s the Great Depression and World War II, while the G3s came of age during the turbulent 1960s and 1970s. The G4s transitioned to adulthood in a 1990s' post-industrial society (Côté and Allahar 1996). During this time, the US economy developed from a manufacturing to a service-based economy, coupled with upward educational and occupational mobility and shifts in social norms and values such as increased individualism and materialism. Parents' attitudes towards their children have also undergone a change, with contemporary parents placing less emphasis on obedience and conformity, as children's autonomy and independence have become more valued. Bengtson and colleagues identify these changes in opportunity structures and values in the US as a period effect to help explain the general upward trend in aspirations and self-esteem in the LSOG sample as well as the increase in individualism and materialism that they discovered.

Thus *How Families Still Matter* highlights the importance of viewing families in a larger social context in order to understand and be able to provide explanations for the effects that social change has had on families. Families do not exist in hermetically sealed worlds but are rather made up of individuals whose lives stretch beyond the family. Families, in other words, are an integral part of an ever-changing society and need to be examined in this context.

A further interesting feature of the LSOG data is that they allow comparisons of different generations in the same families, thus offering not only an insight into changes in families overall, but how the same families have changed over time (cf. Bengtson 2001: 10). Thus, for example, Bengtson and colleagues can make assertions about the strength of intergenerational transmissions of values because they can show that children hold largely similar values to their parents. Arguably they could have gone further with their data by examining more closely developments within particular families or particular types of family. For example, it would be interesting to compare how LSOG families that have experienced divorce might differ from those that have not. Instead, they have chosen to stay on the aggregate level. Perhaps

they have done so in order to strengthen their argument about family solidarity, for it is on the aggregate level that this argument holds best, in other
words that *overall* the families studied seem to be doing better over time when
it comes to aspirations and self-esteem. It is important, therefore, when evaluating the findings of any particular study, to be mindful of the way that
research questions are framed and of the argument that the authors wish to
make. Although it is unrealistic to expect any one study to explore all the
possible questions that their data could answer, it is the reader's task to consider other potential ways of framing the question, as well as combining the
data, and of how these might affect the subsequent findings.

Conclusion

The findings presented by Bengtson and colleagues provide a strong case for
the argument that, in general, family change is not a sign of 'decline' but of
the durability of families. Although some aspects of family change, such as
parental divorce, have had negative effects on individual family members,
overall the families in the LSOG study have been shown to be resilient and
adaptive in the face of the social changes around them. The authors propose
that it is precisely these adaptations that have enabled families to actually
remain important. Seen in this light, family change is *essential* for the survival
of families as a social institution.

The most appropriate way of studying change is to employ a longitudinal
research design. The three main methodological issues related to longitudinal
research that have here been considered in light of the LSOG study are representativeness, attrition and providing plausible accounts of social change.
Bengtson and colleagues provide evidence to show that their data, though not
representative, can lead to careful generalizations. I have further argued that
this is not the only criterion for quality in the social sciences, and have examined the ways in which *How Families Still Matter* provides an important contribution to theorizing about family change. Rather than merely examining the
individual effects of divorce and maternal employment, Bengtson and colleagues understand these as elements of a more complex picture of family
change, the aggregate of which shows that families are in many respects doing
better today than they were 30 years ago. I have also discussed the importance
of paying attention to attrition and sample selection bias when conducting longitudinal research. Although the LSOG has suffered from a degree of systematic attrition, it would appear that this has not significantly affected the findings.

The final issue discussed in this chapter has been the importance of being
able to contextualize data appropriately in order to provide a plausible
account of social change and its effects on the lives of individuals. In the case

of the LSOG, this has meant identifying key period effects that may have had an impact on the outcomes studied. By painting a picture of the changing sociohistorical context that the LSOG sample has experienced, Bengtson and colleagues not only make the argument that demographic shifts such as rising rates of divorce and maternal employment cannot be viewed in isolation, but also provide some flavour of the lived lives behind the numbers.

More research on how these patterns are played out in everyday life is however required, calling for a mixed methods approach (cf. Ruspini 1999: 220; see also Chapter 3). Combining qualitative and quantitative approaches is here understood not in terms of 'triangulation' but in terms of providing contextualized multidimensional accounts that enable us to appreciate better the complexity of social change (Mason 2006). Qualitative approaches could add to the present findings by seeking answers to questions such as how these macrosocial changes are experienced and interpreted by individuals in their everyday lives. What are the processes at work within these families? Microlevel research could further explore the interaction between family members and their social contexts. How do families interact with each other and their surroundings in these changing social environments? Family members are also friends, students, employees and community members, and all of these networks (and more) will have an impact on how they live and interpret their lives – not just families. More recently, major *qualitative* longitudinal studies have gained prominence and funding, such as the UK Timescapes study which is discussed in Chapter 1. These studies are important in gaining understanding of how individuals over time interpret and give meaning to social and individual change.

How Families Still Matter offers powerful evidence that the importance of family relationships and family life is not in decline. For the LSOG sample, families have continued to play an important part in intergenerational transmission of aspirations and values, and, despite increases in parental divorce and maternal employment, the younger generations outperform their elders when it comes to self-esteem. In other words, Bengtson and colleagues show that the portrait of contemporary family life that the 'family decline' thesis paints is probably overly pessimistic. In the face of major demographic shifts, families continue to matter.

Additional Reading

The issue of how contemporary young adults are faring is examined from a slightly different angle in *The Frontier of Adulthood: Theory, Research and Public Policy* (2005) by Settersten et al. Drawing on longitudinal data from the US, Canada and Western Europe they argue that transitions to adulthood are changing by becoming more prolonged, ambiguous and diverse. Smart and Neale's significant study *Family Fragments?* (1999) used qualitative longitudinal data to examine how divorce was experienced by parents and how their parenting practices evolved over time. *Methods of Life Course Research: Qualitative and Quantitative Approaches* (1998), edited by Giele and Elder, offers some interesting chapters on how different longitudinal studies have been conducted and how qualitative and quantitative approaches have been combined in studying the life course. Further longitudinal studies are introduced in the collection edited by Phelps et al., *Looking at Lives: American Longitudinal Studies of the Twentieth Century* (2002).

Acknowledgements

My sincere thanks go to Vern Bengtson for comments on an earlier version of this chapter and to Fiona Devine and Sue Heath for their helpful comments and keen editorial eye.

References

Ahern, K. and R. Le Brocque (2005) 'Methodological issues in the effects of attrition: simple solutions for social scientists', *Field Methods*, 17: 53–69.

Bengtson, V.L. (2001) 'The Burgess Award Lecture: beyond the nuclear family: the increasing importance of multigenerational bonds', *Journal of Marriage and the Family*, 63: 1–16.

Bengtson, V.L., T.J. Biblarz and R.E.L. Roberts (2002) *How Families Still Matter: A Longitudinal Study of Youth in Two Generations*, Cambridge: Cambridge University Press.

Bengtson, V.L. and R.E.L. Roberts (1991) 'Intergenerational solidarity in aging families: an example of formal theory construction', *Journal of Marriage and the Family*, 53: 856–70.

Biblarz, T.J., V.L. Bengtson and A. Bucur (1996) 'Social mobility across three generations', *Journal of Marriage and the Family*, 58: 188–200.

Coltrane, S. and M. Adams (2003) 'The social construction of the divorce "problem": morality, child victims, and the politics of gender', *Family Relations*, 52: 363–72.

Côté, J.E. and A.L. Allahar (1996) *Generation On Hold: Coming of Age in the Late Twentieth Century*, New York: New York University Press.

Cowan, P.A. (1993) 'The sky is falling, but Popenoe's analysis won't help us do anything about it', *Journal of Marriage and the Family*, 55: 548–53.

Dale, A. (2006) 'Quality issues with survey research', *International Journal of Social Research Methodology*, 9: 143–58.

Duncan, G.J. and G. Kalton (1987) 'Issues of design and analysis of surveys across time', *International Statistical Review*, 55: 97–117.

Elder, G.H. Jr (1974) *Children of the Great Depression: Social Change in Life Experience*, Chicago, IL: University of Chicago Press.

Farrington, D.P., B. Gallagher, L. Morley, Raymond J. St. Ledger and D.J. West (1990) 'Minimizing attrition in longitudinal research: methods of tracing and securing cooperation in a 24-year follow-up study', in D. Magnusson and L.R. Bergman (eds) *Data Quality in Longitudinal Research*, Cambridge: Cambridge University Press.

Feng, D., R. Giarrusso, V.L. Bengtson and N. Frye (1999) 'Intergenerational transmission of marital quality and marital instability', *Journal of Marriage and the Family*, 61: 451–63.

Finch, J. and J. Mason (1993) *Negotiating Family Responsibilities*, London: Tavistock/ Routledge.

Fox, J. and K. Fogelman (1990) 'New possibilities for longitudinal studies of intergenerational factors in child health and development', in D. Magnusson and L.R. Bergman (eds) *Data Quality in Longitudinal Research*, Cambridge: Cambridge University Press.

Frees, E.W. (2004) *Longitudinal and Panel Data: Analysis and Application in the Social Sciences*, Cambridge: Cambridge University Press.

Furstenberg, F.F. Jr (1999a) 'Is the modern family a threat to children's health?', *Society*, 36: 31–7.

Furstenberg, F.F. Jr (1999b) 'Children and family change: discourse between social scientists and the media', *Contemporary Sociology*, 28: 10–17.

Furstenberg, F.F. Jr. and M.J. Hughes (1995) 'Social capital and successful development among at-risk youth', *Journal of Marriage and the Family*, 57: 580–92.

Furstenberg, F.F. Jr., J.A. Levine and J. Brooks-Gunn (1990) 'The children of teenage mothers: patterns of early childbearing in two generations', *Family Planning Perspectives*, 22: 54–61.

Gatz, M., V.L. Bengtson and M. Blum (1990) 'Caregiving families', in J.E. Birren and K.W. Schale (eds) *Handbook of the Psychology of Ageing*, 3rd edn, New York: Academic Press.

Giele, J.Z. and G.H. Elder Jr (1998) *Methods of Life Course Research: Qualitative and Quantitative Approaches*, Thousand Oaks, CA: Sage.

Glass, J., V.L. Bengtson and C.C. Dunham (1986) 'Attitude similarity in three-generation families: socialization, status inheritance or reciprocal influence?', *American Sociological Review*, 51: 685–98.

Glenn, N.D. (1993) 'A plea for objective assessment of the notion of family decline', *Journal of Marriage and the Family*, 55: 542–4.

Goodwin, J. and R. Horowitz (2002) 'Introduction: the methodological strengths and dilemmas of qualitative sociology', *Qualitative Sociology*, 25: 33–47.

Hallinan, M.T. (1998) 'Sociology and the goal of generalization', *Contemporary Sociology*, 27: 21–4.

Hauser, R.M. (2005) 'Survey response in the long run: the Wisconsin Longitudinal Study', *Field Methods* 17: 3–29.

Houseknecht, S.K. and J. Sastry (1996) 'Family "decline" and child well-being: a comparative assessment', *Journal of Marriage and the Family*, 58, 726–39.

Karney, B.R. and T.N. Bradbury (1995) 'The longitudinal course of marital quality and stability: a review of theory, method, and research', *Psychological Bulletin*, 118: 3–34.

Karney, B.R., M.A. Kreitz and K.E. Sweeney (2004) 'Obstacles to ethnic diversity in marital research: on the failure of good intentions', *Journal of Social and Personal Relationships* 21: 509–26.

Lewis, J. (2001) 'Is marriage the answer to the problems of family change?', *Political Quarterly*, 71: 437–45.

Mannheim, K. (1952) *Essays on the Sociology of Knowledge*, London: Routledge.

Mason, J. (2002) *Qualitative Researching*, 2nd edn, London: Sage.

Mason, J. (2006) 'Mixing methods in a qualitatively driven way', *Qualitative Research*, 6: 9–25.

Mayer, K.U. and J. Huinink (1990) 'Age, period, and cohort in the study of the life course: a comparison of classical A-P-C-analysis with event history analysis or farewell to Lexis?', in D. Magnusson and L.R. Bergman (eds) *Data Quality in Longitudinal Research*, Cambridge: Cambridge University Press.

Mellins, C.A., M.J. Blum, S.L. Boyd-Davis and M. Gatz (1993) 'Family network perspectives on caregiving', *Generations*, Winter/Spring: 21–4.

Menard, S. (2002) *Longitudinal Research*, 2nd edn, Thousand Oaks, CA: Sage.

Miller, R.B. and D.W. Wright (1995) 'Detecting and correcting attrition bias in longitudinal family research', *Journal of Marriage and the Family*, 57: 921–9.

Mills, T.L. (1999) 'When grandchildren grow up: role transition and family solidarity among baby boomer grandchildren and their grandparents', *Journal of Ageing Studies*, 13: 219–39.

Murphy, M. (1990) 'Minimizing attrition in longitudinal studies: means or end?', in D. Magnusson and L.R. Bergman (eds) *Data Quality in Longitudinal Research*, Cambridge: Cambridge University Press.

Parrott, T.M. and V.L. Bengtson (1999) 'The effects of earlier intergenerational affection, normative expectations, and family conflict on contemporary exchanges of help and support', *Research on Ageing*, 21: 73–105.

Phelps, E., F.F. Furtsenberg and A. Colby (eds) (2002) *Looking at Lives: American Longitudinal Studies of the Twentieth Century*, New York: Russell Sage.

Popenoe, D. (1993a) 'American family decline, 1960–1990: a review and appraisal', *Journal of Marriage and the Family*, 55: 527–55.

Popenoe, D. (1993b) 'The national family wars', *Journal of Marriage and the Family*, 55: 553–5.

Popenoe, D. (2006) 'Marriage and family in the Scandinavian experience', *Society*, 43: 68–72.

Pyke, K.D. and V.L. Bengtson (1996) 'Caring more or less: individualistic and collectivist systems of family eldercare', *Journal of Marriage and the Family*, 58: 379–92.

Ribbens McCarthy, J., R. Edwards and V. Gillies (2003) *Making Families: Moral Tales of Parenting and Step-Parenting*, Durham: sociologypress.

Richards, L.N. and C. Schmeige (1993) 'Problems and strengths of single parent families: implications for practice and policy', *Family Relations*, 42: 277–85.

Roberts, R.E.L. and V.L. Bengtson (1996) 'Affective ties to parents in early adulthood and self-esteem across 20 years', *Social Psychology Quarterly*, 59: 96–106.

Ruspini, E. (1999) 'Longitudinal research and the analysis of social change', *Quality & Quantity* 33: 219–27.

Schmeeckle, M. (2001) 'Rethinking the ties that bind: adult perception of step, ex-step, and biological parents', PhD dissertation, University of Southern California, Los Angeles.

Scott, J. (1997) 'Changing households in Britain: do families still matter?', *Sociological Review*, 45: 591–620.

Settersten, R.A. Jr, F.F. Fursternberg and R.G. Rumbaut (eds) (2005) *The Frontier of Adulthood: Theory, Research and Public Policy*, Chicago, IL: Chicago University Press.

Silverstein, M., X. Chen and K. Heller (1996) 'Too much of a good thing? Intergenerational social support and the psychological well-being of older parents', *Journal of Marriage and the Family*, 58: 970–82.

Smart, C. (2007) *Personal Life: New Directions in Sociological Thinking*, Cambridge: Polity Press.

Smart, C. and B. Neale (1999) *Family Fragments?*, Cambridge: Polity Press.

Stacey, J. (1993) 'Good riddance to "the family": a response to David Popenoe', *Journal of Marriage and the Family*, 55, 545–7.

Stacey, J. (1996) *In the Name of the Family: Rethinking Family Values in the Postmodern Age*, Boston, MA: Beacon Press.

Trivellato, U. (1999) 'Issues in the design and analysis of panel studies: a cursory review', *Quality & Quantity* 33: 339–52.

Troll, L.E. (1996) 'Modified-extended families over time: discontinuity in parts, continuity', in V.L. Bengtson (ed.) *Adulthood and Aging: Research on Continuities and Discontinuities*, New York: Springer.

Waite, L.J. (2000) 'The family as a social organization: key ideas for the twenty-first century', *Contemporary Sociology*, 29: 463–9.

Wallerstein, J.S., J.M. Lewis and S. Blakeslee (2000) *The Unexpected Legacy of Divorce: The 25 Year Landmark Study*, New York: Hyperion.

Williams. M. (2000) 'Interpretivism and generalisation', *Sociology*, 34: 209–24.

Index

215